D1486810

Readings in
GIFTED
AND
TALENTED
EDUCATION

Special Learning Corporation
42 Boston Post Rd. Guilford, Connecticut 06437

SPECIAL LEARNING CORPORATION

Publisher's Message:

The Special Education Series is the first comprehensive series designed for special education courses of study. It is also the first series to offer such a wide variety of high quality books. In addition, the series will be expanded and up-dated each year. No other publications in the area of special education can equal this. We stress high quality content, a superb advisory and consulting group, and special features that help in understanding the course of study. In addition we believe we must also publish in very small enrollment areas in order to establish the credibility and strength of our series. We realize the enrollments in courses of study such as Autism, Visually Handicapped Education, or Diagnosis and Placement are not large. Nevertheless, we believe there is a need for course books in these areas and books that are kept up-to-date on an annual basis! Special Learning Corporation's goal is to publish the highest quality materials for the college and university courses of study. With your comments and support we will continue to do this.

John P. Quirk

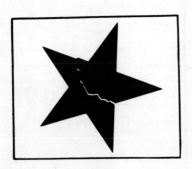

First Edition
1 2 3 4

ISBN No.   0-89568-013-0

SPECIAL EDUCATION SERIES

* ● Abnormal Psychology: The Problems of
    Disordered Emotional and Behavioral
    Development
  ● Administration of Special Education
  ● Autism
* ● Behavior Modification
    Biological Bases of Learning Disabilities
    Brain Impairments
  ● Career and Vocational Education for the
    Handicapped
  ● Child Abuse
* ● Child Psychology
  ● Classroom Teacher and the Special Child
* ● Counseling Parents of Exceptional Children
    Creative Arts
  ● Curriculum Development for the Gifted
    Curriculum and Materials
* ● Deaf Education
    Developmental Disabilities
* ● Developmental Psychology: The Problems of
    Disordered Mental Development
* ● Diagnosis and Placement
  ● Down's Syndrome
  ● Dyslexia
* ● Early Childhood Education
  ● Educable Mentally Handicapped
* ● Emotional and Behavioral Disorders
    Exceptional Parents
  ● Foundations of Gifted Education
* ● Gifted Education
* ● Human Growth and Development of the
    Exceptional Individual

  ● Hyperactivity
* ● Individualized Education Programs
  ● Instructional Media and Special Education
  ● Language and Writing Disorders
  ● Law and the Exceptional Child: Due Process
* ● Learning Disabilities
  ● Learning Theory
* ● Mainstreaming
* ● Mental Retardation
  ● Motor Disorders
    Multiple Handicapped Education
    Occupational Therapy
  ● Perception and Memory Disorders
* ● Physically Handicapped Education
* ● Pre-School Education for the Handicapped
* ● Psychology of Exceptional Children
  ● Reading Disorders
    Reading Skill Development
    Research and Development
* ● Severely and Profoundly Handicapped
    Social Learning
* ● Special Education
  ● Special Olympics
* ● Speech and Hearing
    Testing and Diagnosis
  ● Three Models of Learning Disabilities
  ● Trainable Mentally Handicapped
  ● Visually Handicapped Education
  ● Vocational Training for the Mentally Retarded

  ●   Published Titles   *Major Course Areas

GIFTED AND TALENTED EDUCATION

CONTENTS

4. Creative Teaching Techniques For The Gifted Child

Focus II   144

The Creativity of Gifted Children

TOPIC MATRIX

Readings in Gifted Education provides the college student in special education a comprehensive overview of the subject. The book is designed to follow a basic course of study.

COURSE OUTLINE:

Education of the Gifted Child	Readings in Gifted Education	Related Special Learning Corporation Readers
I. Introduction to the Education of the Gifted	I. Perspective on Gifted Education	I. Readings in Special Education
II. Instructional Provisions for the Gifted	II. Program Curriculum and Materials—Methodology	II. Psychology of Exceptional Children
III. Instructional Approaches for the Gifted	III. Teaching: Mainstreaming vs. Separate Programming	
IV. Fostering Creativity	IV. Creative Teaching Techniques for the Gifted Child	

PREFACE

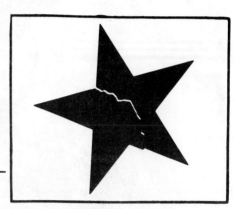

The gifted child. Certainly this child is exceptional but is the child handicapped? Many educators feel education for gifted and talented children is necessary but not as important as education for the retarded, deaf, blind and severely handicapped. Why? Because it is assumed that because children are exceptionally intelligent and talented they have no major problems in learning and developing. Gifted and talented children have similar problems of emotional coping, peer pressure, parental protectiveness, and social and academic needs. More and more programs and materials are being developed for the gifted; through diagnosis and identification better ways of helping are being developed at an earlier age. The future for these children will be strengthened by better diagnosis, parental understanding, and teacher-training.

Perspective on Gifted Education: Identification

Man is eternally short of his goal, always in search of attaining something better. Perhaps it is more efficient shelter, greater warmth, more nourishing food, or longer life. In each of these goals he is particularly dependent on intelligence. Unlike animals who adapt themselves to specific environments, man adapts the environment to himself. In doing so, he does not rely on strength, but on intellect. Therefore, it becomes clear that it is crucial for man to encourage the developement of advanced thinking and reasoning. Unfortunately, only in recent years has the majority of society begun to realize the vast amount of potential in this country, among the young, and the reality of how much of this is virtually untapped. The plight of the gifted child placed in an educational setting void of proper stimulation of creative thinking, is now emerging as a paramount mistake in the present educational structure. The situation for the gifted has not been a particularly easy one throughout history. As early as the days of Plato, the belief that we could attain the ultimate in social harmony through a selective process resulting in only the wisest becoming rulers, never saw fulfillment, and throughout the Roman era, only those born into wealthy families received extensive education. This mode of thinking persisted into the Middle Ages, when a class selective process for educating individuals was applied rather than searching out true intellectuals irregardless of class. Although the Renaissance saw the resurgence of Platonic concepts of education, there was no visible effort to widely develop individual talents or intellects.

Early educational thought in America was dominated by European thinking, including the belief that all children's minds were exactly the same, to be instructed in the same way. In fact, a popular thought was that a thin line separated genius and insanity. Despite the fact that Thomas Jefferson proposed special provisions for gifted students in 1779, it is recognized that the first systematic approach to provide for the gifted began in St. Louis in 1868. This involved a system of flexible promotions, with the school population being promoted when appropriate, at five-week intervals. Soon to follow were several other programs for the gifted in major cities throughout the United States. One monumental change took place in 1898 when ability grouping for bright students was begun. For the first time emphasis was placed on broadening the student's experiences rather than encouraging them to progress more rapidly through the curriculum, a much more effective approach in the encouragement of the gifted child.

For our society to realize its fullest potential, the limits placed on gifted children by improper educational planning and methodology must be dissolved. As man continues to alter his environment to suit his needs, he will continue to rely on the highest level of intellect in his society, which are the gifted children of today.

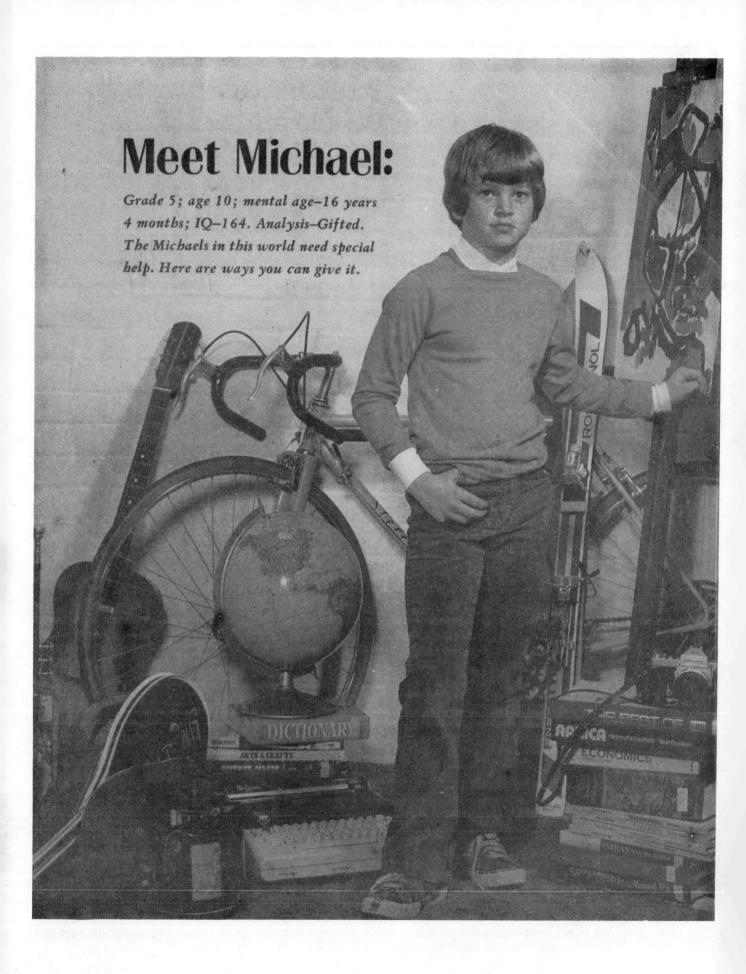

Meet Michael:

Grade 5; age 10; mental age–16 years
4 months; IQ–164. Analysis–Gifted.
The Michaels in this world need special
help. Here are ways you can give it.

Who Are The Gifted?

Who are the gifted and talented? Some say they are the top 2% of the population, the top 5%, the top 10%; those with IQs over 140, over 135, over 130, over 120; those scoring in the top 5% on tests of creativity; and so on. The definitions are as varied as the educational programs serving them. For our purposes, let's say that gifted and talented children are those who are clearly superior to their peers in academic excellence, creative talent, or both.

Specific tests of intelligence, creativity, and achievement are frequently used for identification purposes. However, you can identify gifted kids without formalized testing by using a talent behavior checklist. The one below will not only help you identify the gifted in your class, but also will give you a better understanding of what giftedness and talent is all about.

Identifying characteristics

These are the common identification methods most schools use. Past and present performance is also carefully considered.

____ Consultants on the gifted/creative

____ Report card grades

____ Teacher judgment

____ Self-identification

____ Peer identification

____ Parent identification

____ Psychological evaluation, individual IQ, Stanford Binet, or Wechsler

____ Achievement tests scores, two years or more above chronological age

____ Early school entrance

____ Grade skipping

____ Honors classes eligibility

____ Community agency recommendations—YMCA, scouts, religious education classes

In addition, the following characteristics are normally evident. Gifted children . . .

____ Are curious

____ Have a large vocabulary

____ Have long memories

____ Sometimes learn to read alone

____ Have a keen sense of humor

____ Are persistent

____ Like to collect things

____ Are independent

____ Are creative and imaginative

____ Are healthy and well coordinated, but some may be delicate

____ May be bigger and stronger than average

____ Sustain interest in one or more fields over the years

____ Initiate their own activities

____ Develop earlier

____ Learn easily

____ Have a keen sense of humor

____ Enjoy complicated games

____ Are interested and concerned about world problems

____ Analyze themselves, are often self-critical

____ Like older children when very young

____ Are original

____ Set high goals and ideals

____ Are leaders

____ Have talent(s) in art, music, writing, drama, dance

____ Use scientific methods of research

____ See relationships and draw sound generalizations

____ Produce work which is fresh, vital, and unique

____ Create new ideas, substances, and processes

____ Invent and build new mechanical devices

____ Often run counter to tradition

____ Continually question the status quo

____ Do the unexpected

____ Apply learning from one situation to different ones

____ Solve problems on a superior level, divergently, innovatively

____ May appear different

____ Enjoy reading, especially biography

The checklist is reprinted from The National Association for Creative Children and Adults, Copyright 1976 by Ann Fabe Isaacs. Used by permission.

Why Special Attention?

Ann Fabe Isaacs has been a champion of the gifted and talented for many years. Founder of the National Association for Gifted Children and former editor of its Gifted Child Quarterly, *her most recent endeavor is the creation of the National Association for Creative Children and Adults, and editor of* Creative Children and Adults Quarterly. *Her discussion of why the gifted need special attention should motivate us all to action.*

It is a gift to be gifted. When properly nourished, inspired, and motivated, this gift can be one of joy and productivity. However, the attitude that has prevailed and persisted among both educators and the public is that the gifted can get along without special help. Let's examine that attitude by comparing them to the fine vegetables harvested from a garden. What vegetable garden has ever grown the biggest and best plants all by itself? Good strains of seed are needed, as well as careful planting, good cultivation, adequate sun, sufficient water and nourishment.

Without this special attention, there are some rather puny and average vegetables at best.

When people say that the gifted will get along by themselves, they perhaps are thinking that creative boys and girls will survive in the classroom, grow to maturity, recede into society, and function as average adults. If that is what we want from them and for them, yes, they can get along. But if we want them to live on a productively creative level for the future and to serve as catalysts for the world's population in general, we need to think about how best to educate and motivate them.

We must go beyond their immediate needs and give them the motivation and inspiration to put it all together—to learn the creative joys of not only producing, but of giving and sharing their talents as well.

Because the decisions now being made on educating the gifted will influence everyone's future, it is crucial we identify these boys and girls as early as possible and help

them learn how to function comfortably. They need to know that they are gifted and talented, to learn how to handle it, cope with it, how to make it blossom for themselves and for others.

In-depth studies of the writings of highly creative people show the ultrasensitivity and complexity of their lives and suggest they suffered in trying to come to grips with their talents. Today's talented people have these same problems and the schools and teachers must be ready to help. Classroom teachers, having once identified their talented pupils, must provide for them in the classroom. They must plan daily activities that are challenging and mind-stretching and develop positive attitudes for the future.

While most of us aren't gifted, we must realize that we all have a tremendous stake in educating those who are. If we give them the help needed to develop wholesomely and to share their talents, we can look forward to more productive problem solving in the face of the challenges of this last quarter of the twentieth century.

How You Can Design a Program

Do-it-yourself ideas

Ken Bierly, resource teacher and director of the gifted program at McCornack School, Eugene, Oregon, suggests guidelines for organizing your classroom to create time for special activities.

No special program for gifted and talented children in your class? Worry not. Within your classroom you can find ways to reach them. Use these 10 all-by-yourself ideas to gain the extra time and talent it takes to try something new.

Use extra people in your classroom. Children from other classrooms or schools, reliable parents, aides, senior citizens, college students, student teachers, unemployed neighborhood volunteers, guest speakers, members of your family, former students—all are possible sources of help. (Those with the same special interests and talents as those of your gifted pupils are particularly valuable.) Make a list of possible volunteer functions; then train one volunteer to supervise your program.

Create a G/T learning center. Devote the center to a traditional subject area or to a topic such as "how to . . ." or to a "hands on area." Use the center for a variety of enrichment activities and independent study challenges. Perhaps some of your creative volunteers can suggest activities.

You-Choose-It time. Set aside a time, 10 to 30 minutes each week, to be used as free time for students to work on something of their own choosing—that not only gives them a chance to select their activities but also leaves you free to meet with individual students when they need assistance with their projects.

Conference time. Give individual help while the rest of the class is reading, doing art, and so on.

Outside class time. This may be for the superdedicated only, but it is extremely effective. Use lunchtime, before or after school, weekends, your planning time, time while most of the class is in a special subject to meet individually or in small groups.

Independent learning packets. Create or locate minilessons and encourage kids to make some, too. Put them into a "Pandora's Box" or post several as an after-regular-assignment opportunity.

Self-contained back-to-back program. Divide your class into two or more groups, make assignments for each group, and then work with one group at a time. This technique drastically reduces student-teacher ratios.

Honor pass. In return for a specified amount of productive classwork, students earn building mobility and access to a wide variety of resources. Honor-pass students enjoy widened horizons and retain these special privileges only as long as they use and respect the time.

Commando team. Time out from regular classwork is given individuals or ad hoc groups to attempt completion of difficult assignments.

Start slowly. Begin with one student doing a special project and expand as you gain mastery and the group becomes more interested.

The mentor idea

In these days of tight budgets how can we provide for the one-to-one relationships between gifted youth and adults that are so necessary? Jo Ann Sorrensen, career guidance teacher in the public schools of Claremont, California, suggests the mentor idea using community volunteers.

First we worked with students to explore and define interests. Interest checklists and articles and pictures on projects done by others were given to get them started. We brainstormed, setting the time for three minutes and having students toss in ideas as fast as they could. Many students knew right away what they wanted to do. Others, who found it harder, were provided small group and individual counseling sessions.

Mobile van

For a large district or several small districts, a mobile van may be the answer, says Ronald F. Howells, teacher of gifted students in Martin County, Florida.

Our gifted and talented kids keep on truckin' in their portable classroom. A mobile van brings a teacher and materials to 50 gifted students in five schools. The van has two work-research areas and can comfortably seat 10 pupils. It is a classroom complete with audiovisual equip-

Once we had a list of student interests, we sent out a call to the community for volunteers to work on a one-to-one basis as mentors. Finding them was relatively easy. They included a college history professor, an architectural design student, a student of interior design, a lawyer, a nationally known horsewoman, a magician. We timidly asked the mentors to meet with students once or twice, to be available for telephone consultation, and perhaps to arrange for the students to visit them at their places of work. Most emphasized that they would meet only the minimum of times suggested, but as they became involved with students, many spent a great deal more time than was required.

Once students and mentors were matched, they were asked to submit a project plan signed by both. Projects

ment, bulletin and chalkboards, storage shelves, closet, and combination teacher-driver. A large table fastened to the floor and surrounded with built-in seating is used for discussions and as a work area.

The van arrives at a school and kids enter the van. Ideas are generated by students and teacher, plans are made, assignments are given. Then students move back to their classrooms to utilize the school's resources and facilities to complete the assignments.

Using the van as a base of operations, the kids have developed many different

would be experimental, creative, problem solving, a search of literature on a subject, perfection of a skill, or any other type proposed and accepted.

By February projects were ready to be shared with fellow students. They included displays, oral and written reports, two performances, and an audiovisual presentation. Pupils also exhibited and explained their projects at the school open house.

In addition, students used their projects to set up learning centers for younger gifted students. One that was very successful was a magic center, developed by a young magician who had learned something of the history of magic and had developed considerable showmanship. He set up some magic equipment and taught several tricks.

The mentor program challenged, and inspired, our gifted kids. It's worth a try.

projects. A group of first and second graders constructed a planetarium. This effort was combined with a fourth-grade project on the moon landing of Apollo II. Most of the research, taping, and construction was conducted on the van, then assembled in the auditorium for shows to the entire school community.

The van is an essential part of our gifted program. Not only does it serve as a means of transportation and a classroom, but it has also become the symbol of something very special to the students it serves and to their parents.

Mix and match

Judith S. Wooster, teacher at Green Acres School, Kenmore, New York, public schools, recommends you pick elements from each column to make your program.

Who	How to group	Program type	Where	When

Generally gifted/talented
Academically gifted/talented
Gifted with strength in:
  math
  reading
  any content area
  leadership
  motivation
  creativity
  psychomotor—dance,
  athletics, movement,
  mechanical
  arts—visual, performing
Gifted with weakness in
any of the above
Ethnic gifted
	Multiage—primary or
	intermediate
	Student pairing
	Student and adult pairing—
	in or out of school
	Homogeneous—
	all or part of the time
	Integrated/mainstreamed
	with articulated program—
	all or part of the time
	Independent study project
	Interest based
	Alternative schools
	Early entrance
		Counselor
		Mentor/tutor
		Itinerant resource person
		Learning centers
		Minicourses, seminars
		Community-focused
		Resource room
		Parent volunteer
		Community
		Continuous progress
		Library
		Great books
		Field trip/travel
		Acceleration (faster than
		curriculum)
		Enrichment (broadening
		the curriculum)
		Differentiated curriculum
		Skills/process base
		Advanced placement
			Gym
			Library
			Art or music room
			Coatroom
			Cafeteria—
			student or faculty
			Tent
			Playground
			CD shelter
			Hallway
			Principal's office
			Home EC room
			Shop
			Kitchen
			Classroom
			Loft
			Part of any above
			Community
				Before school
				After school
				Saturdays
				Summer
				Vacations
				During day
				  study hall
				  activity time
				  altered schedule
				  block scheduling
				  released time
				Year-round school

27 challenging activities

Ken Bierly

EACH child in your class has special gifts and talents. Four or five have talent clusters that enable them to excel academically or creatively. One or two of the 30 have that rare combination of ability and temperament which society labels as giftedness. How to meet these needs?

Your curriculum should include two thrusts—one to assist the gifted to use their talents while sharing and getting along with others, the second to help every child develop and enjoy his unique abilities. The following activities can be organized without extra aides or funds. Some are particularly for the gifted, others can be used with every youngster in your class.

Elementary, My Dear Watson (intermediate)—Challenge your G/T kids to solve a famous mystery by reading them a Holmes tale in the original words of Sir Arthur Conan Doyle. Read the story in two parts. First, read until all the facts are given then stop and let young detectives discuss possible solutions. After theories have been proposed read the conclusion. Do this several times a year to help students develop increased powers of observation and reasoning.

Fingerprint Blowups (all levels)— The fact that each person's fingerprints are unique is a starter for unusual individual or group projects. Using a stamp pad, fingerprint your students. Make sure the print is clear and clean. Transfer the print onto large paper with an opaque projector so the finished print is about a meter in diameter. In addition to a great art display, prints can launch a memory game where students try to match fingerprints with owners. Assignments can be signed with a print as well as a name, and a study of identification procedures used by law enforcement agencies can be initiated.

Reduce-a-Book (all levels)—Every elementary school library contains books with concepts of interest to primary children but with words too difficult for the primary child to read. Challenge gifted students to reduce a difficult book to words primary children can read. Have the stu-

dent select a book, study it, become familiar with its setting, plot, style, concepts. Teacher assistance may be necessary during this process. Also help the translator by providing help with primary vocabulary and syntax. The last step is for the student to rewrite the book retaining essential elements of the original in a scaled-down version.

Letters Around the World (all levels)— Help your G/T students write better letters and design more thoughtful questions. Ask each student to list famous people well known for achievements in sports, politics, medicine, religion, music, entertainment, and so on. Suggest that although it's impossible to talk to these people in person, it is possible to talk to them through the written word. Have each student choose a celebrity and write that person a letter. It should contain two sections: (1) an information section telling who the student is, where he or she lives, what purpose the student has for writing, and whatever other information the student wants to include; and (2) an inquiry section in which the student asks three

questions. Each question should be of interest to the student, pertain to the major field of the celebrity, and should be a question not easily answered from readily available sources. It should require the respondent to compare, predict, hypothesize, infer, evaluate, estimate, or perform some other higher order thinking process in order to answer.

Carnivorous Plant Mascot (intermediate)—Tell the class that you are buying a carnivorous plant and that the student who learns most about its care and characteristics will earn the right to become its foster parent. These inexpensive plants can be obtained through local florists, and they do best with lots of moisture and sunshine. As the student gets to know the plant, provide encouragement to pursue related topics.

Newspaper Stakeout (all levels)— Help your G/T students develop the discipline of a daily routine by having them keep daily track of something reported in the local newspaper. Some items, such as food prices, stock quotations, weather information, can be graphed. Other items lend themselves to tabulation—ratio of births to deaths, number of fire runs correlated to daily weather conditions, and so on. Another type of daily tracking is to clip all letters to the editor on a certain issue and become familiar with the various viewpoints. After daily tracking has gone on for a month or so, encourage students to take some action—write a letter to the editor, predict future fluctuations of stock, identify a store with consistently lower prices and try to find out why.

How People Make Decisions (all levels)— A decision occurs when a person chooses one alternative over another. On what bases are such choices made? Challenge students to identify many ways that people make decisions—trial and error, superstition, authority of another, financial considerations, pleasure versus pain, physical force, religious beliefs, recommendation of another, reciprocity, and experimentation. Ask a student to record each decision made during a chosen day and then match each decision to the criterion used to make that choice.

Have him think through the rationale for each and decide what alternative criteria could have been used. If some decisions were based on multiple criteria, which weighed the most heavily? This activity will enable youngsters to realize that there are many ways to make decisions and will encourage them to think through, and become more aware of, the criteria they use.

Lip Sync (all levels)—Much of the music, lyrics, and dialogue you hear on television is prerecorded with the singer, musician, or speaker pantomiming so that movements are synchronized with the sound track. Use this technique to help students develop listening, performing, and coordination skills. Have your student choose a song, poem, instrumental piece, comedy routine, or some other prerecorded piece. Your student-performer memorizes the piece, then performs it with props to create the illusion that he or she is actually speaking the words or playing the music.

Classroom Data Taker (all levels)—Teach your G/T kids to take many kinds of classroom data that can be useful to you or to the group. A simple technique is to identify some behavior or event and have the student record the number of times it occurs, for example, the number of times you use pronouns in your chalkboard writing. Or a gifted primary student might keep a chart showing how many times the class correctly pronounces an unknown word by using word attack skills. Another type of data recording is note taking. School announcements, speakers who come to class, assemblies—all provide material for developing the technique of recording essential elements of a message.

Herb Garden (all levels)—An herb can be defined as any seed plant whose stem withers away after each season's growth, and which is used as a medicine, spice, or food. Ask an expert to visit your class and help you set up an herb garden. Find an interested student to become its caretaker and you're in for months of enjoyment. Try parsley, chives, oregano, and peppermint. These plants can lead into studies of their history, uses, and unique characteristics. Plants will perfume the classroom and will provide a tasty addition to food prepared by students in school or at home.

Encoder-Decoder (all levels)—Encourage G/T students to practice the essential skills of encoding and decoding by learning and using a standard signaling system, such as Morse code, smoke signals, hand signing, or semaphore. With a little research your students will uncover some interesting facts about the uses of these coding systems. For instance, we usually associate semaphore signaling with ships but it is also used on railroads!

Ten-Power Adventures (all levels)—Simple, ten-power hand lens microscopes are widely used by scientists to enter the miniature world hidden from the naked eye. Once your curious students discover the potential of the hand lens, they will use it constantly, both indoors and outside. You will be surprised how different a human eye, a snowflake, or an ant leg appears when magnified ten times. Use these adventures to stimulate some interesting artwork—the little world made big.

Cooperative Bulletin-Board Display (all levels)—Collaborate with an interested student to design a creative, child-oriented bulletin board. Some ideas include a display of everyone's birthstones, illustrations by students of a favorite scene from a

"Gifted programs are *not* undemocratic. The absence of them is."

favorite book, a matching game with names of class members and teacher and their baby pictures, signs of the zodiac and their meanings, a blank sheet of butcher paper with string-hung pencils and an invitation to doodle, a large map of your school's attendance area with color-headed pins so students can locate and identify their own and friends' houses and other points of interest.

Pandora's Box (all levels)—Bring a large cardboard box to class to serve as a file box for manila folders. Find some used folders and reverse them so that the top tabs are free of writing. Use this as an idea file for academic and enrichment activities for school and home. Students will enjoy clipping ideas from magazines, newspapers, discarded texts, idea books, and so on. Include both student and teacher ideas. This will encourage student interest in curriculum and will create a high level of involvement in classroom activities.

Coping with Territorialism (intermediate) —Get a paperback edition of *The Territorial Imperative*, Robert Ardrey (Dell, 1971), and invite a G/T student to read it, take notes in margins, and underline important sentences. Care should be taken to explain that such markings are appropriate only when the book is one's private property. Ask the student to use the notes and underlinings to construct a short, one-paragraph summary of each chapter. Sit down with the student over lunch or after school and discuss the book and its implications. Together, design an experiment or research project that the student could do relating information in the book to the student's everyday life. The student might record examples of territorialism on the playground, clip newspaper articles which describe territorialism among nations, or perhaps construct a chart of territorial animal behaviors and see if classmates can observe such behaviors around the community. Studying territorial instincts and behaviors can help children understand and cope with these behaviors in the human species.

DNA Model (all levels)—DNA, or deoxyribonucleic acid if you prefer, is the building block of all known life. Yet many of us know very little about this mysterious molecule. Help an interested student find articles and pictures of the DNA phenomenon. A good place to start is an article, "Exploring the New Biology," *National Geographic*, September 1976. Then, using either gumdrops and straws, Tinker Toys, or plastic foam balls and doweling rods, build a model of the DNA double helix. If you can't obtain materials to make a model, suggest a large drawing of the life-building molecule. If your student has prepared a written or taped account of the nature and significance of DNA, display it near the model or drawing so that others can learn from the displayed project.

In a Nutshell (all levels)—Give each student a walnut. Tell them to eat the meat and hollow the shell, separating the two halves intact. Invite them to think of as many interesting and unusual items as they can which will fit inside the shell allowing the two halves to be closed and fastened with a rubber band. Such items as a small seed, a paper-punch circle, a baby button will start your youngsters thinking small!

Spock's Favorite Subject (intermediate)— Mr. Spock, the famous character in the television series "Star Trek," prided himself in his attempt to be a totally logical individual. Logic can be as fascinating to youngsters as it is to Spock. Obtain a beginner's book on logic such as *Basic Logic*, Raymond J. McCall (Barnes and Noble, 1965). Suggest that a G/T student advanced in math and reading first skim the book to become familiar with it. Discuss with the student the meaning of a syllogism such as the classic,

Every man is mortal.

John is man.

Therefore, John is mortal.

Ask the student to read the book and attempt some of the exercises in logic at the end of the last chapter. Then encourage him to translate the contents into a presentation the class would enjoy, set up a debate, study fallacies, watch a "Star Trek" episode to see what kinds of formal, deductive reasoning Spock employs.

Classroom Legislative Committee (all levels)—Committees in the state or national legislature spend much time considering the potential consequences of proposed legislation. Students can profit from developing this skill of anticipating potential outcomes. Ask them to submit in writing suggested changes in existing school, community, state, or national laws. Choose a class legislative committee and give members the responsibility of reviewing several reasonable suggestions. Have the committee list five to 10 major negative potential consequences and the same number of positive potential consequences. On the basis of these deliberations ask the committee to identify several suggestions which in their opinion would result in the most desirable and the least desirable consequences. Invite the group to submit these suggestions to the appropriate body for consideration—the student council, city government, state, or national legislature. Some student may want to gather data on the degree of increased awareness of potential consequences in the personal decisions of committee members.

Philosophical Society (all levels)—Ben Franklin started a Philosophical Society in Philadelphia to gather bookish people together to read and discuss great literature. Are there students in your class who would enjoy such an adventure? Pick three or four and try this. Secretly choose five or six classic books, all of which deal with a single theme or concept. Obtain enough copies of each selection for each member of your society. Have the students read and discuss one book each month, evaluating characters, plot, style, mood, theme, and so on. Then as each new book is read, challenge the group to compare it to the ones read before and try to guess the theme which ties them all together. At the end of the last session reveal the theme. Whether or not students have already discovered it, they will come up with many of their own.

Community Guide for Kids (intermediate) —Many communities publish a resource guide describing community agencies and opportunities. Seldom do these guides include resources for young people. Challenge your kids to create such a community service guide. It could be a simple duplicated booklet listing names and addresses of bicycle repair shops, good book stores, firms that give free samples, recipes for paper-mache, rainy-day crafts, toy stores with competitive prices, and clothing stores that carry the latest fads. Or it

could be a full-blown, printed version with advertisements and illustrations.
Famous Sayings and Slogans (intermediate)—Buy or borrow a copy of *Bartlett's Familiar Quotations* for the classroom. Set aside a space on the chalkboard and ask a student to be in charge of picking a different student each week to write a favorite quotation on the board. After several weeks of quotes from the book, invite students to make up their own and then choose one to go on the board along with the author's name. For a related art activity, bring to class a poster with a quotation and picture illustrating the saying. Then have kids create their own either by illustrating a familiar quotation or one they have made up.
An Oatmeal Box Can Be? (primary)—Creativity can also be defined as the ability to see and use unusual relationships. To help youngsters do this, give each an empty oatmeal box and ask them to use their imaginations to make the boxes into something both unusual and useful. Offer clues such as earmuffs, one-stringed guitar, or castle tower for dolls.
The Six Simple Machines (all levels)—All complex machines are combinations of the six simple machines—the wheel and axle, level, inclined plane, wedge, screw, and pulley. Make up a spirit master duplicating book with each page devoted to drawings of objects and tools which use one of the simple machines. Then bring to class some complicated objects, such as a watch, typewriter, sink faucet, or scissors, and play the game of Machine-ups. Choose six individuals or teams representing each of the six simple machines. As you present each item you've brought, any individual or team stands up if he thinks the object works on the principle of the machine he represents. Follow up with a six simple machines bulletin-board display. The concept that complicated things are made up of combinations of simpler things is an important one.
Digging for Word Roots (all levels)—The history of words, etymology, is a fascinating topic. Etymologists are word detectives who uncover layer after layer of change until the roots of modern words can be examined. Spark interest in word origin by featuring a certain word to be researched during spare minutes or between assignments. Your students will be inter-

ested to know, for example, that the word *woodchuck* was the Pilgrims' version of the American Indian word *otchock*. The Latin word *manus,* meaning hand, is the source for words *manufacture, manifold, emancipate,* and even *manners* (original meaning—how to use your hands).
Pizza Portmanteaus (all levels)—Lewis Carroll made portmanteaus famous with his poem, "Jabberwocky." A portmanteau is made by combining two words in both form and meaning. Smoke and fog become smog. Have fun with portmanteaus by having students (1) write several characteristics which describe themselves and combine these into descriptive portmanteaus, and (2) identify their favorite pizza ingredients and create portmanteaus for these combination delicacies. Adolescents might read, *Understanding Media: The Extensions of Man,* Marshall McLuhan (McGraw-Hill, 1964) and analyze the basis for McLuhan's word variations.
Three Magic Keys (all levels)—Some G/T children need to improve skills which will enable them to get along with peers and adults. These key behaviors will help:
1. Put things in the positive. Instead of saying, "Don't touch my eraser," children can learn to say, "Please ask me before you touch my things." Instead of "You can't play with us," they can say, "We'd like to play by ourselves for awhile." By using such positive statements yourself and by expecting students to do the same you will help make the entire class climate more positive, productive, and friendly.
2. Check the message. We constantly give verbal and nonverbal messages to each other. Often these messages are not received or are misunderstood. One way to combat this problem is to check your understanding of another's message either by paraphrasing the message in your own words or by asking the sender to repeat it.
3. React to specific behaviors. Instead of writing a person off because he made fun of you, isolate the behavior that bothers you and react to that. You might tell the person that his making fun of you makes you want to avoid him, or you might ask him to play somewhere else if he wants to make fun of people. Whatever action you take, remember that everyone wants to be liked. Obnoxious behaviors can only be changed when we are made aware of them.

Another Chance for Learning-The Assessment Class

Peggy L. Escovar

The word assessment in education typically has come to represent the often cursory practice of a stranger pulling a child out of his classroom, putting him into an equally unknown "testing room," and asking him to respond to long lists of uninteresting questions and tasks. This interaction usually takes no more than one hour, after which the stranger must then compile this brief sample of behavior, whether totally satisfactory or not, and make definitive conclusions about the child's future potential for learning and his most appropriate educational placement.

It is true that along with teacher observations this process may be adequate to assess the achievements and needs of many children in our schools. However, as educators and advocates for every child in our classrooms we must ask ourselves: What about the child who refuses to play the testing game? Or the one who is terrified of strangers? Or the one who has subtle speech, language, or muscular problems? Or the one who is experiencing emotional problems? Or the one who cannot or will not sit attentively for more than a few minutes? How about the child who has had years of conditioning at home that tests or other school activities are not really important? These types of cases underscore the absurdity of the standard testing situation for some children.

RATIONALE FOR THE ASSESSMENT CLASS

Housed in The Pennsylvania State University campus as part of a project coordinated by the Central Intermediate Unit of Pennsylvania, the assessment class is designed to work with children who need a more in-depth and varied assessment. The unique feature of this class is the working premise that some children need an assessment that is more than a brief sampling of behaviors. Assessment is viewed as a complex process in which environmental, medical, and emotional factors are examined. The interaction of many variables, including teacher and situational factors, is studied, and workable hypotheses are derived on what makes children respond as they do. In many ways this class provides a place for children to show their teachers what they really can and cannot do *over time*.

The fact that the assessment is not the sampling of one time behaviors provides two obvious advantages. First, the validity of the conclusions reached is enhanced since behavior is observed over time in a multiplicity of situations. Second, the reliability of scores obtained initially can be verified against similar criteria during later testing and observations. Combined, these two advantages lead to a more thorough understanding of the child and his or her problems.

DESIGN OF THE ASSESSMENT CLASS

The assessment class is designed as a relatively short term (10 to 20 week) diagnostic assessment and teaching program serving local school district personnel. The children may range in age from 5 to 10 years and are bused in daily from surrounding areas within a radius of approximately 15 to 20 miles.

The children may be referred by teachers, principals, psychologists, or parents and are chosen on the basis of diagnostic need and available space. The class size varies from five to seven pupils during each 10 week period. Although in rare cases a child may stay beyond 20 weeks, most children are back in the public schools within 12 weeks.

The assessment class can be considered a self contained classroom in that children come every day and stay the regular six hour school day, but it is not considered a categorical classroom serving one speciality, such as the mentally retarded, the emotionally disturbed, or the learning disabled. The class is designed for any child whose case raises questions about the validity of prior testing, possible emotional involvements, or the relative effectiveness of past teaching strategies. In essence, it was created to give these very special children a second chance at learning.

THE STAFF

The two most important factors that determine the opportunity to conduct educational assessment are teacher time and know-how. The assessment class is staffed by a master teacher, an instructional advisor, and a teacher's aide and is used extensively as a practicum site for graduate and undergraduate students of the Department of Special Education at The Pennsylvania State University. A one to one teacher-pupil ratio allows for individual tutoring sessions an average of 10 hours per week.

Reprinted from, *Teaching Exceptional Children*, Fall 1976. Copyright ©1976 by The Council for Exceptional Children.

1. PERSPECTIVE

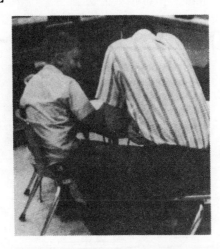

Useful information and mutual respect are benefits of one to one instruction.

Teaching machines are often used to promote motivation and repetition.

THE DIAGNOSTIC EDUCATIONAL PROCESS

When a referral requesting assessment class enrollment is received, the instructional advisor begins a thorough background search, which includes:

Visiting the family at home and interviewing both parents, if possible.

Obtaining all medical, social, and educational information.

Observing the child in his present class placement.

Conferring with appropriate school personnel.

During a staff meeting that includes the assessment class staff and the child's present teacher, counselor, or principal, the information obtained during the background search is discussed and a decision on acceptance is mutually made. If the child is accepted, target dates for entrance and exit are established.

In most cases, a child is accompanied by his mother on his first day in the class. At this time the instructional advisor explains in detail the process involved in assessment and the responsibilities of staff members who will be working with the child. An invitation is extended to the parents to visit the class anytime and to participate in various parent programs.

During the next two to six weeks, a working rapport between the new student and his teachers is established, and academic, social-emotional, speech and language, and physical behaviors are examined. Throughout the assessment period, emphasis is placed on creating an environment in which the true abilities and potentials of the child can be assessed adequately and fairly.

Formal testing information is always done in a one to one situation, usually by a person who has spent several days, or in some cases weeks, obtaining the child's trust and respect. Often it takes time to establish rules and expectancies, and even more time is needed for many children to realize that adults can provide reinforcement and friendship.

Informal teacher-designed assessment measures are then used to obtain a further breakdown in areas of deficit. For example, if a child shows difficulty in discriminating similarities and differences, the teacher may vary the formal testing setting by using objects in the environment, by questioning the child unobtrusively in play situations, by having another person present the material, or by noting whether the child's error was one of vocabulary rather than concept.

In other words, informal assessment is used to verify validity of the results of prior formal testing in the give and t of the real world. During this more informal assessment, teacher may often attempt to teach the skill while obtain additional information regarding the child's rate of learni reinforcement needs, short and long term retention, abilit generalize, need for repetition, and personal attitude tow learning. Accurate information of this depth can only be lected within an accepting environment and over an exten period of time.

For some children the assessment data are collected and v dated in the first 2 weeks. For others up to 20 weeks are ne sary, with the first 10 weeks concentrated on behavior mana ment and the second 10 week period focused on acade assessment.

After assessment data in a certain subject area are compi strengths and weaknesses are identified and objectives written. The process of matching the child's learning charac istics to the appropriate instructional material and teach technique is then undertaken. At this stage the teacher kn what types of material will most interest the child, and rea made materials can be adapted accordingly. Often in sub areas such as reading and math, several programs, includ those used in the child's home school, are tried and evaluat

Before the arrival of the target exit date, the school person of the child's home school are contacted and invited to visit assessment class. A meeting (or "staffing," as it is sometir called) is held to review all the assessment findings and the r ommendations on materials and methods that were most s cessful. A behavior management program is often an impor part of this discussion. Particular attention is paid to the tra tional school setting where one teacher is responsible for la group instruction. The assessment team advises staff as to best use of data in this situation.

Occasionally a tutor or community agency is contacte provide supplemental volunteer help. The instructional ad sor follows up on the progress the child makes when he retu to his new or regular placement and helps the teacher ad procedures that were found to be successful in the assessm class.

PARENT INVOLVEMENT

An important part of the assessment comes from the contributions of parents, who become involved and learn about their child in a variety of ways, including:

Home visits made by both the master teacher and instructional advisor.

Frequent (at least twice monthly) classroom visits, during which the parent observes behind a one-way mirror.

Parent notebooks, which are started during the first week of the child's stay. These notebooks are the weekly communication link with the assessment class and contain all relevant information such as assessment findings, behavior observations, lists of specific strengths and weaknesses, behavioral objectives, and specific suggestions for home involvement.

Behavior management programs, which are initiated on an individual basis and usually are done through a programed, workbook approach.

Parents often find that the specific knowledge they acquire about their child helps them to accept weaknesses while maximizing the child's many strengths. In addition, this involvement complements the parents' understanding of educational concerns and placement considerations for handicapped children in general.

CONCLUSION

Unlike the usual one or two hour assessment packages typically used by schools, the assessment class concept offers a short term, intensive investigation of the whole child. This approach gives a child the chance to demonstrate his various learning strengths, as well as weaknesses, over time. Assessment thus becomes more valid and more reliable. The final goal of the class is to provide the child, his parents, and his teacher with information on the best way to enhance the learning process.

It is recognized that this assessment class, because of its location within a university, is perhaps in an ideal situation—one that cannot be replicated easily in school systems that are not located near a college or university. The concept, however, is a workable one if the teacher is well trained in the use of diagnostic measures, has access to and knowledge of materials, has an aide or access to volunteers, and if the class is small enough to be transported on a short term basis.

Determining how a child learns and how best to remediate his problems is not an easy task. It becomes an impossible task if the examiner must do so in one hour only. For some children, an assessment class is the only fair answer.

THE UNFAVORED GIFTED FEW

It is ironic that in setting up the Office
of the Gifted and Talented the Federal Government made it a part
of the Bureau of Education for the Handicapped.

Gene I. Maeroff

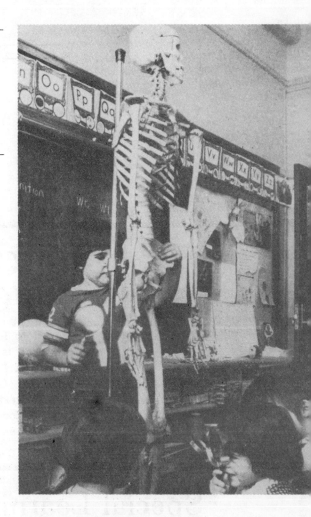

*S*tudents discussing a
skeleton's joints at
Brooklyn's P.S. 208,
which participates
in a program for in-
tellectually gifted
children between
the ages of 4 and 7.

Every day he would cry, shamed by a
teacher who chided him for being different and ridiculed by classmates who
tormented him for being "peculiar."

Several months later, David was enrolled in a school that has a program
for children like him.

What set David apart from the other
children was not a physical handicap or
mental deficiency but superlative intelligence. He is one of one million to two
million gifted children in the United
States who represent 2 percent to 4 percent of the nation's elementary and secondary school pupils, and their plight is
finally beginning to get the attention
that was denied for so long. They are,
said Sidney P. Marland Jr., the former
United States Commissioner of Education, among "our most neglected" students. According to Julian C. Stanley
Jr., a psychologist who founded the
Study of Mathematically Precocious
Youth at Johns Hopkins University in
Baltimore, most of what passes as
education for the gifted in the United
States is, "even at best, potentially
dangerous" because youngsters are
held back instead of being permitted to
move ahead as fast as they are able.

- "The Unfavored Gifted Few," Gene I. Maeroff, *The New York Times Magazine*, August 21, 1977. ©1977 The New York
Times Company.

For gifted children, knowledge is its own reward. Creativity is often their hallmark. From the very beginning, they are unlike other children in the classroom. Their attention span is longer, their learning rate is faster, their potential for abstraction is greater, their sensitivity is keener and their need for exploration in depth is overwhelming. Their drive for perfection makes them fearful of mistakes, and they are themselves discomfited by mental capabilities they possess but do not yet fully understand.

New and challenging educational approaches are needed for teaching the gifted, but change has come slowly in the more than five years since Marland, now president of the College Entrance Examination Board, compiled his report in response to a Congressional mandate. Dorothy A. Sisk, director of the Federal Government's Office of the Gifted and Talented, which was created as a result of the Marland report, estimates that no more than 4 percent of the nation's gifted are fully getting the special educational services they require.

Some, like John Tucker, have been lucky enough to attend schools that are willing to give them extra attention. When John was just 2½ years old and able to identify the makes of automobiles, his parents thought he was distinguishing the cars by their shapes. It was not long, though, before they realized that their son had taught himself to read by learning to sound out letters and words on "Sesame Street" and "The Electric Company." And by the time he was 4, John was reading books for an hour every morning and two hours every evening.

Now that he has turned 7, John is accomplishing feats that make his parents, neither of whom is a college graduate, forget that he is only a second grader in his neighborhood school in Catonsville, Md. He is reading on the level of a high school student and doing mathematical problems given a youngster entering junior high.

Yet even John's public school is reluctant to allow him to skip a grade, which his parents think would be appropriate. And for many parents of gifted children, it is not uncommon for them to encounter school officials who do not recognize the children's special intellectual abilities.

Last year at this time, for example, Mr. and Mrs. Armand DeToro of suburban Chicago tried to get the local public school to accept their son, Jeffrey, as an early entrant for the following fall. Only 4 years old, Jeffrey was extremely verbal and could already read and do arithmetical calculations. The teacher

Prekindergarten child doing a math problem at an experimental preschool at the University of Washington, Seattle.

who examined Jeffrey turned down the request for early entrance. She acknowledged that Jeffrey could read, but said that he had no comprehension of what he was reading.

So, Jeffrey, who is now 5 years old, will be starting school this fall. While he was waiting to be old enough to begin kindergarten, Jeffrey spent a good part of each week in the public library pursuing personal research projects in astronomy and geography. His parents had his I.Q. tested and found it to be more than 180. (Most educators feel that the gifted range begins somewhere above 130.)

Being gifted can be a liability, and it is ironic that in setting up the Office of the Gifted and Talented the Federal Government made it a part of the Bureau of Education for the Handicapped. The office has only $2.5 million to spend annually on the gifted. There is another $4 million available for the gifted through the Elementary and Secondary Education Act and a few smaller programs, yielding a grand total of $6.5 million in Federal moneys for the gifted. (Each year, the same Department of Health, Education and Welfare allots $2 billion for the education of the economically disadvantaged and $600 million for the education of the handicapped.) Thus, even if a school were to

recognize its gifted children, special programs might not be instituted simply because of a lack of funds.

Champions of increased funding for the gifted face several formidable hurdles: the charge of "elitism"; the emphasis on inclusion, not exclusion, in our schools; the belief that gifted children can make it on their own.

Egalitarianism is the order of the day and the idea of giving extra help to those who are already ahead of the pack strikes critics as being akin to allowing 7-foot Kareem Abdul-Jabbar to wear stilts on the basketball court. Many parents of the gifted, intimidated by this mood, are resigned to accept and be grateful for small favors.

"One of the problems in stimulating support for education of the gifted," Sisk says, "is the inherent feeling of parents that it is not quite appropriate to demand programs for their children. If those same parents had children with defects, they would be willing to seek every bit of professional and educational help for their children."

The attitude is not new. Lewis M. Terman, the pioneer in education of the gifted, who began a long-term study of gifted children in 1921, remarked al-

Learning liquid measurements. The preschool is trying to refine methods for the early identification and education of gifted youngsters ranging in age from 2 to 5.

1. PERSPECTIVE

most 50 years ago that "it is a curious fact that special classes for bright children are strenuously opposed by a few of the country's leading educational authorities. Their opposition seems to derive from an extreme democratic bias which minimizes native inequalities of endowment and scents the danger of class favoritism in every departure from the plan of a single curriculum for the entire school population."

Even in Newton, Mass., which has one of the country's leading public school systems, the Angier Elementary School encountered objections when it wanted to have a mathematics laboratory to supplement classroom work for gifted children. The P.T.A. provided $500 for the project this spring, but only on the condition that the laboratory not be limited to the gifted.

All across the country, the emphasis is on inclusion, not exclusion, and an upshot of this has been to expand the definition of a gifted child; the new label is "gifted and talented" — so as to throw the net as wide as possible. The broadened definition therefore includes the intellectually gifted as well as students whose exceptional performance or potential is in a single academic field, in creative or productive thinking, in the visual or performing arts, in "psychosocial" skills (group leadership) or in "kinesthetic" ability (dance and athletics).

Most educators working in the field of the gifted accept the widened version of gifted and talented, some because they truly believe that the older, strictly intellectual definition is wrong in its narrowness. Others find the new emphasis distasteful, but are willing to live with it if it makes the idea of aiding the intellectually gifted more palatable. Indicative of the official outlook is the fact that of the 55 nationwide projects to which the Federal Office of the Gifted and Talented is contributing, only two are purely for the intellectually gifted.

Adding to the problem of winning support for the intellectually gifted is the persistent belief in many circles that children of extraordinary intelligence should be able to make it on their own. "I feel that the gifted child, despite the concern of many parents, is well able to take care of himself," says Bruno Bettelheim, the psychologist. "If he isn't, then he isn't gifted."

Advocates of aid for the intellectually gifted reject this argument. They maintain that there must be stimulation for the gifted and that there is even some evidence that failure to nurture intellectual ability can cause it to wither. "We are increasingly being stripped of

the comfortable notion that a bright mind will make it on its own," Marland wrote in his report to Congress. "Intellectual and creative talent cannot survive educational neglect and apathy."

Helen Rosenthal, who teaches in Public School 208 in Brooklyn, one of nine New York City schools that participated in the remarkable program — funded by the Astor Foundation — for 500 intellectually gifted children between the ages of 4 and 7, has witnessed the ravages of the neglect and apathy described by Marland. David was one of her pupils.

[ ]

A special policy statement by the New York State Board of Regents last year warned that the continued failure of local school districts to mount programs for the gifted is leading to frustration and boredom, making underachievers of such children and prompting some to drop out of school. The dropout phenomenon has been documented by several studies, including one in the Midwest that found that gifted children drop out at a rate anywhere from three to five times greater than the rest of the population.

John Tucker is used to teachers explaining to him facts and figures that he has read and understood. Once, during an individual tutoring session, his arithmetic teacher introduced a fe Greek symbols to him in the context a problem, explaining at length wha the letters were. John, a shy chil merely nodded assent; he alread knew the entire Greek alphabet, havir come across it in one of his books a memorized it.

Eric Jablow of Brooklyn discovere early what being gifted meant. H showed an unusually strong interest arithmetic in the first grade and d voured assignments as quickly as h teacher could supply them. But th teacher was loath to provide Eric wit work that was much more than a yea or two beyond the rest of the class.

"The teacher gave me a little mo advanced problems," Eric recall "but not that much more advance problems that probably would hav come under the heading of second-c third-grade mathematics. But I sti was uninterested. From then on, I wa extremely bored with mathematic . . . [My parents and I] felt that if I d not get into more advanced studi soon, I would get so frustrated wit math that I would lose all interest schooling."

Yet another difficulty seems to be tl haphazard way in which the educa tional system goes about identifyir the intellectually gifted, especiall among girls and minority children

reschoolers listening to music. The attention span of gifted children is longer than others their age, their learning rate is faster.

ON RECOGNIZING A YOUNG EINSTEIN

Even the young Albert Einstein was not immediately recognized as intellectually gifted. All too often, a child's extraordinary intelligence is overlooked as the signs go undetected or are misinterpreted. A gifted youngster who is shy may not allow his talents to flourish and one who is bored may be falsely labeled as lazy. Parents who train themselves to be aware of the traits and behavior of the gifted will be better able to insure that their own gifted children do not get shortchanged in a system that is not geared to the needs of the exceptional.

A toddler who exhibits precociousness should be carefully watched. By drawing comparisons with other children of the same age, parents may see that their own youngsters are speaking in more complex sentences and using a larger vocabulary. Gifted children may also be reading earlier and showing an unusual amount of curiosity. They tend to be especially sensitive and creative, recognizing cause-and-effect relationships to which their peers are largely oblivious.

Once they enter school, gifted children often perform difficult tasks more easily than their classmates, and are able to do work equivalent to that being done by children at least a year or two older than they. A child who is getting very good grades and registering achievement test scores well above average may be gifted, though sometimes boredom or negative feelings may prevent a gifted child from displaying his or her potential.

Gifted students in the upper elementary and junior high school grades are capable of work well beyond their grade level, and if their special abilities have not come to light by that age, there are probably signs that they are not being sufficiently challenged. One gifted girl was finally identified because not

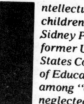

ntellectually gifted children are, said Sidney P. Marland Jr., former United States Commissioner of Education, among "our most neglected" students.

only was she getting 100's on her tests, but also she was filling the margins of the tests with doodles that she drew after completing the examinations well ahead of her classmates.

Parents who suspect their children are gifted should ask the school to administer an individual intelligence test and perhaps a creativity test as well. If the school refuses, parents should take their children to private psychologists for the testing. But it is most important that parents should try to work within the system

and get the cooperation of school officials, rather than become belligerent. The child stands to be the loser if the teacher and principal feel threatened by the family.

What is vital is that the parents of a gifted child recognize that they have a special responsibility to work with the youngster and do all they can to help him or her. "The parents of a bright child need to spend as much time nurturing the child's talents as they would meeting the needs of a handicapped child," said William C. George, associate director of the Study of Mathematically Precocious Youth at Johns Hopkins University.

Parents of other gifted children are natural allies and a lot can be achieved by forming advocacy groups and working together.

Careful preparations should be made for meetings with school officials, and the more that parents can do to document the case on behalf of their children, the greater the likelihood of success. Parents should learn about the kinds of programs that exist for gifted children around the country and be able to propose some possibilities for their own youngsters. "Don't blunder in and don't be put off by the argument that your child is exceptional and nothing can be done for him," George said.

Advice and assistance for parents of the gifted is available from several sources, including the following organizations:

The Association for the Gifted
Council for Exceptional Children
1920 Association Drive
Reston, Va. 22091
Leadership Training Institute
316 W. Second Street
Los Angeles, Calif. 90012

Office of the Gifted and Talented
United States Office of Education
400 Sixth Street, S.W.
Washington, D.C. 20202

both sexes. Such children may be left to languish in inappropriate classroom settings throughout their years in school.

Demonstrating the magnitude of the problem was a survey by the United States Office of Education in which more than half of the school administrators claimed that there

were no gifted children in their schools, a dubious contention in light of the belief that the intellectually gifted are distributed fairly evenly throughout the population. "Many states circumvent having to serve gifted kids by simply not identifying them as gifted," says Sisk.

Terman found a half-cen-

tury ago that teachers were not skilled in identifying the gifted, and Julian Stanley of Johns Hopkins thinks that matters have not improved greatly. The university's mathematics department recently sponsored a contest for the ablest 11th graders in metropolitan Baltimore, and asked high school teachers to

1. PERSPECTIVE

recommend candidates. Missing from the list of nominees were 19 students who several years earlier had been high scorers in the annual "talent search" by the Study of Mathematically Precocious Youth (S.M.P.Y.) at Johns Hopkins.

Stanley invited these youngsters who were not nominated by their teachers to join the competition, and they won five of the top 12 spots, including first place. "Apparently, students who would score high in such a contest tend to be relatively invisible in their math classes," he said. "They are not perceived as being truly outstanding. The subject matter isn't advanced enough to reveal their brilliance."

[ ]

Educators debate the best way to aid the gifted, if they are to be served at all. One basic approach is called "acceleration"; another is "enrichment." There is an inevitable overlap between the two. Acceleration involves letting a student work at a higher grade level — for example, giving sixth-grade books to a fourth grader or even advancing him into a sixth-grade class. Enrichment calls for keeping a student on grade level, but giving him assignments and experiences that enable him to go into greater depth on subjects than his less gifted peers. Stanley is a leading advocate of acceleration, and S.M.P.Y. is one of the nation's most important vehicles for identifying the mathematically able and steering them in the proper direction.

Each year, Stanley and his small staff ask teachers and principals in Maryland and surrounding states to nominate outstanding seventh graders. The youngsters are given the Scholastic Aptitude Test, which is normally used for college admissions purposes. Stanley has found that the S.A.T. is valuable in predicting which students can most benefit from the radical acceleration of their mathematical education.

One balmy day last spring, in Shriver Hall Auditorium on the Johns Hopkins campus, 190 11- and 12-year-olds — whose scores on the S.A.T. surpassed those of the average college-bound high school student — gathered for what has become an annual ceremony. There were all the trappings of a commencement exercise as children showed up in their Sunday best, accompanied by beaming parents with younger brothers and sisters in tow. Flashbulbs popped and waves of applause rolled across the audience as youngsters marched to the stage to get rolled-up certificates that had the appearance of diplomas. It was an old-fashioned celebration of intellect, almost a subversive activity in a day when tests are being assailed for their nonegalitarian role in ranking and sorting.

Chi-Bin Chien, the 11-year-old son of Taiwanese immigrants, was the star of the afternoon. This serious-looking, bespectacled child scored 750 on the mathematics portion of the S.A.T. and 710 on the verbal portion, placing him ahead of 97 percent of the high school students who take the tests, which have a ceiling of 800.

Like 80 other gifted students who have been identified by S.M.P.Y. since 1972, Chi-Bin is expected to begin college early. Six of the eight S.M.P.Y.-sponsored students who are now college seniors, none older than 18, were among the 550 persons in the entire country to win National Science Foundation fellowships this year. Eric Jablow was guided into college at 11½ by S.M.P.Y., straight out of the sixth grade, and is now a 15-year-old Brooklyn College graduate and one of the N.S.F. recipients. He has almost a perfect "A" average and will enter Princeton in the fall to pursue a Ph.D. in mathematics.

The vast majority of students identified through S.M.P.Y. do not go directly into college, however, and the program tries to help them find opportunities more suitable to their needs. Some skip a grade or two; some take a few courses with older students; some take part-time study in college, and some get special tutoring to give them a greater challenge.

Although S.M.P.Y. is a catalyst, not a teaching program, it does provide a limited amount of instruction. Older S.M.P.Y. students are matched with younger ones for tutoring, and there are Saturday and summer workshops for students. A number of workshops that S.M.P.Y. developed are being replicated elsewhere in the United States. This summer, the seventh graders honored recently at Johns Hopkins were given a seven-week course that brought them to the level of a high school student who has already completed plane geometry and the second year of algebra.

Once students have mastered the usual work for their age, they often are confronted by another obstacle — resistance to acceleration by those who fear it will lead to emotional maladjustment. As it is, negative stereotypes haunt the gifted almost everywhere. Even the New York State Board of Regents in its policy statement spoke of the gifted as "loners" or "eccentric."

Many gifted children feel that image is incorrect and that the solicitude is misplaced. Says Joseph Bates, who was a freshman at Johns Hopkins at 13 and is now a 21-year-old doctoral candidate at Cornell, "I didn't go to high school, so I'm not terribly certain exactly what's there. But it seems to me that college offers many of the same things that high school offers. If you're ready for the academics, I think you should have the opportunity to skip. . . . When I first went to Hopkins, I entered a freshman class with freshmen. The freshmen assume everyone else is their age. They're trying to get into the courses and experience college for the first time, so I didn't feel out of place in skipping four grades and going into college. I met friends. . . .

"I find that the ages of my friends vary tremendously. I have friends who are 24 whom I get along with very well and I have friends who are 16 whom I

Tots at Seattle's experimental preschool are exposed in small groups to an informal curriculum that includes science, language, dramatics and art.

participating in many of the physical activities that all children their age need to build coordination in their bodies. To a visitor, it looks like a nursery school until he observes the children doing things that are atypical for their age. A 4-year-old is reading "Little House on the Prairie." A group of youngsters is making graphs, measuring and recording the heights and weights of their pets. Another group is studying ecology, talking about people's need for shelter and what kinds of protection houses must provide in various climates. Some have been given costumes and props, and will be asked to make up characters and stories. Still another group has a container of water into which substances are being immersed to see which will dissolve.

It was this school that a

suburban Westchester County couple recently visited in their cross-country search for a school for their 2½-year-old son. "We wrote to Senator Javits, who referred us to Dorothy Sisk, who told us about the experimental preschool at the University of Washington," says the child's mother, a physician. She and the boy's father, a college professor, are considering relocating so they can send their son to the school, one of the few of its kind.

The child, still in diapers and barely three feet tall, is already reading and speaking English, French, Hebrew, Yiddish and Spanish, languages spoken by his parents. He has dabbled in Danish. He is studying music theory — he would like to play the guitar but is not big enough to hold the instrument — and he is carrying out basic scientific experi-

get along with. . . . There are some things you can say I missed. When I was at Hopkins, I did not date much. I didn't go out with girls much. But when I was at Hopkins, I didn't feel ready for that. I was into my studies and I enjoyed my time at Hopkins. Now, I am a lot more interested in that and I have time. I have time for meeting girls and going out."

While Joseph may be untypical, and there are enough tales of maladjustment to offset his favorable experience, there is no assurance that some of the misfits might not have had as unpleasant a time had they remained with children of their age.

☐

Any comprehensive description of the nation's treatment of its gifted tends to be a portrait of frustration illuminated by glimmers of hope. Legislatures in Delaware and Massachusetts have ordered the implementation of programs for every gifted child, but in Dela-

ware there is no financial aid and in Massachusetts there is no enforcement. Pennsylvania and some other states have put regulations on the books, but have not fully implemented them.

Yet, there are solid signs of progress, such as the Center for the Study of Gifted Children at the University of Washington in Seattle, which is trying to refine methods for the early identification and education of intellectually gifted youngsters of pre-kindergarten age. In a two-story, wooden house in the middle of the campus, the university is operating an experimental preschool for 30 children ranging in age from 2 to 5.

The tots attend the school each day, getting exposed in small groups to an informal curriculum that covers science, arithmetic, social studies, language, dramatics and art. They circulate through the six first-floor rooms

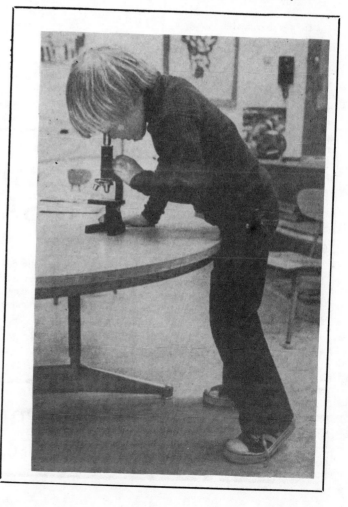

1. PERSPECTIVE

ments. "It's hard to fit all this into the schedule of a little boy who still has to nap every afternoon," his mother says, laughing. She is concerned about providing him with a setting in which he can have peer stimulation and proper social development.

They are willing to move, even if it is only for the two remaining pre-school years, because they can find nothing for their child in New York and in other parts of the country in which they have looked. Their frustration is enormous, having already been told by a member of their local school board in Westchester that "it is not the responsibility or the function of public schools to deal with such children."

Two Approaches to Identification of Gifted Students

JOSEPH S. RENZULLI
LINDA H. SMITH

Abstract: This investigation compared the efficiency and effectiveness of traditional and case study approaches to the identification of academically gifted students in the elementary grades. Time and cost analyses were carried out, as was an examination of the usefulness of various types of information included in case study formats. The results suggest that the case study approach is generally superior to the traditional approach because of its consideration of multiple sources of information. The case study approach was effective in identifying gifted minority students and was found to be less costly and time consuming than others have suggested.

JOSEPH S. RENZULLI *is Associate Director, Bureau of Educational Research, and* LINDA H. SMITH *is Instructor and Research Associate, Department of Educational Psychology, University of Connecticut, Storrs.*

O NE of the continuing concerns in programing for gifted students is the efficiency and effectiveness of various methods that are used in the identification process. Until recently, giftedness was viewed almost entirely in terms of high measured intelligence. Thus, comparative studies of identification procedures have traditionally used individual intelligence tests as the ultimate criterion measure for judging the efficiency and effectiveness of alternative approaches to identification (Pegnato & Birch, 1959; Martinson & Lessinger, 1960; Baldwin, 1962; Blosser, 1963). In recent years, however, giftedness has come to be viewed as a concept that is much broader than solely high intelligence (Renzulli, 1973; Gallagher, 1975; Sato, 1974). Consequently, a wider variety of identification procedures have been developed.

In view of this broadened conception of giftedness, the use of individual intelligence tests as the ultimate criterion in comparative studies is a questionable practice because it is obviously biased against identification procedures that do not rely heavily on measures of intelligence. The purpose of this study, therefore, was to compare two general approaches to identification using an alternative criterion measure to judge efficiency and effectiveness. The study also investigated the cost of the two approaches and the usefulness of certain types of information that are used in identification.

Description of Identification Procedures

Data from seven school districts that were initiating programs for gifted students in grades one, three, and five were gathered and analyzed in order to obtain basic information relating to the development of appropriate methods and techniques for identifying

"Two Approaches to Identification of Gifted Students," Joseph S. Renzulli, Linda H. Smith, *Exceptional Children*, Vol. 43 No. 6, May 1977. ©1977 The Council for Exceptional Children.

1. PERSPECTIVE

academically gifted students. Three of these school districts, referred to as Districts 1, 2, and 3, used what will be known in this article as the traditional approach. Essentially, this method consisted of (a) administering group ability tests to all students in the grades from which program participants would be selected and (b) administering an individual intelligence test to all students whose score was above a certain level on the group test.

The remaining four districts participating in the study used case study approaches as the main means for identifying program participants. Three of the case study approaches were adopted from formats developed in Florida, California, and Illinois, while the fourth district used a format that was developed by project personnel. These districts will be referred to as Districts 4, 5, 6, and 7, respectively.

Although the various case study approaches differ somewhat in the particular types of information and instruments that they include, most of the formats include data that can be classified into the following categories:

1. Information based on aptitude and/or achievement test scores.
2. Information based on ratings by present and/or past teachers.
3. Past performance information included in students' cumulative record folders.
4. Information based on parent ratings.
5. Information based on student self ratings.

The procedures for actually carrying out the case study approaches also tended to remain rather uniform from district to district. The required information on each child was gathered by professional and clerical personnel and then submitted to a selection committee for review and assessment.

Comparison of Efficiency

One of the major objectives of this study was to investigate the efficiency of various approaches to the identification of academically gifted students. Efficiency is defined as (a) the amount of time (in terms of professional and clerical staff/hours) that was devoted to identification activity and (b) the cost in dollars for carrying out these activities. An additional dimension of efficiency is concerned with the usefulness of particular types of information that were gathered for purposes of making selection decisions.

Time and Cost Analysis

Copies of an instrument entitled the *Log for Recording Preselection Activities* were provided to all persons involved in the identification process. These persons were requested to record their time according to a predetermined classification system that consisted of such tasks or activities as reviewing student records and compiling information, individual testing, group testing, and completing rating scales. Using salary and fringe benefit information that was entered in the logs, all time entries were multiplied by adjusted hourly pay rates.

The time and cost information derived from this procedure is summarized in Table 1. Inspection of this table reveals some interesting comparisons between the traditional and case study approaches. Although the traditional approach is supposed to be relatively mechanical (i.e., preselection is based on a group test cutoff score followed by an individual intelligence test), the authors note that there were small differences between the two approaches with regard to the amount of project teacher's time devoted to identification activity. In addition, a relatively large amount of administrator's time was spent in identification related activity in the districts using the traditional approach. As might be expected, time devoted to identification by regular classroom teachers and secretaries was significantly higher in most of the districts using the case study approach.

The total number of hours devoted to identification in the districts employing the traditional approach ranged from 305 hours to 455 hours; the mean for the three districts was 373 hours. A proportionate range was found when these figures were converted to dollar amounts. In the four districts using the case study approach, it can be seen that with the exception of District 7, there was also a fair amount of consistency in the number of hours expended on identification activities. The range in total hours was between 106 (District 5) and 151.75 (District 6), with costs being proportionate to the differences in hours.

As far as District 7 was concerned, the disproportionate amount of time devoted to identification activity was generally accounted for by the large number of hours recorded by school administrators. These individuals were responsible for developing a case study format prior to actually engaging in the screening and selection process. This devel-

TABLE 1

Summary of Time and Cost in Identifying Gifted Students by Means of Traditional and Case Study Approaches

Type of Approach	Project Teacher		Administrators		Secretaries		Teachers		State Psychologist		Total	
	Hours	Cost	Hours	Cost	Hours	Cost	Hours	Cost	Hours	Cost	Hours	Cost
Traditional												
District 1	104.75	817.05	16.50	208.89	—	—	12.75	107.01	171.00	1710.00	305.00	2842.95
District 2	139.00	1615.18	16.00	201.44	—	—	72.05	584.65	132.00	320.00	359.00	3721.27
District 3	47.50	480.70	250.50	2677.34	26.00	49.40	5.00	37.45	126.00	1260.00	455.00	4504.39
Mean	97.08	970.78	94.33	1029.22	8.67	16.47	29.93	243.04	143.00	1430.00	373.00	3689.70
Case Studies												
District 4	109.50	1158.51	—	—	7.00	27.79	23.00	200.24	—	—	139.50	1386.54
District 5	66.00	620.40	4.25	50.31	—	—	35.75	319.29	—	—	106.00	990.00
District 6	53.25	626.75	16.25	224.40	35.00	160.53	47.25	406.36	—	—	151.75	1418.05
District 7	197.00	[a]	482.75	[a]	66.50	[a]	148.50	[a]	—	—	894.75	[a]
Mean [b]	106.44	801.89	125.81	91.57	27.13	62.77	63.63	308.63	—	—	323.00	1264.85

[a] Could not be calculated because information on salaries and overhead costs was not submitted.
[b] Mean costs are calculated on the basis of three districts.

opmental activity, in addition to the involvement of a second school building (and therefore double administrator time in such activities as staff meetings, etc.), may explain why such a large amount of time was required for identification activity in District 7.

In an attempt to evaluate the efficiency of alternative approaches to identification, time and cost figures were analyzed in relation to the ratio between the total number of students who had been screened and selected. The word screened is used here to describe any youngsters for whom data had been gathered, regardless of whether or not that youngster was ultimately selected for the program. Table 2 presents a breakdown of the number of students screened, the number of students selected, the ratio between these two figures, and the cost and hours spent per selected student. Inspection of this table shows that the mean ratio of screened to selected students was slightly lower for those districts using the traditional approach. The significance of this difference is minimized however, when considering the relative cost of screening students using the traditional versus case study approach. Whereas the mean cost per screened student in the traditional districts was $16.64, the average cost for the case study districts in which information on salaries was submitted was only $5.23.

Usefulness of Case Study Information

In an attempt to investigate the usefulness of various types of information that constitute the four case study formats, all selection committee members were asked to indicate the value of each type of data in making his or her individual decisions in selecting students for program participation. Following this rating, each committee member was asked to estimate the value or usefulness of each type of information in influencing the group decision making process (i.e., the decision of the selection committee as a whole).

In three of the four case study districts, scores on some type of intelligence or achievement test were rated as one of the most highly useful types of information in making selection decisions. In the fourth district (District 7), intelligence test scores received the lowest usefulness rating and achievement tests received the second lowest rating. This major discrepancy between District 7 and the other three case study districts may have been due in part to the fact that District 7 served a large

1. PERSPECTIVE

proportion of minority group youngsters, and it is generally acknowledged that intelligence and achievement tests are not as valid for this group as they are for the population in general.

One type of information that was judged to be highly useful by a large number of selection committee members was ratings supplied by students' current teachers and information included in students' cumulative records or obtained through interviews with previous teachers. Health and family background information was judged to be of little value in making selection decisions, as was information supplied by parents through the use of questionnaires or rating scales. Peer nomination information, which was gathered in District 7, received the highest usefulness rating by individuals and was also considered to be the most influential type of information in helping the total group to arrive at decisions.

Comparison of Effectiveness

The second major area of inquiry in evaluating the identification process had to do with the effectiveness of the respective approaches. Effectiveness was concerned with whether or not the most appropriate selections were made in placing students into gifted programs. Since individually administered tests of intelligence constituted one of the identification approaches being evaluated, the criteria for effectiveness consisted of followup ratings by regular classroom teachers and project teachers. Ratings were based on the degree to which teachers thought students were appropriately placed.

The results of this inquiry are presented in Table 3. By comparing the proportions at the bottoms of the columns for the two groups of regular classroom teachers, the authors note that there was a fair amount of consistency in making judgments regarding placement. In both traditional and case study districts, regular classroom teachers estimated that approximately 85% of the youngsters "definitely should be in the program."

A somewhat different picture emerges when a comparison of the overall ratings by the project teachers in districts using the traditional selection approach is made with those by project teachers in districts using the case study approach. Here it is found that approximately 79% of the youngsters in traditional approach districts were judged as: "def-

initely should be in the program," whereas the figure for case study districts was 92% of the students. The difference between these percentages was found to be statistically significant, and thus a significantly greater amount of certainty about placement in the case study districts so far as the project teachers were concerned can be noted.

Discussion and Conclusions

Several conclusions appear to be warranted as a result of the findings discussed in the preceding sections of this article. The first and perhaps most important general conclusion is that the identification process should be based on a variety of types of information that reflect several indicators of a youngster's superior performance or potential for superior performance in a program that is specifically designed to enhance academic ability.

This conclusion is based on two general trends that emerged from the data. First, the collection of a wide variety of information about a particular youngster does not seem to present any hardships as far as time and costs are concerned. Indeed, the case study approach costs approximately one-third as much as the traditional approach, which in its pure form requires only one type of information—intelligence test scores. However, persons who served on selection committees in the case study districts pointed out the need for some type of information that is based on standardized tests of intelligence or academic aptitude. Thus, it seems clear that certain features of both the traditional and case study approaches are optimally desirable in a comprehensive identification system.

Another conclusion related to the efficiency issue deals with the number of students that must be processed in order to make final selections. Although it has been suggested that the case study approach will result in an unmanageable number of nominees, such was not the case in the data obtained in this study. The ratio of students screened to those selected was only slightly higher in districts employing the case study approach, and thus, it seems safe to conclude that a case study approach is feasible as far as time and cost are concerned.

An additional finding that lends support to the case study approach is that it appears to be more sensitive to identifying academically

TABLE 2

**Summary of Number of Students Screened and Selected as Gifted by Means
of Traditional and Case Study Approaches**

Type of Approach	No. of students screened	No. of students selected	Ratio of screened to selected	Cost per selected student (in dollars)	Hours spent per selected student
Traditional					
District 1	225	31	7.26:1	91.70	9.84
District 2	220	24	9.17:1	155.05	14.96
District 3	221	40	5.53:1	112.62	11.38
Mean	222	31.67	7.32:1	119.79	12.06
Case studies					
District 4	217	25	8.68:1	55.46	5.58
District 5	308	28	11.00:1	35.36	3.79
District 6	233	45	5.18:1	31.51	3.37
District 7	267	51	12.29:1	[a]	17.54
Mean [b]	256.25	37.25	9.29:1	40.78	7.57

[a] *Could not be calculated because information on salaries and overhead costs was not submitted.*
[b] *Mean costs are calculated on the basis of three districts.*

able students in schools that serve minority group populations. A high level of effectiveness emerged in the followup ratings that were received from District 7, and this finding, coupled with extremely favorable comments regarding the identification of minority group children, suggests that a system based on diversified sources of information will help to take account of differences in youngsters' backgrounds in general. In other words, all types of differences in youngsters' backgrounds (e.g., racial, ethnic, socioeconomic, demographic) can be considered in a multiinformational approach, but such is not the case when identification rests solely on intelligence test scores. As greater efforts are made to expand the number of programs for gifted students, it will be important to have an identification system that is flexible enough to take account of population differences within states and within school districts that serve youngsters with a variety of backgrounds.

Relating to specific procedures for carrying out the identification process, an analysis of the value or usefulness of various types of information in making selection decisions suggests that the opinions of past and present teachers are an important consideration in identification. Peer nominations appeared to be a valuable source of information but, since this technique was used in only one case study district, its usefulness must be viewed as a tentative conclusion at this time. Finally, in view of the role that project teachers play in identification, it seems clear that some special arrangements must be made to allow these persons released time for identification activity.

TABLE 3
Number and Percentage of Students Identified by Regular Classroom Teachers
and Project Teachers as Qualified to be in Gifted Program

	Type of teacher			
	Regular Classroom		Project	
District	Number	Percentage	Number	Percentage
Traditional districts				
District 1				
Grade 1	3	100	9	82
Grade 3	6	75	7	88
Grade 5	7	100	7	70
District 2				
Grade 1	5	83	5	83
Grade 3	6	86	6	100
Grade 5	5	100	2	22
District 3				
Grade 1	4	80	4	80
Grade 3	3	60	7	88
Grade 5	6	100	8	100
Total Number & Average percent	49	88.33	55	79.22
Case study districts				
District 4				
Grade 1	6	100	6	100
Grade 3	5	100	6	100
Grade 5	8	80	7	88
District 5				
Grade 1	6	100	6	100
Grade 3	6	86	6	100
Grade 5	1	100	1	100
District 6				
Grade 1	9	69	10	77
Grade 3	15	88	14	82
Grade 5	14	93	13	87
District 7				
Grade 1	15	88	17	100
Grade 3	9	75	13	81
Grade 5	7	56	16	94
Total Number & Average percent	101	86.42	115	92.42

Don't make me walk when I want to fly

An open letter from a gifted child

"Don't Make Me Walk When I Want to Fly," John Scott, *Instructor*, No. 5 Vol. LXXXVI, January 1977. ©1977 The Instructor Publications, Inc.

1. PERSPECTIVE

MY NAME IS JOHN. I'm 16, and I have two younger brothers, Mark and Todd. On our school records, a green clip identifies all of us as *Ex Chs*, which for years mystified me, but which you know stands for Exceptional Child—the smarty pants variety.

My parents were told that my IQ is in the 160s and that my brothers weren't far behind. School was easy, and I was in the top five percent on SAT scores. Maybe I'm innately bright, but I have another theory as to why I became an *Ex Ch*.

Here's how I explain myself. I was born right after my grandfather's death, and my grandmother became a great influence in my life. At first it was almost full time. She spent her waking hours reading, showing, telling, taking me places—the latter starting when I was less than one year old.

Influence number two was almost as potent. My aunt is a reviewer of children's books. From the day I was born, boxes of books arrived at my grandmother's house. I can honestly say that I can't remember when I couldn't read. My grandmother thinks I recognized words at two, and it's probably true, for both my brothers did. Anyway, I spent hours on my grandmother's lap following along as she read, and I guess I learned automatically.

The other major contributors to my early life were my mother and father. My dad is a carpenter, and early he taught me how to use tools, how to measure exactly, how to be thrifty and neat in what I made. Under him, I developed precise skills. He's also an outdoor man and spent many hours with my brothers and me gardening, hiking, and camping. I learned innumerable lessons from my father, who is a truly great guy in a thousand ways.

My mother gave me order and oughtness in a low-key sort of way. I can never remember not folding my clothing neatly at night. Changing my clothes after school was automatic, and they got hung up, too. My brothers and I shared a room and each guy made his own bed—a hard, fast rule. Even on weekends when we got up ahead of our parents to watch cartoons, no one dared look at TV if his bed wasn't made. From my mother I also learned the rules of politeness—how to meet grown-ups, how to accept gifts. Don't knock it. This training gave me a lot of confidence.

It wasn't until I went to kindergarten that I realized I knew more or thought more complexly than other kids. Sunday school had been sort of vague. I would sit and read the Sunday school papers, but I honestly didn't know that the other kids couldn't read them.

In kindy I was a marked kid. I handed out papers for the teacher, read stories to the other kids, and once I even marked papers for the first-grade teacher. I didn't learn much except an important lesson that I've been learning ever since: One's peers are suspicious and resentful of you when you do things more quickly or better than they do. I soon found ways to hide or play down what I know, and I find myself still doing it today.

Since this is a letter for teachers, I want to tell you mostly what happened in school. Unlike many schools, it *did* try to take care of the *Ex Chs* in a variety of ways.

SKIPPING

I'm sorry to report that I got skipped twice. After my kindergarten performance, the first-grade teacher didn't want me. (Maybe it was those papers that I marked.)

Anyway, the principal convinced my parents I should start the next year in second grade.

At first I found myself behind the others in both motor and formal skills. I didn't write as small and neatly as they did, and had to do a lot of practicing at home for the first couple of months. Also, the kids who had been in first grade knew how to do their workbook exercises and they had less trouble sitting at their desks for long periods of time. Yet, I soon noticed that my classmates, who I was in awe of because they were older, made some pretty simple judgments and decisions which the teacher accepted. I learned to keep quiet.

My second skipping came after I was in fourth grade for two months. I felt the teacher wanted to get rid of her *Ex Ch* so she pushed me off on the fifth-grade teacher. It was the best break of my elementary years. I'll tell you why later—but I paid for it in high school.

Absolutely, I don't recommend skipping for *Ex Chs*. It may be an immediate solution, but it's a long-range detriment. It's no fun being 13, 14, and 15 in tenth, eleventh, and twelfth grades.

ENRICHMENT

If schools don't skip *Ex Chs*, then they have to provide more of the stuff that's called enrichment. Schools aren't set up for innovative enrichment—they could learn a lesson from my grandmother—but I'll describe what happened. A student interested in science or math was accommodated fairly easily. There were kits for them to build, experiments to do, advanced workbooks in math, and so on. Unfortunately, I was interested in books, social situations, aesthetics, and languages; so I was more of a problem. The school didn't have kits for me.

For example, in the summer between second and third grades, I met a Spanish boy. That fall I asked the principal I could learn Spanish, but he turned me down because there was no teacher to help me, and he wouldn't let me do it on my own. I think the prospect of a seven-year-old third grader learning Spanish independently may have been too much for him to accept.

LANGUAGE AND COMMUNICATION

My fifth-grade teacher was an elderly lady near retirement. She was a jewel, and I cried at her funeral last year. She may have had no training in what to do with an *Ex Ch*, but she was a natural. First, she talked to me about anything and everything. She introduced me to old-fashioned diagraming which I found to be great fun. We played games, with her trying to concoct a sentence that I couldn't diagram. She brought me Latin books and I would stay after school and talk Latin to her. Latin was the only other language she had ever learned, but from that experience I learned that I have a knack for languages. Today, I speak fairly fluent Spanish, French, and German, having learned the first two in high school and teaching myself the latter with the use of tapes, records, and self-study books.

She gave me Lamb's *Tales from Shakespeare*, then took me to see Hamlet and I became a disciple of the Bard . . . and was she ever sneaky! She insisted I train my memory and gave me passages of Shakespeare to memorize. I fell for it, seeing myself as the next John Gielgud. Today I'm grateful. Memorizing is not only a wonderful tool, it gives comfort and support in lonely moments.

She built my vocabulary by introducing me to complex words, and in our private conversations we used them freely—you never heard such talk! You may have sensed that she and I were almost clandestine in our special relationship. In front of others she treated me like them and I understood. Fifth grade was my happiest year, and I never had a better teacher.

SPECIAL EFFORTS

While I was in fifth grade, a new young principal who cared about Ex Chs came to our school. He set out to identify us and give us special things to do. Some of his projects were what I called, so-whats, but my brothers loved them. I didn't, but I respected him so much that I did them anyway. For example, he taught us how to estimate the height of a flagpole by measuring its shadow. He showed us how to estimate the number of bricks used to build our school. Today I amuse myself in boring situations by doing so-whats. In high school courses that were dull, I'd figure how many bricks would be needed to box in the room. Doodling is another good so-what. I find I can keep myself out of a lot of trouble by doodling.

The principal organized chess games and encouraged games such as Monopoly and 3-D checkers. He liked games and I think we all learned from playing them.

SPECIAL PROJECTS

By the time I was in sixth grade, the principal had convinced someone in authority that there should be a resource teacher to set up special projects for Ex Chs. He meant well, but we were better off when he was taking care of us.

Don't think me a snob, but the person who thinks up Ex Ch projects better be a former Ex Ch. Our resource teacher wasn't and didn't have much of a sense of humor. In October I was assigned a research project on Columbus. (Original idea, wasn't it?) The whole thing was pretty boring, but I did it and got into a lot of trouble. As part of the assignment was to do a piece of original writing, I wrote a funny (to me) soap-opera skit. My plot was that Isabella and Christopher were having an affair. Ferdinand discovered it and sent Chris off on the high seas. Further, Ferdy got his revenge by using Isabella's money to finance the project. The teacher went into shock and called my parents.

RESPONSIBILITY

My brothers and I were encouraged to earn our own money. I started with a paper route and soon had both brothers

---

Do you have to be gifted to teach the gifted?

INSTRUCTOR Teacher Awareness Questionnaire

What characteristics should teachers of gifted and talented (G/T) children have? To participate in this study, complete and mail the preaddressed, postpaid questionnaire below. Please answer ALL the questions. It isn't necessary to include your name and address. However, if you do, we will send you a bibliography of materials on gifted and talented children. All information will remain confidential. No names will be used in compiling the data. Watch future issues of INSTRUCTOR for study results.

Position _____ (a) Years taught _____ (b) age _____

(c) Degrees held: Bachelor's____ Master's____ M+30____ EdD/PhD____

Academic Average: (d) High School A_____ B_____ C_____ D_____

(e) Undergrad A__ B__ C__ D__ (f) Graduate A__ B__ C__ D__

Would you have wanted John (see article page 68) in your class? Yes No

Have you ever taught a G/T child? Yes No

Have you ever taught a group of G/T children? Yes No

Would you like to teach G/T children? Yes No

G/T children should be provided special programs. Yes No

Do you think G/T children should be taught in a:
Separate homogeneous group   Mixed group   Combination of both

(g) If you were told that starting next week you would be teaching G/T children, rate yourself on a one (poor) to six (outstanding) scale on how well you would be able to meet their needs.   1 2 3 4 5 6

(h) Were you ever identified by someone else as a gifted and/or talented child?   I was G/T   I was not G/T   I don't know

There are many definitions of gifted and talented and over the years the terms used to identify these children have changed. Give us yours. (Indicate whether it's a personal definition or a formal definition used by your school.) _____
_____
_____

On a one (unimportant) to six (important) scale, rate the following items as you perceive their importance by circling the number you select. On a space at the end of the number scale, rate yourself on the same item by writing in a number from one (poor) to six (outstanding).

Teachers of gifted and/or talented children should have:

1. Knowledge of nature and needs of G/T children, understanding how they think and learn as compared to other children.   1 2 3 4 5 6 _____

2. Knowledge of current research and information about G/T children.   1 2 3 4 5 6 _____

3. Special coursework and preparation in G/T.   1 2 3 4 5 6 _____

4. Skill with wide variety of teaching methods.   1 2 3 4 5 6 _____

5. Skill at testing and evaluating G/T children.   1 2 3 4 5 6 _____

6. Ability to study self and children and use the results to improve teaching.   1 2 3 4 5 6 _____

7. Skill in the psychology and practice of effectively working with groups (group dynamics).   1 2 3 4 5 6 _____

8. Supervised experience teaching G/T children.   1 2 3 4 5 6 _____

involved. We had it down pat, both distribution and collection. We paid our father a dollar to drive us to deliver Sunday papers.

Once we mastered paper delivery, we began looking for a way to earn greater profits. Since we had our own tools, which our father had taught us how to care for and use, we opened a gardening service. Throughout junior and senior high school we had all the lawns we could care for. Of course there were some family donations but most of the $3,100 I had in my savings account when I graduated from high school I had earned.

AESTHETICS

Starting in sixth grade (my parents had reservations, and I told none of my friends) I enrolled in ballet class. Today I don't want to be a ballet dancer and I'm through my John Gielgud period, but the ballet class was a great experience. I enjoyed the expressive movement, the music, the costumes, and even learned how to do some choreography.

I experimented on my grandmother's piano and took enough lessons to give me a limited facility. My tastes in music differ from my brothers; so my father helped me fix my own equipment in the headboard of my bed, and I listen with earphones.

THE FUTURE

As maybe you can guess, I hope to be a writer and am studying toward that end in college. I think I would also like to teach literature or languages in college.

In conclusion, I'd have to say that I came out of elementary school relatively unscathed. No teacher was ever really mean to me, and my fifth-grade teacher and the principal were great—I group them with my parents and grandmother in a special closed set.

But elementary school could have been a lot better. I spent a lot of time standing still, doodling, and pretending. Undoubtedly, the teachers had a lot of other children who needed their attention more than I did.

I want to finish with an idea and a question. The idea is, if you have an *Ex Ch* in your room, remember he has problems of his own. Be supportive, even protective, and never put him down in front of his peers. Help him fly when the world around him is walking.

The question—would you have wanted me in *your* room?

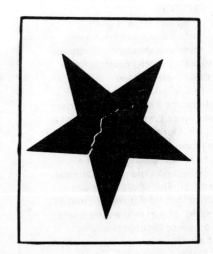

Prodigy From Plum Tree

Allen Rankin

WHEN Jim and Judy Hall took their firstborn child, Joe, home to the peaceful Blue Ridge hamlet of Plumtree, N.C., ten years ago, they expected to settle down quietly. But the physiological mysteries that produce genius—indeed the miracle of life itself—swiftly changed all that. At 14 months, Joe sprang his first major surprise. Exploring the floor, he found and popped into his mouth a felt-point pen. To show him that pens were not to be eaten but written with, his mother wrote the letters a b c on a tablet. Joe took the pen and copied the letters in a remarkably good and steady hand. Judy Hall, not sure she had really seen what she thought she had,

Clearly a potential genius, Joe was also a gravely ill little boy

then wrote the whole alphabet. Her infant son, not to be outdone, copied that, too—every letter of it!

Soon Joe was writing the entire alphabet from memory. Well before he was two, he drew a very good picture of a cat and under it wrote c a t. "Look at that!" exclaimed an aunt, pointing out the feat to a visiting schoolteacher. "Yes, I see it," said the teacher. "But," she added, "of course he can't do that." This was to be a typical reaction to Joseph Hall performances. People refused to believe what they were seeing or hearing.

Toward the end of his third year, Joe was reading everything he could lay hands on, including a high-school science textbook. And he was asking a hundred questions a minute about his favorite subjects, space and electronics.

Pride and Alarm. Before long, he had discovered the piano, and was playing chords and harmonious passages. His father, who is band director for county high schools, put off giving him his first piano lesson until the morning of his fifth birthday. A few months later, the little prodigy had mastered the simpler works of Bach, Beethoven and Mozart, and was composing some rather elaborate music of his own!

By now Jim and Judy Hall's pride was tinged with genuine alarm. How could they cope with a child who was physically and emotionally five years old but already had the original and probing mind of an adult scientist-artist?

A psychologist friend told them that Joe might well become another Mozart or Einstein if he could get the *right* training in his formative period. But who knew what that was?

"Prodigy from Plum Tree," Allen Rankin, *The Reader's Digest*, Vol. 109 No. 652, August 1976. ©1976 The Reader's Digest Association.

An educator suggested that they move to a big city that would have special programs for gifted children, concluding: "There's nothing in a little place like Plumtree for a boy like Joe."

The Halls disagreed. "There's nothing here for Joe," Judy argued, "except maybe his best chance to have a normal childhood. He'll have a long time to be smart, but not much longer to be a little boy."

Then, suddenly, it seemed that Joe's time might be shorter than anyone had thought. He had begun suffering from acute weakness and faintness. The diagnosis was leukemia.

Stunned, the Halls tried to keep the facts about the disease away from Joe, but he read up on leukemia and later even discussed the technical aspects of his treatment with Dr. Richard Patterson, head of the children's cancer program at the Bowman Gray School of Medicine in Winston-Salem.

One night, the five-year-old said to his mother, "I suppose my statistical chances don't look too promising, do they?" That night, and for many nights thereafter, he asked Judy to sit at his bedside and keep him company until he fell asleep.

Now the situation had changed. The Halls agreed that Joe must live and learn as much and as fast as possible. Like other parents of superkids, they soon found, however, that there is still comparatively little financial and psychological help for exceptionally gifted children.

Fearing that Joe, who longed to go to school, might not live to arrive there at age six, Judy wangled permission for him to "audit" the first grade at five. But Joe, by this time an eager student of astronomy, was bored nearly to tears.

Off the Scale. Judy managed to get him transferred to another school and skipped to the second grade. Joe loved his new teacher, Lola Young, who let him lecture the class on the wonders of planets and stars. And when the results of a standard intelligence test leaked out, the citizens of Plumtree, some of whom were hostile toward the "Know-It-All Kid," realized what a prodigy was in their midst. Most experts consider an I.Q. score of 175 or 180 an indication of top-level intelli-gence. Joe's score soared up the test scale, and he was assigned an I.Q. of 200!

"This means that in intellect this mountain child is probably far rarer than a one-in-a-million phenome-non," later commented Richard Stahl, director of the program for gifted and talented children at Ap-palachian State University.

Meanwhile, Jim and Judy Hall, who had long wondered why a boy like Joe had happened to *them*, were learning some interesting—if not too helpful—facts about giftedness:

• A gifted person might be de-scribed as an individual whose genes and control chemicals happen to ar-range themselves in lucky patterns during his conception, and thus com-bine the highest abilities of parents and/or ancestors, enabling him to excel in the proper environment.

• Potential geniuses are often firstborn children (as was Joe) or are the offspring of at least one "older" parent (Jim had been 35 when Joe was conceived).

• Super-giftedness crops up in families of every walk, race or social stratum.

• When a child's brilliance soars to an I.Q. of 180, or more, he is likely to suffer from being "too different" and to be unable to fulfill his bright promise—*unless* he gets an accele-rated education, is exposed to special enrichment programs at the normal grade level or is put in touch with minds as brilliant as his own.

Shadow of Leukemia. Joe's par-ents did all they could to make their gravely ill prodigy's days interesting. Further straining a budget weak-ened by medical bills, they bought him *some* of the books he begged for, the best chemistry set they could find and a splendid new grand piano. To make ends meet, Jim raised most of the vegetables and beef the family ate, and Judy canned hundreds of jars of produce.

Between spells of illness, Joe, at six, became a frequent pianist with the high-school bands his father di-rected. He won a county-wide talent contest with an impressive original composition titled "Five Thousand Miles of the Universe."

A reporter asked him, "What are you going to be when you grow up?"

"I don't know," the little boy re-plied, then added quietly, "I'm not sure I'm going to be anything."

Joe's sixth summer was bad. Sick much of the time, he was as restless as a caged animal. He had exhausted the resources of the local library and was making constant demands for more reading matter than the family could possibly afford. Desperate, Judy hoisted an SOS to the Army, the Navy, the Air Force, NASA, the Atomic Energy Commission and The Reader's Digest. "Do you have any technical material you can send Joe?" she wrote. "Anything at all!"

A week later, an Army staff car pulled up at the Halls' door and three officers got out, staggering un-der the weight of 400 pounds of technical manuals on subjects from the space program to guerrilla warfare.

Joe was ecstatic and, for a while, so was his mother. "I thought that 400 pounds of stuff would entertain him all summer," she says. Joe went through it in three weeks. Reprints of scientific articles from The Digest and brochures from NASA and the AEC were also quickly exhausted.

In March 1975, Wernher von Braun, the rocket wizard, sent a copy of his book *History of Rocketry and Space Travel*. Delighted, Joe raced through the volume—and spied an error. "If that Saturn V had been powered by J-2 engines," he wrote von Braun, "it would never have gotten off the ground." The great scientist sent back thanks. "You detected a mistake that had crept through all the painstaking proof-reading!"

That summer, the Halls received a visit from another super-bright young man—29-year-old Pat Gunkel, a researcher with New York's brainy Hudson Institute. "Talk? recalls Judy Hall happily. "You should have heard those two talk! About galaxies and time and rela-tivity and eternity. It was as though neither of them had ever had any-one to talk to before!"

A Place for Joe. About that time his mother heard of a new School for Gifted Children sponsored by Appalachian State University, in Boone, just 39 miles from Plumtree. Offering college-like courses on six consecutive Saturdays, this enrich-ment program, limited as it is, fills such a local need that 580 of the smartest kids in nine surrounding counties, ranging from preschool to ninth grade, were enrolled. But Joe's mind, says director Richard Stahl, "was simply too far ahead of most of the others at the school. Exploding with a thousand things, he was as disruptive as a bomb in the classes he chose."

Looking for a place where Joe might fit in, Stahl took him to a regular college-sophomore class in astronomy. This didn't work out much better. "Wow!" said one college student. "He doesn't belong in sophomore astronomy. Put him in graduate school."

In the end, Joe, today age ten, returned to Plumtree. I met him there recently—a slightly built, plucky little boy whose wise blue eyes twinkle mischievously behind horn-rimmed glasses.

He confided his belief that flying saucers are real and are "manned" by robots. His gadget-cluttered room serves as headquarters for the Joseph Hall UFO Research and Investigation Committee. The one-boy "committee" sends out a neatly mimeographed technical questionnaire to people all over the world who have reported sighting a UFO. He has received scores of completed forms from sighters—plus some 2000 letters from other precocious children or their parents.

Joe still has problems aplenty. Though he has skipped two years of school, he must endure a sixth-grade classroom that probably lags 10 or 12 years behind his learning capacity. That is, it lags in subjects he *likes;* in those he scorns as "unimportant," he's no better than his slowest classmates.

Still, despite this, Joe is as normal as any potential genius could possibly be. He loves to romp and whoop in the woods, to play baseball, to bedevil his three younger brothers and to be teased by them. He is explosively enthusiastic about his parents, his friends and his dog, Poochie. In other words, he is having a happy childhood and, as his mother notes, "Nobody can take that away from him."

Furthermore, Jim and Judy believe that if Joe had not had the extra drive, grit and zest for life that are the legacy of most superior children, he would not have won the fight, so far, against leukemia. Dr. Patterson adds, "Of the several hundred kids I've treated, Joe is one of eight or ten who have been in remission for five years or longer."

In comparison to this, any musings about whether he will become a great concert artist or an astronomer fade into insignificance. "Whatever the future brings," says Judy Hall quietly, "Jim and I have had Joe with us long enough to be forever grateful for that miracle, and for all the special wonder, joys and challenges he has already brought us."

THE GIFTED CHILD IN THE UNITED STATES AND ABROAD

Joe Khatena
Marshall University

The gifted movement began in the United States, we might say, with the interest, curiosity and industry of one of our very talented psychologists, Lewis M. Terman, in the early years of this century. His studies of mental tests and precocious children led eventually to two major contributions, namely, the construction and use of the *Stanford Binet* and the *Gentic Studies of Genius,* a monumental longitudinal study of more than 1,500 gifted Californian urban children from kindergarten through high school, followed through mid-life and reported in five volumes by Terman and his associates (e.g. Terman, 1925; Terman & Oden, 1959).

There is much we have learned from his sustained research about the intellectually gifted who as a group:

came from superior intellectual, physical and environmental
backgrounds, and generally maintain this superiority;

tended to be many-sided intellectually, emotionally stable,
and well adjusted, maintaining these with little incidence
of serious problems;

had normal marriages and sexual adjustment;

showed in general a low mortality rate;

were normal to superior in social intelligence, interests and
play activities, averaging better than most people on
nearly every personality trait;

were well in advance of their age mates in educational achievement
and benefitted by acceleration with almost no occurrence of
failure in school subjects generally obtaining A grades; and

went to college such that 70 percent became college graduates
(a third with academic distinction), 63 percent went to
graduate school, and 17 percent obtained doctoral degrees.

However, among the several variables that tend to reduce the generalizability of his findings are three relating to instrumentation. *First,* is the fact that IQ was used as the sole criterion for the iden-

"The Gifted Child in the United States and Abroad," Joe Khatena, *The Gifted Child Quarterly*, Vol. XXI No. 3, Fall 1977. ©1977 The National Association for Gifted Children.

tification of gifted children about which Catherine Cox Miles (1960) cites Terman as challenging educators, sociologists and psychologists to produce if they could:

> "..... another concept as effective as the IQ for delimiting of a group of talent to include the most successful students, the best achievers in the world, and...in the world of human relationships and human endeavor generally" (P. 51).

Second, is the fact that the *Stanford Binet* used to determine IQ is biased in favor of the verbally gifted, and so responsible for leaving out potentially non verbally low socio-economically gifted students from selection.

And *third,* the *Stanford Binet* was not constructed to include the screening of divergent thinking so that creatively gifted students were eliminated from selection.

Of course at the time the Terman studies began (1921) there were no effective intellectual measures that could yield a better index of superior abilities than IQ. But that IQ as an index of intelligence persists in being deified in some quarters, it is necessary to underscore Taylor's critical observation (1959) that "intelligence" is a concept created by western culture that stresses its important values, and that intelligence tests in our culture "essentially concerned themselves with how fast relatively unimportant problems can be solved without making errors," whereas in another culture, "intelligence might be a measure more in terms of how adequately important problems can be solved making all the errors necessary and without regard for time (P. 54).

MANY KINDS OF GIFTEDNESS

A recognition of the presence of many kinds of giftedness by the United States Office of Education in its recent report (Educating the Gifted, 1972) rather than the one kind identified by IQ is a reflection of the change in thought that occurred about giftedness over the past two decades or so. These have been identified as general intellectual ability, creative or productive thinking, specific academic aptitude, leadership ability, visual and performing arts abilities and psychomotor abilities.

General Intellectual Ability

Regarding general intellectual ability, thought on the subject has moved from general intelligence first defined in terms of Mental Age or MA by Alfred Binet and T. Simon (1905) in France, through Intelligence Quotient or IQ defined as a single index of general intelligence by Lewis Terman (1916) to an IQ differentiated as verbal, performance and global by David Wechsler (1966) in the United States.

Perception of intelligence as a univariate phenomenon moved towards perception of intelligence as a multivariate phenomenon, with major contributions coming from England and America. Through simple factorial analyses Charles Spearman (1927) in England derived his two factor theory of intelligence which saw general intellectual functioning as governed by some general mental

1. PERSPECTIVE

energy or "g" that entered into the functioning of a number of specific abilities called "s". Sir Cyril Burt (1949) and P. E. Vernon (1951) expanded this conception of intelligence into hierarchical models of human abilities. Both subscribe to the concept of Spearman's "g' as entering into all human mental functioning. *Burt's model* consists of a series of successive dichotomies: the first dichotomy emerges from the head of the hierarchy, the human mind, as the *relations* level or "g" and *practical* level (which includes psychomotor, mechanical and spatial abilities); these dichotomize to the next lower level or *associations* level, which again subdivide into the levels of perception and sensation. *Vernon's model* is headed by "g" which subdivides into two sets of major group factors, namely, verbal-educational or v:ed and kinesthetic motor or K:m factors with the latter being equivalent to Burt's "practical factor." The major factors subdivide into minor factors such that v:ed subdivides into verbal, numerical and educational factors while K:m subdivides into practical, spatial, mechanical and physical factors. These then divide still further into specific factors.

In America, L. L. Thurstone (1938) by using factor analyses discovered that certain grouping of test responses occurred with no presence of "g", and a limited number of elementary factors. This led him to conceive intelligence as consisting of about a dozen or so group factors which he named Primary Mental Abilities most important of which labeled as Verbal, Number, Spatial, Relations, Word Fluency, Memory, and Reasoning. He did find that the primary factors related to each other as a result of further work with his tests and explains this relationship as a function of a "second-order factor".

The expanding concept of intellectual functioning found fullest expression in Guilford's comprehensive theoretical three dimensional model which he called the Structure of Intellect (Guildford, 1967). Ths model consists of five kinds of mental *operations* (cognition, memory, divergent production, convergent production, and evaluation), four kinds of *contents* (figural, symbolic, semantic, and behavioral), and six kinds of informational forms or *products* (units, classes, relations, systems, transformations, and implications), making a total of 120 possible intellectual abilities each different from the rest by its unique combination of mental operation, content and product used. Not only did Guilford's model articulate the multi-faceted nature of ability but also included the dimension of "divergent thinking" (more loosely called creativity) as one of five major thinking operations hitherto omitted by others from their models and measures of intelligence.

Creative or Productive Thinking

In the main creative thinking abilities and their measurement have derived from the works of Guilford (1967) and Torrance (1962, 1974) and their associates. Relative to the Structure of Intellect, Guilford defines creative thinking in terms of divergent thinking, redefinition and transformation abilities. Torrance defines creativity as a process of becoming sensitive to problems, deficiencies, gaps in knowledge, missing elements, disharmony, and so on; identifying the difficulty; searching for solutions, making guesses, or formulating hypotheses about the deficiencies; testing and retesting these hypotheses and possibly modifying and retesting them; finally communicating the results (Torrance, 1974).

Their tests of creative thinking in general give major roles to four creative thinking abilities: *fluency* (the ability to produce many ideas to a given task), *flexibility* (the ability to produce different kinds of ideas that show shifts in thinking), *originality* (the ability to produce ideas that are unusual, remote and clever), and *elaboration* (the ability to add details to a basic idea produced). To these four creative thinking abilities Torrance and his associates (1975) have added *synthesis* (the ability to combine two or more figures into a related whole picture) and *closure* (the ability to dely completing a task long enough to make the mental leaps that make possible the production of original ideas). It should be noted that while Guilford tries to measure fluency, flexibility, originality and elaboration in a way that requires a person to do many test tasks, each setting out to give information about one of the 24 divergent thinking abilities, Torrance tries to measure the same four abilities in a way that requires a person to do several complex tasks each designed to make a person show all these abilities at one and the same time.

Specific Academic Aptitude

This appears to relate to the ability to do one or more academic subjects like language, mathematics, science and social studies. In terms of the Vernon model for instance, much "g" functioning is required to enter into the verbal-educational component of intellect and may call into play one or more of the specific abilities. If the Guilford model is preferred, one or more of the five mental operations may be called to action relative to the kind of content (symbolic and semantic), and product required.

If by specific academic aptitude is meant the potential to do better in certain subject areas than others, then measures of intellectual abilities generally and the sub-tests of these measures specifically may be used to predict aptitude. However, if by specific academic aptitude is meant performance in one or more academic subjects, then a direct approach of evaluating scores obtained in the subject should be the approach. It may be that a combination of these two would fetch the best indices of relevant ability, in which an IQ test and a measure of achievement may be concurrently administered.

Leadership Ability

To possess leadership ability a person needs to be bright, to have understanding of people, to have a feel for the way people behave in groups, to be sensitive to change, and to be able to creatively and skilfully handle them. In short, such ability requires what Thorndike called "social intelligence". The behavioral component of the Structure of Intellect offers a good explanation of leadership potential as it relates to the single individual assessed where *behavioral content* relates essentially to non-verbal information involving attitudes, needs, desires, moods, intentions, perceptions, thoughts and the like. Acting together with the five mental operations and six product categories, the behavioral component of intellect offers a good assessment model of leadership ability. However, since leadership involves not only the leader but the led, some appraisal of the dynamics of social relations seems to offer a fruitful direction to take. Sociometry as developed by Moreno could be used as a valuable tool to evaluate the social status of the individual in the contest of his group relative to the choice of a leader for a specific assignment. Together these two approaches might provide reasonably good evidence of leadership potential.

Visual and Performing Arts Ability

Ability in these dimensions are more appropriately considered as abilities in one or more of the areas in the Fine Arts, and not some single ability that necessarily enters into all activities defined as visual and performing arts. By visual arts we probably mean, drawing, painting, sculptor, designing, musical composition in written form, and all other related forms of art whose products can be observed; by performing arts we probably mean music, dance, oratory, drama, and all other related forms of art that require performance.

Abilities that are required for superior production or performance are not easily measurable; few if any psychological measures are available at present for the purpose; and much reliance has to be placed on observable behavior and products to determine if a person is gifted in the visual and performing arts.

Common to all these art forms is *creativity,* a processing and an energizing agent that differs in degree for its operation depending upon the form of art used. Specific to each art form are highly specialized knowledge and skills that must be acquired by a person before he can express himself in that medium; and often because it takes time to acquire these, it is not unusual to find screening of young children for talent in the arts in terms of potential, difficult. Of course we do find children of exceptional talent that manifests itself early as in the performance of child prodiges in music--but this is quite rare.

For the most part the best way to identify the gifted in these special areas would be through observation by those expert in the field of their products and performances with relevant and important criteria set up for such purpose. Such experts should be alerted to look out for not only superior ability to reproduce but also ability to be innovative and the tendency to break away from the more conventional nature of the art forms. It would be of great value to screen for creative potential as well since the information so obtained would give useful clues about the way in which a person's talent in the visual and performing arts would probably develop.

Psychomotor Ability

Psychomotor ability or abilities involve the combined function of body and mind, the "practical intelligence" of Thorndike or Burt; or the kinesthetic-motor (k:m) abilities of Vernon' hierarchical model of intelligence that involve such factors as practical, mechanical, spatial and physical factors; or the Figural dimension of Guilford's Structure of Intellect. Abilities such as these are found in people who are good handymen, mechanics, engineers, draftsmen, clerks, truck drivers, airplane pilots, footballers, athletes, and the like.

If one uses Vernon's model of intelligence then "g" enters into all of psychomotor activity to a greater or lesser extent with highly specialized skills that are involved in a particular psychomotor performance. If one uses the Guilford model, then the Figural dimension as it is processed by the five mental operations and six product categories are involved.

To find out who are gifted in the psychomotor areas, there are a number of good tests available. Where educated observation of psychomotor abilities can be made it should be made. Thi becomes a necessity when no measures are available; besides, it is also a valuable complement to the assessment procedures for the identification of psychomotor ability.

Identification of the Gifted in the United States and Abroad

In the United States while aware of the presence of many kinds of talent in our midst that could be called gifted we have had a special bias for the "intellectually gifted" as the sole category of giftedness, possibly traceable to the mental test movement that began in the first decade of this century and possibly from the term "genius" as derived from high IQ levels as measured by the *Stanford Binet* and the Terman *Genetic Studies of Genius*. Change of thought about the "intellectually gifted" was to a large extent initiated by the changing conceptual models of intellectual abilities precipitated by various advocates into the United States Office of Education recognition in 1972 of six categories of giftedness, namely, general intellectual ability, creative or productive thinking, specific academic aptitude, leadership ability, visual and performing arts abilities and psychomotor abilities.

Generally, and where applicable, in other countries, the official emphasis in the main is still on the "intellectually gifted" with some minor recognition given to talent as manifested in the fine arts. The Binet conception of intelligence and the IQ index of intellectual ability have great prestige abroad, and much reliance is placed upon t and achievement exams for the identification of the gifted, though at times less formal observational screening procedures are used. There has been some growing interest and recognition given to the identification of creative potential abroad, but this is unofficial and negligible. When we stop to think how recent the official recognition in the United States of the six categories of giftedness is, we can better understand the position regarding this abroad.

Government Provision For The Education of The Gifted

Although our knowledge of the gifted and talented and what we can do for them has increased over the years it has not been without considerable frustration over the obstructionism of a public education system that is essentially geared to a philosophy of egalitarianism. The first really significant step to counteract this problem took the form of an Act of Congress of the United States to include in the Elementary Education Amendments of 1969, signed into law on 13th April, 1970, provisions for gifted and talented Education of Gifted and Talented Report, 1972). This required the Commissioner of Education to determine the extent to which special educational assistance programs were necessary or useful to meet the needs of gifted and talented children, to evaluate how existing federal educational assistance programs can be more effectively used to meet these needs, and to recommend new programs, if any, needed to meet these needs; further, the Commissioner was to report his findings together with the recommendations not later than one year after the enactment of this act (Section 806c of Public Law 91-

1. PERSPECTIVE

230)

In 1972, Commissioner Marland launched the Federal Program for the gifted and talented details of which can be found in the report itself and in my earlier presentation on this subject (Khatena, 1976). Much of his directions have been translated into action. Some features of immediate interest are:

(a) establishment of the CEC/TAG Educational Resource Information Center in Reston, Virginia that collects and disseminates information on the gifted with the aid of its computer services;

(b) funding in 1976 of a graduate training program in the area of the gifted conducted by a consortium of universities headed by Columbia University such that graduate fellows may work with some of the best known scholars in the field whose universities have programs towards degrees in the area of the gifted.

(c) increased state government involvement in providing special educational opportunities for the gifted, either directly via their school systems or Federal and local special projects, with some states enacting laws for the educational advancement of their gifted, and in the appointment of personnel to actualize the law

(d) greater university involvement in providing training of facilitators of the gifted, from single course programs to certification and degree programs; and

(e) continued conduct of leadership training institutes in various locations in the United States for the preparation of professional personnel to assume leadership positions in the advancement of provisions for the gifted in their state and colleges.

Conditions abroad do not quite match the efforts in the United States to provide superior educational opportunity to the gifted. In fact the latest release by the USOE of Application for Grants Under Gifted and Talented Program (CFDA no. 13.562) with April 27, 1977 as the closing date for applications defines the gifted and talent and their need for differentiated education or services beyond those provided by the regular school system to the average student in order to realize these potentialities. It also requires comprehensive screening for the identification of these different kinds of giftedness and in such a way that subjects in each category of giftedness stand an equal chance of selection. Further, that identification of a single category of giftedness is appropriate for a special program related to it.

However, among the most progressive countries abroad relative to the provision of special educational opportunities for the gifted are

England, Israel, India, Brazil, Czechoslovakia, Mexico, Syria, and Turkey (Gibson & Chennels, 1976).

(a) *England.* Foremost among these countries is England (and closest to the kind of efforts that exist in the United States) and in addition to various experimental projects, government support comes by way of scholarships, special classes or schools, with opportunities for the gifted to attend the best Universities in the land.

(b) *Israel.* A department for the gifted was established in 1971. Up to 50 percent financial support is given to all programs for the gifted so as to keep fees paid to attend these programs at a relatively low level. There is funding of large and small experimental projects as well. Regional activities for the gifted are encouraged. There is also the development of post secondary boarding schools for the disadvantaged able. Anticipated expansion in 1976 of educational opportunities for the gifted was preceeded by various pilot experiments. Further, government funds and scholarships are available for the advancement of the gifted in the country.

(c) *India.* Government support and commitment in India comes mainly through scholarship especially since 1963. Gifted students are awarded scholarships to attend various projects conducted in the country as for instance, through the National Science Talent Search (1963), the National Rural Talent Search (1971/1972), and the Government of India Merit Scholar in Residential Schools.

(d) *Brazil.* In 1973, a government decree created the National Center for Special Education with the purpose of expanding and improving facilities for teaching exceptional children including the gifted through eleven years of schooling within the regular school. Funds are provided for this by the government through one of its agencies like the Association for the Protection of Gifted Children.

(e) *Czechoslovakia.* The government there supports most of the special educational opportunities given though at times a small fee had to be paid by pupils who for instance attend the People's School of Art.

(f) *Mexico.* Government support is by way of scholarships given to the needy gifted. The aim is to provide special opportunities to all the gifted in Mexico.

(g) *Turkey.* In Turkey the Code of February 16, 1975 clearly defines support of the gifted, and efforts towards this end have been going on since 1948 and includes experimentation, research, grants from TUBITAK or the Government Research Center, special classes (1950/60) and scholarships.

Another group of countries have no committed national or Federal support. However, variation in support exists at the regional, state and local levels ranging from none to some special programs and schools for the gifted. Among these countries are Australia, Canada, Ghana, Kenya, Malaysia, New Zealand, Nigeria, South Africa, Tobago and Trinidad.

Three countries whose governments recognize the need to provide special opportunities for the education of the gifted are Kuwait,

1. PERSPECTIVE

Syria, and Sri Lanka. However, their programs, in the main, are in the planning stage.

A *fourth group of countries* have governments that do not support or are apathetic towards the needs of the gifted. Among these countries are Denmark, France, Italy and the Netherlands.

A number of factors have influenced the directions that these countries have taken among which are the nature of the political organizations of the country, the degree of their commitment to egalitarianism, the hostility towards an elitism, the relative status of these countries as developing nations, and their economy and wealth.

Educational Opportunities Provided In The United States And Abroad

The educational opportunities provided in the United States and other countries concerned for the gifted vary from special provisions within the regular school to special schools; from grade acceleration to enrichment of the learning environment in the form of enriched curriculum materials and physical surroundings; from development of intellectual and academic abilities relative to language arts, science and mathematics to development of talent in the fine arts and sports to which may be added the provisions for correspondence courses and tutoring, placement in advanced grades and classes, and independent study.

More peculiar to the United States, the provision of educational opportunities have also concentrated on discovering and using superior methodological approaches, on creating psychological climates conducive to optimum learning, on allowing high school students to attend college courses while still in school, on sensitivity training, on individualized instruction through such means as team teaching and non graded plans, on arranging for separate classes with specially trained teachers, supervisors and consultants, special attention to the emotional and social adjustment, and curriculum through programs which emphasize higher level thought (Education of the Gifted & Talented Report, 1972; ERIC--CEC/TAG Selective Bibliography, 1973).

A growing awareness and acceptance of the importance of developing creative and productive thinking of gifted individuals are becoming more noticeable in the United States, and to a lesser extent for instance in England, Australia and Israel.

Contributions Of National Associations To The Gifted Movement

Another very viable influence takes the form of the contributions and activities of national associations. The Association for the Gifted in *Canada* formed in 1975 for instance has set itself the prime function of spurring legislation for the gifted. The National Association for Gifted Children of *France* formed in 1971 levels itself at stirring the French Government, which shuns support for the gifted for fear of being accused of elitism, to do something for the gifted. It organized creativity workshops in 1972 and formed chess clubs in 1974 for gifted children. The National Association for Gifted Children of the *United Kingdom* is more than 20 years old and has championed the cause of the gifted in significant ways, and has recently made some very valuable contributions by organizing the

First World Conference in 1975.

The Association for the Gifted and the National Association for Gifted Children of the *United States* are among the chief and loudest voices of support for the gifted, drawing their strength from parents and professionals all over the country. They influence thought to a far greater extent and in many more ways in the United States than do similar bodies elsewhere in the world through national or regional workshops, conferences, and annual conventions; and through participation at USOE organized conferences they have urged special provisions for the Gifted that culminated in the significant legislation of 1970. Both organizations reach their membership in the United States and other subscribing countries, TAG through its newsletter *Talents and Gifts,* and NAGC through its journal the GIFTED CHILD QUARTERLY. Together the message that gifted children are neglected and should be specially provided with unique educational opportunities ring loud and clear. The GIFTED CHILD QUARTERLY in addition is also the leading journal in its field and provides direction for thought and research on matters pertaining to the gifted.

Other developments of interest is the First World Conference held in London, 1975. It was organized by the NAGC of the United Kingdom with the aim of trying to bring together those concerned about the welfare of the gifted from all over the world. In this they were very successful and must be credited with initiative, foresight and industry that has resulted in the establishment of the World Council for the Gifted, the production of a fine book of the proceedings of the Conference entitled *Gifted Children: Looking To Their Future* (Gibson & Chennells, 1976), numerous benefits of contact, and dissemination of knowledge on the gifted whose significance cannot be easily measured.

One direct consequence of the establishment of the World Council has been the emergence of a Second World conference that will be held in August, 1977, in San Francisco, that in its planning has involved the participation of nearly all organizations as well as personnel of the Office of the Gifted in Washington, D.C.

The efforts of all these bodies both national and international towards the cause of the gifted are bound to make significant impact all over the world in time, and we cannot help but anticipate with excitement and pleasure the spread of interest and action universally.

Summary Conclusions And Implications

This presentation has attempted to link up Terman's studies of the gifted to the development of thought that led to conceptions of many kinds of giftedness, namely, general intellectual ability, creative and productive thinking ability, specific academic aptitude, leadership ability, visual and performing arts ability and psychomotor ability. Further the extent to which education of the gifted is provided by the governments of the United States and by other countries of the world was outlined. In addition, educational opportunities found in the United States and abroad were summarized. The contributions of national associations to the gifted movement and the significance of some of their productions were

1. PERSPECTIVE

discussed.

Some very significant steps have been taken in the United States and some smaller but no less important ones have been taken in a few countries elsewhere that recognize the gifted and talented as people who deserve our very special attention and nurture that can only lead to the fuller realization of their potential and unique productions which must enhance their immediate social-cultural group at first, and the rest of the world next.

What, we may ask, are some of the goals we need to set for ourselves in the United States? Here are a few that I think are pertinent:

1. Concerning identification, we still need to formulate procedures that we can use to identify all six USOE categories of giftedness. As it stands now we have but areas of abilities that do not lend themselves to psychological measurement, in which case we will need to consider at least setting up appropriate criteria which can be used with as little bias as possible by observers for selection purposes.

2. We need to move away from the prejudice of considering only the intellectually gifted and academically able as those with exceptional talent and to regard other forms of superior ability as defined by the USOE categories of giftedness.

3. Programs, educational materials and techniques need to have injected into them principles of innovation, flexibility and invention that will allow participants the greatest use of their creative abilities and imagination towards productive learning and self-involvement.

4. Enrichment should be thought of more in terms of specific needs and arrangements for specific development and accelerated learning rather than in more general terms as is customary in the educational system.

5. Acquisition of information from the United States by countries elsewhere about the gifted would be of great value and I see the ERIC--CEC/TAG Clearinghouse as the best facilitator of this. Dissemination of information regarding the availability of its computerized services and some of its low cost publications among the countries of the world would be an extremely valuable service to the cause of the gifted.

6. A closer communication network among the various associations for the gifted can only lead to major thrusts in the advancement of the cause of the gifted, and we should strive for this.

7. The value of having local associations for the gifted affiliated as well with the national organizations while maintaining their own autonomy will no doubt lead all kinds of benefits to the gifted at the local level. This too should be our concern.

8. Research on the gifted dormant for more than a decade has received fresh impetus by the passage of the 1970 Act, certain financial support from the Office of the Gifted, by the effervescence of activity relating to the gifted all over the country, and by the

scholarship of professionals in the gifted movement today. We can expect a fresh blossoming of thought on the gifted in the near future and should both encourage and support it.

9. Already efforts to study the gifted relative to creative energies at work, and to environmental impediment, and the disadvantaged gifted are well under way. These should also find increasing interest.

10. Further, some research directions that are receiving attention are variables affecting the full development of gifted women, the retarding effects of emotional disturbance on the creative energies of the gifted, and the problems affecting the gifted handicapped. These deserve our concern and should be given much encouragement.

In conclusion, the United States is in a position of leadership on matters pertaining to the gifted: in legislation, in measurement, in innovative educational facilities, projects and programs, in storage and retrieval of information through its computerized services, in books and journals, and so on, the United States has much to share with other countries of the world.

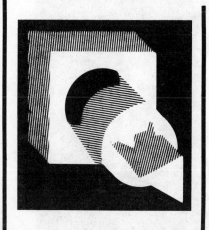

Les enfants terrifiques!

"Every time a child is born into the world it's Nature's attempt to make a perfect human being. Well, we've seen Nature pushing and contriving for some time now. We all know she's interested in quantity; but I think she's interested in quality, too." So wrote Thornton Wilder in *Our Town.* It's not nice to contradict Pulitzer Prize winners or fool around with Mother Nature, even though, as we all know, she's produced a string of spectacular clinkers lately. Let's put them aside for a moment, and dwell instead on a few of her more splendid achievements, eight to be exact. Any like these in your home?

Royal Game Player

Robert LeDonne, here facing a forty-year-old opponent with guarded confidence, is only six. Yet, according to Bruce Pandolfini, his official coach at New York's Marshall Chess Club, "Robert has the potential to be the greatest chess player ever. He is now the best player of his age in the recorded history of the game." Currently, Robert holds the Second Grade Championship of the Metropolitan Area and remains the youngest child in the U.S. to give successful chess exhibitions. Fascinated by games and numbers from the time he turned four, Robert took up chess after seeing the Fischer-Spassky matches on TV. He learned the moves in a day, and within weeks had beaten all the children in his Woodcliff Lake, New Jersey, neighborhood. In more formidable competition Robert tries to take winning and losing in stride, but occasionally an important defeat provokes a quiver of his lips and a plaintive, "I want to see my daddy."

"Les Enfants Terrifiques!" Esquire, Vol. LXXXI No. 3, March 1974. ©1974 Esquire, Inc.

Ice-Skating Team

Joel and Gale Fuhrman (right) are nineteen and fourteen. They are also brother and sister and the youngest pair skaters in world competition. In 1973, they placed second in the U.S. National Figure Skating Championships and thirteenth in the World Championships. Their goal, however, is the gold medal in the '76 Olympics. To this end they have set themselves a grueling schedule. Weekdays it begins at five-forty-five a.m. when they drive from their home in Yonkers to the Sky Rink in Manhattan. Here they put in three and a half hours on the ice before Joel drops Gale at Professional Children's School and goes on to N.Y.U. They spend their weekends in Wilmington, Delaware, training eight hours a day with a coach. If all this leaves little time for other activities, Joel and Gale don't mind. "There's only one first place," they say, "and we want it."

Television Star

During the past two years, Mason Reese (left), age seven and a third-grader in a New York Montessori school, has become known to the public as that wrinkled, chubby kid in TV commercials. He's made nine so far, six of which have won awards. Mason himself won a Clio for the Best Performance by a Male Actor, 1973, for his Underwood Spread commercial ("It's like a borgasmord"). Last September he was signed by WNBC-TV to report on children's events and his interviews now appear irregularly on the six o'clock news. He is also a sought-after guest on the talk shows. For his work Mason has earned a healthy five-figure bank account, kept intact by his parents. However his real ambition, he says, "is to be a magician" and currently he is perfecting "the trick where you turn all the confetti in the glass into flowers."

Computer Scientist

When he was fourteen, two years ago, Michael Landy (above) "dropped out" of high school to become the youngest freshman in more than forty years to enter Columbia University's School of Engineering and Applied Science. At that time, Michael was a sophomore at Hightstown High in New Jersey and had completed all the math courses that the school offered, plus two semesters of calculus at Princeton University (with grades of A and A plus). It is not surprising, then, that Michael, who has just turned seventeen, will graduate from Columbia in June, enter the Master's program in computer sciences at Stanford in the fall, and complete the requirements for his Ph.D. in 1976—"if everything goes according to plan," he adds. "Who knows, after that maybe I'll take another doctorate."

Karate Expert

Phillip Paley, ten, of Encino, California (right), is a black belt in the Tang Soo Do style of karate. "It's a Korean style," Phillip says, "mostly punching, kicking, different kinds of blocks and some judo throws." Here he demonstrates with a side kick to the chest of his opponent. If not the youngest black belt around, Phillip is the smallest: forty-eight inches tall, fifty pounds. He took up the sport when he was five, "because I was small for my age and was having trouble with a couple of kids. One day my mother and I were driving down the street and we saw a sign for the Chuck Norris Karate School. I asked my father and he said yes." Phillip still goes to class twice a week to practice and instruct other children, among them his younger brother.

Violin Prodigy

Lilit Gampel, fourteen, is the first acknowledged music prodigy in America since Lorin Hollander, two decades ago. A determined youngster with a preference for Beethoven, Dickens, opera, candy and practicing her violin, Lilit began taking lessons when she was six—at her own suggestion. When she was ten, she won the Young Musicians Foundation Competition in Los Angeles, whose previous winners include Van Cliburn and Misha Dichter, and at the age of twelve she was soloist with the New York Philharmonic, the Los Angeles Philharmonic, and the Seattle Symphony. While her parents, both scientists, restrict Lilit's performance schedule so she will not miss much schoolwork (she is an A student at the Lycée Français in Los Angeles), Lilit and her Stradivarius will travel from Hawaii to Alaska this year to keep close to a dozen dates.

Trapeze Artist

Julio Faria (right) is just ten which makes him the youngest aerialist in the U.S. and the envy of every kid who sees him perform in the Circus Vargas with The Flying Farias, a troupe of five led by his father. Julio works with his parents thirty-two feet above the net executing passing leaps and double somersaults with the greatest of ease. One day he hopes to perfect "the big one," the triple somersault. For Julio this means, simply, doing what comes naturally: his father has been a trapeze artist for twenty-five years and his mother comes from a circus family. During 1974, Julio will work a forty-eight-week season. Between performances (two to three most days) he will pursue his correspondence-school lessons, which suits him just fine. "I like it much better staying with the circus than going to school at seven in the morning."

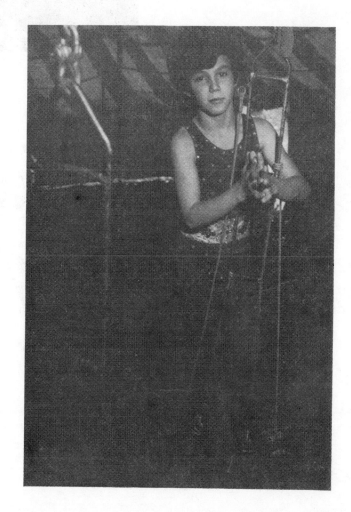

What if Your Child Is Gifted?

By knowing the indicators, parents can spot special talents in
their youngsters and, by taking a few simple steps, can start the
process of bringing these gifts to flower

By DOROTHY A. SISK

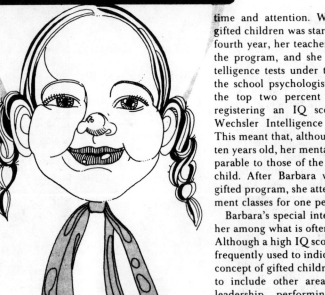

Barbara, aged 12, gobbles up learning. She shifts a stack of papers from the floor beside her cluttered desk, riffles through them for her outline, and then dashes to the school library for yet one more source. She keeps a "to do" list of things she wants to accomplish, books to be read, and what she calls "poem starters," words that spur the imagination. Barbara is also a compulsive reader. "I read at least a book every two or three days. It's like a big thirst. There's so much to read that I just can't waste time."

Barbara is a sixth grader now, but she was adding simple sums at age three and reading before she was four. Her parents viewed these achievements as unusual, but they did not see any reason to refer Barbara to a psychologist or testing expert. Barbara's first-grade teacher was introduced to the youngster's special abilities on the very first day of school when Barbara plowed through the preprimer, primer and first-grade reading book. Fortunately, the teacher didn't mind that she would have one less beginning reading student; instead, she arranged for Barbara to read independently during the regular reading period.

Over the next two years Barbara encountered some resistance from teachers who found—within the crowded classrooms—that Barbara's advanced reading skills and endless questions were too taxing on their time and attention. When a program for gifted children was started during Barbara's fourth year, her teachers nominated her for the program, and she took a series of intelligence tests under the observant eye of the school psychologist. Barbara scored in the top two percent of her age group, registering an IQ score of 140 on the Wechsler Intelligence Test for Children. This meant that, although Barbara was then ten years old, her mental abilities were comparable to those of the average 15-year-old child. After Barbara was admitted to the gifted program, she attended special enrichment classes for one period each day.

Barbara's special intellectual abilities put her among what is often called the "gifted." Although a high IQ score or high grades are frequently used to indicate "giftedness," the concept of gifted children is now expanding to include other areas of talent such as leadership, performing and visual arts, creativity, and psychomotor.

Understanding Giftedness

Almost every child has something that he or she can do better than most children of the same age. A child might speak or read better than other children; he or she could have a special skill such as singing, jumping

"What If Your Child Is Gifted?" Dorothy A. Sisk, *American Education*, Vol. 13 No. 8, October 1977. ©1977 United States Department of Health, Education and Welfare.

rope, or playing the guitar. Still other children encounter great difficulty in trying to master skills that most of their peers possess. For example, at age four, most children can hop on one foot. A few children may be able to hop adeptly on one foot within a small circle, and a few others may not be able to hop at all. For purposes of ability, most children could be classified into one of three groups: average, above average, or below average.

In a formal school setting, children usually fall into one of three learning levels: average learner, above-average learner, or slow learner. But there will also be a small number of students who are so slow that they are referred to as "retarded." Likewise, an equally small group of students is so advanced that these students are called academically "gifted" or "talented."

To get an idea of the statistics of learning ability, you might imagine a hypothetical roomful of 100 children who represent all children in the fifth grade. Based on overall statistical findings, 68 of them are likely to be average learners, 13 above average, 13 below average, three retarded, and three gifted learners.

Identifying the Gifted

Gifted and talented children have always existed, but they have only recently begun to receive attention from state and national education agencies. In 1972, the Office of Gifted and Talented was established within the U.S. Office of Education. In order to identify these children, the Office formulated a working definition of the gifted and talented: children capable of high performance, including those with demonstrated achievement or ability in any one or more of these areas—general intellectual ability, specific academic aptitude, creative or productive thinking, leadership ability, visual and performing arts, or psychomotor ability. Applying this definition, approximately three to five percent of the school-age population—some two to five million children—could be considered gifted and talented.

Obviously, the intellectually gifted child, like Barbara, is the easiest to spot in a school setting. But other forms of giftedness and talent may go unnoticed or be misinterpreted by teachers and parents. Children with giftedness in, say, specific academic aptitude, leadership, visual and performing arts, and creativity may be high achievers in only one subject, with records of underachievement in other areas. Some actually turn off their teachers or classmates by expressing wild or silly ideas. What they share in common is an extraordinary ability to excel in one or more of the gifted categories.

Devotion to One Discipline. Terri is 13, with a physical maturity that makes her look at least five years older. She hungers to be a scientist. Each of her assignments in biology is meticulously done, right down to her notebook of detailed and complicated drawings of dissections. As she carefully pins the legs of a giant grasshopper onto cardboard, she chats happily with her biology teacher. But in her other classes, Terri is often sullen and inattentive. Her work is usually sloppy. She daydreams a lot, keeps to herself, and doesn't have many friends. Her best friend is Mandy because, as Terri explains, "She likes biology, too." Her teachers understand and respect Terri's passion for biology, but they are equally concerned about how she is neglecting the rest of her schooling.

A Natural Born Leader. "Ted is always planning something," his father says wearily. "Two months ago, I got a call from our town mayor. He wanted to know if I approved of Ted's latest campaign to convert an empty downtown lot into a baseball field. Imagine my surprise! The only word I had heard from Ted about the campaign was over dinner several months ago, when, out of the blue, he asked me what I thought about turning vacant space into community play areas. I said it sounded like a fine idea. Then he asked me some questions about who performed certain jobs in our city government.

"That was the last I heard until the mayor called. Naturally, I had a talk with Ted that evening. He told me he had convinced his friends that one of the vacant lots downtown would make an excellent playing field. Then he arranged a meeting with a city commissioner, but the commissioner reacted negatively to Ted's idea. Undaunted, Ted then organized his friends to campaign with various business and civic leaders in support of the plan. Well, they won! Right now they're down at the lot helping the city workers sow the grass for the field. Rather remarkable," adds Ted's father, "for a boy of 11, don't you think?"

The Inner-City Artist. Luisa is small for her nine years. She sits quietly kneading her clay into gently flaring flowers to place around the top of a pot. "Her work is far advanced for her age," explains the director of the inner-city art center. "She comes here every afternoon after school and creates something. This class is for young adults, but we welcome her because there is nowhere else she can go—and because she is so full of talent."

Luisa's mind is quick and she loves to read, especially adventure stories. She says she would like to write stories of her own. But she is not encouraged at home. Her family expresses little interest in her schoolwork or her talents. Both of Luisa's parents work at night jobs, and life is hard; they are just thankful that Luisa is no extra trouble. Luisa's teachers are sincerely worried about whether she will have the chance to grow and reach her potential.

Brimming with Talent. Dale is eight and has curly red hair and freckles. He is presently playing the demanding role of Puck in the school production of *A Midsummer Night's Dream.* His mother says that he is a good-natured boy at home and that his sense of humor and sensitivity make him popular with friends. He also works part time for the neighborhood veterinarian. Last week he helped remove porcupine quills from a dog's muzzle. "He vacillates between wanting to be an actor and a veterinarian," says his father. For Dale, socially popular and multitalented, there is the danger of going in many directions at once without any focus.

Playing Up "Being Different." Marsha has spent her 12 years in a section of the city where unemployment and crime are commonplace. One might think that, amid such rough surroundings and with her good mind, Marsha would work hard in school as a way of escaping the area. But no. Marsha seemed quite content with using her head to invent crazy ideas and questions. Nor did her classmates warm to her. They thought her too different, and she seemed to relish playing up her inconformities.

As one example, last winter Marsha's class decided to study the energy problem. The students were supposed to go home, observe how their families waste energy, and then list ways energy might be saved. But Marsha, with a compulsion to be different, came back with a story about being a light bulb in a traffic light along with other light bulbs! She told how, in her role of light bulb, she peered out through the green-yellow-red lights, watching the cars stop and start. She saw thousands of gallons of gasoline going up in smoke. Then one day, all the traffic lights gathered at a huge convention in Miami Beach and decided to coordinate traffic signals everywhere so that cars can move through them without having to stop.

The class found her story very amusing, but it missed her point completely. Then Marsha asked the class Why not have someone design a computer that could plan how to set the lights to keep traffic moving? The class, finally recognizing her idea, voted it the best energy saver. In fact, the students were so excited that they wrote a letter proposing the idea to President Carter. "I suppose Marsha's ideas can pay off, but I just wish she wouldn't come up with so many of them during class discussions," concludes Marsha's exasperated teacher.

Is Your Child Gifted?

As the above examples show, there is no easy formula for identification of gifted children because they vary in ability, physical development, and personality. Often, the difference between a bright child and a gifted child is only one of degree rather than of kind, with encouragement and challenge spelling the difference. Teachers and school psychologists can assist parents who suspect

1. PERSPECTIVE

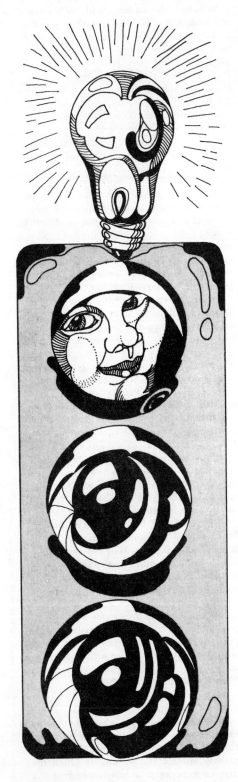

their child is gifted by providing special tests which measure intelligence, aptitude, and even creativity. Parents also might find it useful to jot down their observations of the child in a notebook to help the teacher or psychologist in assessing giftedness and planning a program.

Although there is no easy way to identify a gifted child, certain characteristics appear to set these children apart from their peers:

□ *Early use of advanced vocabulary.* Most children at age two make sentences like: "There's a doggie." A two-year-old who is gifted might say, "There's a brown doggie in the backyard and he's sniffing our flowers."

□ *Keen observation and curiosity.* A gifted child might pursue lines of questioning such as What makes Scotch tape sticky on one side and smooth on the other? How can they make a machine that puts on the sticky part without getting the machine all gummed up? Why doesn't the sticky side stay stuck to the other side when you unroll the tape? A gifted child will also observe details. At a very young age the child might remember where all the toys go on the shelf and replace everything correctly.

□ *Retention of a variety of information.* Gifted children amaze parents and teachers by recalling details of past experiences. For example, one six-year-old returned from a trip to the space museum and reproduced an accurate drawing of a space rocket he had seen.

□ *Periods of intense concentration.* A one-year-old gifted child might sit for five minutes or more listening attentively to a story being read to an older brother or sister. Older gifted children can become totally engrossed in a book or project, becoming oblivious to the events happening around them.

□ *Ability to understand complex concepts, perceive relationships, and think abstractly.* Although an average four-year-old looks through a picture book of baby and mother animals with interest, a gifted four-year-old is more likely to observe concepts such as how much animal mothers and babies look alike except that the baby is smaller. Or, if a fifth-grade class were told to write a paper on what it's like to be poor, most of the children would write, "I would be hungry" or "I wouldn't have enough money." A gifted fifth grader would tend to view the problem more abstractly and might write something like: "Being poor would only be a problem if others were not poor. If everyone else also had very little money, then we would all have less to spend and things would be cheaper."

□ *A broad and changing spectrum of interests.* Gifted children often show an intense interest in a subject, perhaps dinosaurs one month, then turn to a totally different subject like French literature or railroad engines the next.

□ *Strong critical thinking skills and self-criticism.* Gifted children evaluate themselves and others. They notice discrepancies between what people say and what they do. But they are usually most critical of themselves. For example, a gifted child who has just won a swimming race might complain, "I should have beat my time by at least one second."

□ *Characteristics of children gifted in other areas.* Children gifted in visual and performing arts or psychomotor skills will display many of the characteristics just cited as common to intellectually gifted children. In addition, such creatively or physically gifted children demonstrate their talents early. A visually gifted child might draw a man riding a motorcycle while classmates are still struggling to put nose, eyes, and mouth in the right places in drawing a face. Overall, children who have special creative abilities differ from intellectually gifted children in many ways. They are likely to have one or more of these characteristics: a reputation for having wild and silly ideas or ideas that are off the beaten track, a sense of playfulness and relaxation, a strong tendency to be nonconformist and to think independently, and considerable sensitivity to both emotions and problems.

Steps a Parent Can Take

If you suspect that your child is gifted, there are some initial steps you can take: First, meet with your child's teacher. Teachers are often keen observers of giftedness, and a meeting with your child's teacher will give an opportunity for you to compare findings. The teacher may also know about further services offered by the school system. Don't be discouraged if the teacher is unable to help; some school systems have not yet recognized the need to provide special services for the gifted.

Second, meet with the school counselor, psychologist, and administrator—particularly if the classroom teacher is not trained in the identification of gifted children. Bring along your notebook of observations and anecdotes that describe your child's behavior.

Third, investigate community resources. If your school system cannot provide adequate services, local colleges and universities often try to help fill the gap. Get in touch with the education or psychology department of a nearby college or university. They may have a program or know about one given in a local community center. They can also refer parents to specific professionals in the community. Bear in mind that not all communities have programs for the gifted child. In fact, less than four percent of our nation's gifted children receive services of any sort. Many parents have organized effective lobbying groups that are encouraging schools and

Programs for the Gifted

Once your child has been identified as gifted, you should check out what type of program would most benefit the youngster. Programs for gifted children should be geared to the special abilities of the children being served and provide an opportunity for them to interact with each other. One type of service for gifted and talented children is the self-contained class in which all the children are gifted and the teacher is specially trained to work with them. The children are permitted to work at a level corresponding to their mental age rather than their chronological age.

Another type of program has gifted children using resource rooms equipped with materials for exploration and study of subjects not usually covered in the regular classroom. Resource-room teachers generally are specialists in education for the gifted.

A third approach is through independent study programs that can be set up in schools having no special classes or resource teachers. Independent study is usually based on a written contract between student and teacher for the completion of specified work in subject areas of interest to the student.

As a fourth kind of program for the gifted, advanced placement can be offered at the high-school level, allowing a gifted student to attend college or university courses before high-school graduation. Sometimes individual arrangements can be made for admission to college before the senior year, particularly in cases where all high-school requirements have been satisfied.

In still another approach, mentorships are designed to pair gifted and talented children with highly skilled community resource persons, perhaps contact with a professional artist or an apprenticeship with a business firm, bank, hospital, or school agency.

From state to state, gifted and talented education programs vary from a short one-hour-a-week program to an entire special school for the gifted. As teachers and parents become increasingly aware of the needs of gifted children, more school systems are offering a variety of services. If you are the parent of a gifted or talented youngster, you will not only want to provide challenges for the child but also check out these resources in your school and community.

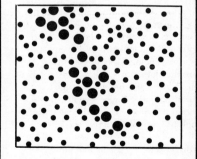

THE GIFTED CHILD

KALI and CHANDRA

For these creative girls, the extraordinary is ordinary

PHYL GARLAND

Constant companions, Kali (l.), her sister, Chandra (r.), and their mother, Mrs. Verta Mae Grosvenor, author of popular soul food cookbook, *Vibration Cooking,* share creative life. All three talented New Yorkers are following literary pursuits.

WHEN Kali Grosvenor was nine years old, back in 1970, she achieved a level of celebrity as a superkid. Her first book, *Poems by Kali,* had been published by a major firm (Doubleday) and was selling at the rate of 1,000 copies a week, a pace that might well have been the envy of more established authors. Actually, she had written the poems at the ages of six and seven when the turbulence of the late '60s had inspired her to set down her thoughts as a little black girl trying to grow up in a most confusing world:

> Lady Bird, Lady Bird
> Fly away Home
> Your house is on fire
> And Rap's on the phone.

Her precocious musings, printed with childish misspellings intact, were reviewed in the New York Times. She appeared as a guest on the Dick Cavett and David Frost television talk shows at an age when most children must be content merely to *watch* TV.

All of that happened four years ago. Today, at the gangly age of 13, Kali has decided that the literary life is not for her.

"It doesn't do anything for me," she explains in her usual quiet, almost deferential manner. "When I write, it's only for myself. I don't like to be famous or whatever, because I don't like

the way people think about it. If you're too involved in being Kali Grosvenor or like somebody important, then your work is going to slack off because you have to keep doing certain things so people will know you."

But superkids will be superkids and thus she has diverted her energies toward a new project, Popcorn Productions, a film collective which she serves as president. Conceived and organized by Kali, it is designed primarily to educate children, as well as interested adults, in cinematic techniques. Currently, it is composed of about 26 members ranging in age from three to 45 and averaging out at 13, according to her estimate. The organizational structure is intentionally loose for, as she says, "I don't want some people to feel superior to others. I want everybody to be somebody." The collective operates, primarily, on a $161 grant she obtained from Trident Productions, a film company, on the strength of a short proposal she drew up and submitted. The funds are being channeled into her first film, titled *Stick 'Em Up* and based on her own script. "It's about a revolution of children who are being oppressed by adults," she comments, gazing through granny glasses perched on a sensitive, honey-colored face of early adolescent beauty. "It takes place in 1984," she says,

crediting a George Orwell novel she admires. "The thing is that the adults, instead of being mothers and fathers, which is what the kids need, act like *owners* to them, so it turns the kids into very adult kinds of people who have to make their own decisions when it's too early for them." Though she is reluctant to reveal the whole plot which, she admits, "I haven't worked out yet completely," the action is replete with rebellious baby-sitters and tiny drudges who sabotage the weekly wash by cutting up the clothes or soaking items in tubs of bleach. While Kali's budget is as modest as her equipment, "just a Super-8 camera with a tape recorder for sound," her softly stated ideas are enough to set adult society a-quaking.

But, then, there always has been something just a little bit different about Kali Grosvenor. Part of it has to do with the fact that she was born in the midst of the civil rights movement during an era when men would learn to walk on the moon. Some of it also has to do with her being a native New Yorker, growing up in the most competitive city of the Western World. Even her schooling has been competitive. Now an eighth grader at Hunter College High School, she gained admission to its selective program by scoring in the upper percentiles on a city-wide test administered to pupils who had demonstrated that they possessed exceptional academic promise. Much more of it is related to her family and her upbringing.

The product of a mixed marriage now dissolved, Kali has been surrounded by creativity since birth. Her father is Robert Grosvenor, a respected sculptor. Her mother, with whom she lives, is Verta Mae, the colorful "geechee girl" from South Carolina who has cooked, written and rapped her way through unconventional career as a "wordsmith" and "culinary anthropologist." Mother and daughter frequently have shared the spotlight since the time four years ago when both became published authors simultaneously. Always at their side has been the third member of this formidable female triumvirate, Kali's 11-year-old sister Chandra, an aspiring writer in her own right and an avid student of dance, astrology and Buddhism. Whenever the three engage in conversation, talk is likely to range from politics to reincarnation, with the children often taking the lead. Yet their mother says, "I don't think they're precocious. I mean they ain't *dumb* but they're not any fantastic kids in school or in the ordinary sense. I guess they *are* different, but they've acted like that ever since I've known them. Since I only have two kids, I thought that was the way *all* children acted."

As their mother's almost constant companions, the girls travel freely through artistic and entertainment circles, particularly on Manhattan's Upper West Side where they live. Actress Josephine Premice, a close friend and neighbor, took charge when Chandra broke her arm, recently, arranging for hospitalization even before Verta was able to hurry home from a school where she was lecturing. Later "Auntie Josephine" introduced Chandra to actor Paul Winfield at her apartment where he signed her cast. The girls speak unselfconsciously of "Auntie Nina" (Simone) and her daughter Lisa, of "Auntie Maya" (Angelou) and "Uncle Calvin" (Lockhart). Chandra, being younger, is more likely to show the extent to which she is impressed, recalling, "I met Richard Roundtree in the elevator at a party once and he put

Equally creative as her older sister, Chandra, 11, works on a class project with two classmates at New York City's Public School No. 75. Although she is not yet published, Chandra is herself a writer and painter. She is also a talented student of dance, astrology, Buddhism and drama.

his arm around me." However, their admiration runs much deeper than mere hero worship. "They have a respect for what people do," says Verta. "They go to the library to request their books and they read them." As a result, when Kali met playwright Alice Childress, she told her how much she and her friends had admired her play *Wedding Band* when it was televised. Once, when the author Toni Morrison phoned their apartment, Kali answered and exclaimed, wide-eyed, "Mommy! *The Bluest Eye* is on the phone!" referring to Ms. Morrison's first novel.

The respect they show others is readily returned, for they are well liked by the adults who have become accustomed to seeing them at book parties, previews, fashion shows and all manner of affairs. Possibly it is because they always behave as children, though without a trace of brattishness. As their mother explains, "If they were just bright and got on everybody's nerves, that would be one thing, but

Starting early as a superkid, Kali, is shown (above) in 1970 autographing a book she had published when she was nine years old. Titled *Poems by Kali*, the book sold some 1,000 copies per week. With her literary fame behind her, Kali has formed her own film collective called Popcorn Productions composed of 26 youngsters who want to learn filming techniques. At left, she chairs a meeting of her film "board."

1. PERSPECTIVE

Cultural pursuits go hand in hand with everyday household chores for the two gifted Grosvenor girls. Chandra attends ballet class every day under the tutelage of Miss Leah Randolph (left) at George Faison Universal Dance Center. Mrs. Grosvenor (below), shows Chandra how to iron amid stimulating surroundings.

I want people to like them too."

This attitude of mutual respect begins in the home where Verta encourages them but does not meddle in their projects, feeling that "If I did, then it wouldn't be their thing." She collected Kali's poems when she first began writing them at kindergarten age simply because they were something her child had created. They were published only at the suggestion of a friend. Interestingly, it was the then nine-year-old Kali who told the publisher, "My mother also writes." This led to publication of Verta's popular *Vibration Cooking*, an offbeat autobiography built around the theme of soulful food. Though Chandra has maintained a "lower profile" than her famous sister, Verta has collected her writings and drawings with equal enthusiasm. A few years ago when Verta was hospitalized for surgery, Chandra sold several of those drawings to neighbors in the East Village, where they then lived, to buy her mother a pair of earrings she still treasures. And while Verta rules her roost with a loud voice, the girls seem to understand the tenderness beneath it for they pitch in readily on the housework and shopping, already having developed a keen eye for bargains.

In spite of their close association, the girls have distinctive and totally different personalities. This was pointed up three years ago when the mother-daughter team was invited to lecture at Yale University, with little Chandra dutifully accompanying them. During a break in their activities there, Chandra joined in play with other children, gaily turning sommersaults on the lawn. Meanwhile, Kali sought out the Yale Library where an adult in charge admonished her at the door, saying, "*Town* children aren't permitted to enter the library." Kali snapped back, "I'm not a *town* children. I'm a visiting *lecturer!*"

"I've never tried to make them the same," says their mother. "They're just different people. Kali's usually been pretty good in school but Chandra had some problems. She had a speech impediment when she was younger and Kali had to interpret for her, but she got over it by herself." Referring to her younger daughter as "a Head Start drop-out," Verta explains, "Yeah, she acted *real*

different when she first went to school. She was on parole in kindergarten and on probation in the first grade, but now she's gotten it all together and has developed a sense of herself."

Throughout the years, Chandra's continuing passion has been homeless animals. Once she brought home a mangy looking stray cat because "it doesn't have any mother or father or sister or brother or cousins." When her mother set the animal loose to forage for itself, Chandra scoured the East Village and managed to recover the pitiful creature. Then there was Conchita, the baby rooster, and a whole family of gerbils who ran loose throughout the apartment until one accidentally drowned in a bucket of scrub water. Chandra determined that it had "committed suicide" and took to her bed in a state of despair.

Chandra's humanitarian inclinations affect the way she reacts to the daily news which she, like her sister and mother, follows with a rare intensity. She recalls, "I was very angry at the Arabs and the Israelis when they started having war, because it was so *stu*pid! I had a dream that I went over there one day, spoke to each side and tried to get them to live like normal. And someone shot me, but, after I had died, they realized I was right. They realized that they shouldn't take somebody's life."

Verta acknowledges Chandra's flair for the dramatic and admits, "I wouldn't be surprised to see her end up on the stage." This is entirely in keeping with Chandra's goal which is "to be an actress, to make it in the big time and be famous." She's even worked out a plan as to how she intends to "make it to Hollywood some day." Says Chandra, "I'm going to call up somebody who's *already* discovered somebody that *wants* to discover somebody else. I'll tell them where they can discover them, give them my address. Then I'll get ready and meet them at the door! I think I'm gonna *leave* when I'm 17!"

Kali, on the other hand, has no desire to seek the spotlight, possibly because she was exposed to it at a very early age. When she insists that her film project should be purely educational with no attempt to transform it into a commercial item, Chandra chides, "That's a whole lot of work to put into something nobody's goin' to see except some people sittin' in the living room."

"Kali's not flamboyant," says their mother. "She's a gentle, almost shy child. But whatever she gives up, Chandra will latch right onto with her dramatic self."

In keeping with her somewhat scholarly nature, Kali now has a new dream, which she insists is far more important than the film collective, her poetry or anything she has done in the past. "The only thing I really want to do right now is to become a teacher," says Kali, "and I want to have my own school. I think too many teachers just teach for the money because that's an easy thing to

Like a typical teen, Kali (c.) walks in drizzle while rapping with Hunter College High School chums Brenda Harris (l.) and Michelle Hardy on their way to lunch.

do. In my school, the teachers would have to be selected. Not everybody who applied for a job would get one. It would have to be a school of *good* teachers."

She has definite ideas as to how she would approach education. "In my school, I would make it *easy* for the students to help themselves. Most schools you go to, you're *forced* to learn, but if the students were *eager* to help themselves, then it wouldn't be forced." Her curriculum would include math (though she admits not liking it), social studies and current events, with students being encouraged to bring in clippings of articles they'd read on their own. In her music class, she'd have "books like about Billie Holiday and Bessie Smith and not just music books." She insists that her proposed school, though private, would provide scholarships for those who could not afford to pay and would be fully integrated. When Kali was six, she wrote: "Were is my head Going . . . its Going Black/thats were." Today, her philosophy is closer to the theme of another early poem of hers that goes:

> WHO AM I
> *love is my color*
> *black is my color*
> *beige is my color*
> *red is my color*
> *yellow is my color*
> *love is my color*

In her school, she would teach black history, but also Chinese, Yugoslav and other types of history. "It would be so that everyone could be comfortable and things like that make a lot of difference. People should learn more about each other because you can be a racist if you only learn about one different type of people. They could learn from each other and people have different needs."

More than recognition, she seeks the gratification of helping someone else to learn. She points to her protégée, Mukie Brown, a three-year-old girl who is a sort of adjunct member of the household. Mukie's mother, Marie Brown, is Verta's editor at Doubleday. Says Kali, "I like it best when I can tell her something and then

days later, she'll do it. It just makes you proud that she remembers it and does it and you know that she's probably going to use it for the rest of her life."

Whether or not Kali and Chandra will undertake greatly dissimilar courses throughout life, so far the bond between them has withstood tests that might have driven adults apart in fits of jealousy or rivalry. For while Kali willingly has relinquished a place in the sun, Chandra has yet to find hers. Yet Chandra expressed her deepest feelings in a card she made for her sister on Kali's 13th birthday. On the front, there is a picture she drew of a small boat with a sail. Inside, the verse reads:

> *As you ride in your little boat, I follow . . .*
> *Day by day you grow, I grow, we grow together.*

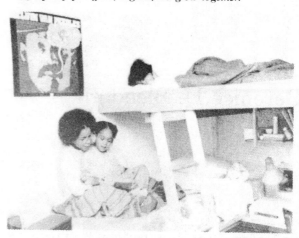

At bedtime, Kali reads to Mukie Brown, 3, daughter of mother's book editor, Marie Brown, and star of Kali's film, *Stick Em Up!* while Chandra sleeps in top bunk.

FUTURE STUDIES FOR THE GIFTED

Berenice D. Bleedorn,

The future is here and we're all in it. What's more, there is an acceleration and heightening in the process of its arrival. In the words of Arthur C. Clarke, "We are living at a time when history is holding its breath, and the present is detatching itself from the past like an iceberg that has broken away from its icy moorings to sail across the boundless ocean." The rate, expectation, and implications of radical change are in the public consciousness. Educators concerned with Gifted and Talented have particular reasons for paying attention to the emerging ways and means of incorporating the study of the future into thinking and learning experiences in the classroom. Bright, creative thinkers of all ages can find challenge and stimulation in intellectualizing on problems and conditions of the future. In the process, they will add an important dimension to their possible leadership role as global citizens.

The purpose of this article is to suggest specific strategies and resources for use in classrooms (also in settings of a personal, social, professional, or business nature,) for the study of the future, a process defined as a "dramatic rapidly growing attempt to identify the forces for change in our society, their interactions, and their probable future courses". (Hinrichs, 1975)

Connection to Creativity and Problem Solving

Practitioners and proponents of creative thinking are pre-conditioned to engage effectively in the strategies of Future Studies. Classroom activities and attitudes from the familiar work of E. Paul Torrance (1970), Frank Williams (1970), Calvin Taylor (1972) and Sidney Parnes (1967) provide a natural base and mind-set for students of all ages to participate productively in futuristic thinking and problem-solving. Guessing causes and consequences, planning and decision-making, generating alternatives (brainstorming, etc.), recognizing relationships, valuing individuality and personal uniqueness, and cultivating awareness and intuitiveness are only a few of the intellectual talents relevant to the practice of both creativity and futurism. The two are inseparable.

Techniques for Future Studies

The Future Studies Department of the Minnesota Scien[ce] Museum in St. Paul sponsors an annual workshop for educat[ors] on - *Exploring the Future*. Their program includes sessions experiences with a variety of futures strategies that are usable readily adaptable for use) at both secondary and element[ary] levels. (The content to which the processes can be applie[d] open to the purposes, imagination and alertness of the teache[r] current issues, and to present and potential interest levels students.)

1. *Future Wheel:* Identify a present trend as the cen[tral] event. (Example: More educational TV programs are becom[ing] available to children and young people.) What are some f[irst] order effects of this trend? What might be some of the sec[ond] order results of each first order effect? Responses from [the] group are recorded and displayed in graphic form on large (2[4 x] 36) newsprint. The central event is written in the center ci[rcle] (hub) of the wheel. First order and second order effects [are] indicated by additional circles attached appropriately to for[m a] network of implications. Students may work in small groups [on a] central trend or event. A variety of predictions will be produ[ced] and may be examined together to determine the degree [of] negative or positive (mark each response "+" or "-") attitu[des] and values reflected in the separate groups. Posting Futu[re] Wheels in a classroom promotes discussion and inquiry.

2. *Relevance Tree:* Decide on an idea or purpose that [a] group would like to support or actualize for improving exp[ec]-tations of the future. Working backwards is logical order f[rom] the goal to the situation as it is at the present, ideas are discus[sed] and recorded in sequence on large newsprint in tree format[.]

3. *Trend Extrapolation:* Use graphs with a time dimensio[n on] the base line and quantity figures on the vertical axis. Chart [data] collected through investigation and interview concerning [the] past; note the recorded trends; extend their directions into [the] future as suggested by the graph.

4. *Cross Impact Matrix:* Use a matrix to speculate on how [a] trend or event might affect another, even when not ostens[ibly] related. Any four or five concerns significant to the fu[ture] (population growth, food supply, weather control, urban tra[nsit,] energy resources, land use, etc.) are arranged on the matrix, [both] vertically and horizontally. Discussion of effects and [rela]-tionships between each of the possible pairings forces [new] insights. As a variation, assign a single group member to ea[ch of] the positions indicated on the matrix, and pair the roles in dy[adic] discussions.

"Future Studies for the Gifted," Bernice D. Bleedorn, *The Gifted Child Quarterly*, Vol. XX No. 4, Winter 1976. ©1976 The National Association for Gifted Children.

5. *Scenarios:* Write fantasized accounts of the long-range future of some matter of social or scientific interest. Describe the ultimate result of the perceived present trend in dramatic, exaggerated, or satirical terms. (Example: Write a scenario on the growing evidence of pollution in the oceans — or our growing dependence on foreign oil.)

6. *Science Fiction:* Read and discuss the provocative fantasies and realities of time and space, technology, and social issues presented in Science Fiction literature, films, TV shows, etc.

7. *Games:* Locate games designed to stimulate creative and futuristic thinking. (Example: *Futuribles: Gaming Together with 288 Possible Futures,* available from Cokesbury, Servid Department, P.O. Box 840, Nashville, Tennessee 37202, for $9.45. It is a card game suitable for High School students or able thinkers of Junior High or Upper Elementary levels.) Guidelines for designing original games are published in *How to Design Educational Games,* Ray Glazier, ABT Associates, Inc., 55 Wheeler St., Cambridge, Mass. 02138.

8. *Immortality Game:* Divide the class into small groups to discuss this fictitious situation — A major drug company is asking for citizen opinion on the marketing of a newly developed product. The drug which has been developed will keep people's bodies from growing older. It can be taken as a pill. It does not affect the ability to think or learn. It simply stabilizes body age. The group is asked to try to arrive at consensus on such questions as; Should everyone (or anyone) be able to buy it? Should the drug be put on the market at all? Who should qualify for using it? Who should decide? What would happen if it were sold and used according to people's choices?

Resources and Links to Leadership

Buckminster Fuller is probably one of the best known futurists. The statement from his book, *I Seem To Be A Verb* (Fuller, 1970) is significant:

I live on earth at present and I don't know what I am.
I know that I am not a category.
I am not a thing — a noun.
I seem to be a verb,
An evolutionary process
An integral function of the universe.

It is a reminder of the personal and global qualities of the process of becoming. Especially for those with special talents and gifts, the process has potential for exceptionality and outreach.

How are educators making the connection with the national scene? Where might they find guidelines for incorporating applications of Futures Studies into learning experiences and thinking processes? One step is to contact the World Future Society, an association for the study of alternative futures. Membership includes a monthly publication, *The Futurist.* It is a journal of forcasts, trends, and ideas about the future. It

information on resources and materials. A few examples of such resources are appropriate to this article:

1. Detailed directions of Futures Studies techniques are described in a 1975 publication by Ronald LaConte, *Teaching Tomorrow Today.* It can be ordered from Bantam Books for $1.25. (666 Fifth Avenue, N.Y. 10019.)

2. Another resource for educators, *Teaching Futures,* was prepared for an Elementary and Secondary Teachers Conference in 1974 and edited by James Stirewalt. The price is $5.00 ($4.50 to members of World Future Society) and can be ordered from their Book Service.

3. A book for juveniles is *Danny Doodle* by Darold Powers. It is described as a "doodling-and-coloring book designed to encourage creativity in children 5 to 10 years old. The child participates in completing the book. The book's purpose is to help children live in a changing world." It is available from the Book Service, World Future Society.

Information regarding materials and membership may be addressed to World Future Society, 4916 St. Elmo Avenue (Bethesda), Washington, D.C. 20014. The World Future Society held its Second General Assembly in Washington, D.C. in June, 1975. A publication based on that meeting is in print and available from their office. A catalogue of additional resources including books, tape cassettes, games, magazines, and learning materials is available. A discount is offered to members.

According to a 1974 World Future Society survey, Education ranks high in special interest topics among people concerned with the future. Other special interest areas are: Human Values, International Affairs, New Technology, Transportation, Biology/Medicine, Cities, Energy and Resource Conservation, Food and Population, Communications, Work and Careers, and Government. Education is one of the areas for which a Special Studies Division has been designed by the Society. Its purpose is to provide opportunities for active participation of members in organizing conferences, seminars, forums, and other meetings. Among the national futurists whose writings relate directly to educational futures are Alvin Toffler (1975), Harold Shane (1973), and Edwin Reischauer (1973).

In addition to the national effort, state organizations are being developed and speakers bureaus organized in a number of settings. Industry, in many places, is directing attention toward the establishing of Futures Studies Departments. Courses in the field of futurism are appearing in college catalogues. Graduate programs in Alternative Futures are being announced. Libraries in many areas are adding countless books and films on futurism to their collections. All of these trends have implications for schooling and career planning for today's children and youth.

THE FEDERAL ROLE IN EDUCATION OF THE GIFTED AND TALENTED

By Jane Case Williams
Deputy Director

OFFICE FOR GIFTED AND TALENTED
U.S. OFFICE OF EDUCATION

In the more than 100 years of its existence, the role played by the U. S. Office of Education in serving the gifted and talented has ranged from nonexistent or peripheral to that of strong advocate and administrator of legislation specific to gifted and talented education. Prior to 1961 there were sporadic publications from USOE, e.g., "Reading for the Gifted", and some research and surveys of program offerings for the gifted in high schools. Between 1961 and 1964 a specialist in the area of "gifted" was employed to develop training programs for the Division of Elementary-Secondary Education; however, in 1964 the Office was reorganized away from emphasis on specialized areas.

A measure of success of this brief attention to gifted education can be noted in the fact that here began the impetus which has succeeded in moving the definition of giftedness away from narrow emphasis on academics and "IQ" toward the broadened approach which is currently accepted for federal programs.

The definition of giftedness for purposes of federal education programs, established in the Commissioner's Report to Congress in 1971, reads:

Gifted and talented children are those identified by professionally qualified persons who by virtue of outstanding abilities, are capable of high performance. These are children who require differentiated educational programs and/or services beyond those normally provided by the regular school program in order to realize their contribution to self and society.

Children capable of high performance include those with demonstrated achievement and/or potential ability in any of the following areas, singly or in combination:

1. general intellectual ability
2. specific academic aptitude
3. creative or productive thinking
4. leadership ability
5. visual and performing arts
6. psychomotor ability

It can be assumed that utilization of these criteria for identification of the gifted and talented will encompass a minimum of 3 to 5 percent of the school population.

Evidence of gifted and talented abilities may be determined by a multiplicity of ways. These procedures should include objective measures and professional evaluation measures which are essential components of identification. Professionally qualified persons include such individuals as teachers, administrators, school psychologists, counselors, curriculum specialists, artists, musicians, and others with special training who are also qualified to appraise pupils' special competencies.

The Congress of the United States expressed its interest and concern by passing a landmark addition to the Elementary and Secondary Education Amendments of 1969 (Public Law 91-230), section 806, "Provisions related to gifted and talented children." This amendment, unanimously passed in the House and Senate, provided for two specific changes in existing legislation. It explicated congressional intent that the gifted and talented student should benefit from Federal education legislation-notably titles III and V of the Elementary and Secondary Education Act and the teacher fellowship provisions of the Higher Education Act of 1956. Section 806 directed the Commissioner of Education to conduct a study to:

1) Determine the extent to which special educational assistance programs are necessary or useful to meet the needs of gifted and talented children.

2) Show which Federal education assistance programs are being used to meet the needs of gifted and talented children.

3) Evaluate how existing Federal educational assistance programs can be more effectively used to meet these needs.

4) Recommend new programs, if any, needed to meet these needs.

This study represented an area of concern for both the Federal and non-Federal sectors, and offered the U.S. Office of Education (USOE) the opportunity to study an educational problem with nationally significant, long-term implications for society.

The study consisted of five major activities:

1) Review of research, other available literature, and expert knowledge.

2) Analysis of the educational data bases available to USOE and the development of a major data base through the "Survey of Leadership in Education of Gifted and Talented Children and Youth" (Advocate Survey).

3) Public hearings by the Regional Assistant Commissioners of Education in each of the 10 HEW regions to interpret regional needs.

4) Studies of programs in representative States with a longstanding statewide support for education of gifted and talented children.

5) Review and analysis of the system for delivery of Office of Education programs to benefit gifted and talented children.

This study began in August 1970 with the development and acceptance of the plan and concluded in June 1971 with the preparation of the final report, based on the findings and documentation from the five major activities.

This study produced recommendations on special programs and suggested priorities in planning individual programs, estimates of the professional support and teacher training required, and adjustments in legal definitions that would enhance the possibility of State and local fiscal support. The major findings of the study — those with particular relevance to the future planning of a federal role on education of the gifted — are:

— A conservative estimate of the gifted and talented population ranges between 1.5 and 2.5 million children out of a total elementary and secondary school population (1970 estimate) of 51.6 million.

— Existing services to the gifted and talented do not reach large and significant subpopulations (e.g. minorities and disadvantaged) and serve only a very small percentage of the gifted and talented population generally.

— Differentiated education for the gifted and talented presently perceived as a very low priority at Federal, State, and most local levels of government and educational administration.

— Although 21 States have legislation to provide resources to school districts for services to the gifted and talented, such legislation in many cases merely represents intent.

— Even where there is a legal or administrative basis for provision of services, funding priorities, crisis concerns, and lack of personnel cause programs for the gifted to be miniscule or theoretical.

— There is an enormous individual and social cost when talent among the Nation's children and youth goes undiscovered and undeveloped. *These students cannot ordinarily excel without assistance.*

— Identification of the gifted is hampered not only by costs of appropriate testing — when these methods are known and adopted — but also by apathy and even hostility among teachers, administrators, guidance counselors and psychologists.

— Gifted and talented children are, in fact, deprived and can suffer psychological damage and permanent impairment of their abilities to function well which is equal to or greater than the similar deprivation suffered by any other population with special needs served by the Office of Education.

— Special services for the gifted and talented will also serve other target populations singled out for attention and support. (such as the disadvantaged)

— Services provided to gifted and talented children can and do produce significant and measurable outcomes.

— States and local communities look to the Federal Government for leadership in this area of education, with or without massive funding.

— The Federal role in delivery of services to the gifted and talented is presently all but nonexistent.

These findings provide ample evidence of the need for action by the U.S. Office of Education to eliminate the widespread neglect of gifted and talented children. Federal leadership in this effort to confirm and maintain provisions for the gifted and talented as a national priority, and to encourage the States to include this priority in their own planning was immediately assumed by the U.S. Office of Education.

The Commissioner of Education, Sidney P. Marland, immediately established the Office for Gifted and Talented. The OGT was to be an advocate office within the U.S. Office of Education for purposes of coordinating activities which could be supported with USOE resources and to encourage investment by the private sector and other public, State and local resources. Dr. Marland stated: "During 1971-72, the Federal government, through the U.S. Office of Education, committed itself to a new and extremely important area of concern -- the education of the gifted child. . . . It is a significant commitment."

To support this commitment a small staff was assembled and housed within the Bureau of Education for the Handicapped — the part of the U.S. Office of Education administratively most parallel to accepted patterns for provision of services to gifted children, and one highly experienced and successful in the delivery of specialized services to specific target populations. Some USOE program funds were made available for national projects benefitting the gifted and talented, e.g., the Education Professions Development Act supported the National-State Leadership Training Institute for the Gifted and Talented; Title V, ESEA, supported several regional interstate projects; career education for gifted and talented was initiated with an institute supported by BOAE. All of these commitments were enhanced by the cooperation of the Regional Commissioners of Education in assigning in each of the ten DHEW regions, a part time Gifted and Talented Program Officer.

In 1974, full recognition of the federal role in education of the gifted and talented was realized with the passage of the Education Amendments of that year. Section 404 (a part of the Special Projects Act) gives statutory authority to administer the programs and projects authorized by the legislation and to coordinate all programs for gifted and talented children and youth which are administered by the Office of Education. This is the initial legislative authority for a program of categorical federal support for education of the gifted and talented.

The legislation provides for the following:

"grants to State educational agencies and local educational agencies to assist in the planning, development, operation, and improvement of programs and projects designed to meet the special educational needs of gifted and talented children at the preschool and elementary and secondary school levels";

"grants to State education agencies for purposes of establishing and maintaining, directly or through grants to institutions of higher education, a program for training educators of the gifted and talented and their supervisors";

"grants to non-profit agencies or institutions for leadership training, including internships with local, State or Federal agencies and other public or private groups";

"contracts for the establishment and operation of model projects for the identification and education of special target populations of gifted and talented children, including such activities as career education, bilingual education, and programs of education for handicapped children and for educationally disadvantaged children";

1. PERSPECTIVE

and

"dissemination to the public of information pertaining to education of the gifted and talented."

A program of research is also authorized; however, this is to be conducted by the National Institute of Education. The legislation authorizes an annual appropriation for the above purposes of $12.25 million for each year of the three-year life of the Special Projects Act. Regulations and program announcement dates as published in the Federal Register may be obtained upon request for the use of potential applicants.

In implementing programs under this authority, the Office of Education is drawing upon the experience and successful approaches used in meeting the special educational needs of other special target populations, as for example, handicapped children and youth who have received enormously increased and improved services through implementation of the Education of the Handicapped Act.

The program of educational assistance for the gifted and talented will employ a catalytic strategy for stimulation and support primarily of state leadership and excellence of programming at points of impact which are critical in the development of a national delivery system for education of gifted and talented children and youth. This is a logical extension of the existing initiative begun in 1971 and 1972 with the Commissioner's Report to Congress on education of the gifted and talented, and the designation of the Office for Gifted and Talented as an unfunded advocate office within the agency. In the intervening two years, this office, working with cooperatively secured public and private sector resources, has initiated a program of national awareness, leadership training and development, State planning, research on special problems in identifying and serving gifted disadvantaged, career education, and development and dissemination of information to a national user network.

With the enormous interest in this program and the stringencies imposed by limited resources, strategies for obtaining maximum benefit from approved projects are important. All projects are funded on a competitive basis — that is, there is no formula distribution of funds. Applications are reviewed on a fully competitive basis by qualified readers from the field and the Office of Education. Awards are made on the basis of review criteria which emphasize the planned coordination of already existing resources within a State or locality, multi-institutional cooperation, high quality, activities which achieve a multiplier effect, dissemination and replication of project outcomes, general effectiveness, and cost efficiency.

It is anticipated that supported programs under this authority as well as other federal and non-federal resources will address continuing needs in the major areas of national concern to which the Office for Gifted and Talented has directed resources to date. These include the following:

State Leadership — The primary target group is educational leadership, especially within the State education agencies, where the focus has been on the development of trained teams from each state which have capability to direct a variety of public resources toward improving educational opportunities for gifted and talented youth. The underlying assumptions are supported by the fact that even the earliest data available to the Office of Education shows a high correlation between State agency efforts and services provided to the gifted and talented populations of those states. Funds

available under the Education Professions Development Act in 1972, 1973, and 1974, have enabled the training of diverse teams and development of State plans for more than two-thirds of the States and Territories as well as some regional and large city teams, and will have reached all fifty-seven by the end of fiscal year 1975. The program of State and Local Education Agency grants authorized under Section 404 will provide for enactment of these plans and the "unlocking" of State and community resources.

Manpower and Training Needs — The absence of programs for the gifted and talented is accompanied by shortages of personnel experienced or trained in the field. Manpower training studies in education have shown the value of short-term institutes for inservice teacher preparations, technical assistance centers of excellence and catalytic funding to, or contracting with colleges and universities to encourage course offerings. Cooperative training efforts will coordinate State planning with provision of resources at institutions of higher education.

A critical need exists also for a nationally distributed cadre of leaders — people who can assume the role of training other leaders, influencing school districts and State education agencies, and developing high quality curricula for the gifted and talented and for the provision of "internship" leadership development opportunities at State and national administrative levels in governmental and non-governmental organizations.

Information Development and Dissemination — In the development of national public awareness and to respond to the heavy flow of information requests, the development and dissemination of information on educating the gifted and talented child has been a concern of all program efforts coordinated by the Office for Gifted and Talented. Every project has been information product oriented and wide distribution is achieved for the resultant publications. This effort has been facilitated by the existence of the ERIC Clearinghouse on Handicapped and Gifted, supported by the National Institute of Education for purposes of acquiring, indexing and retrieving relevant research and related data.

Through the network of States, Regional Offices of Education, services such as the Leadership Training Institute, and national associations of persons involved in education of the gifted and talented, a mechanism can exist for efficient determination of user requirements and dissemination services.

Research and Exemplary Projects — An early history exists of research on the measurement and development of high potential of individuals through education. In recent years, research in education has tended to emphasize special needs of disadvantaged and other target populations without recognizing the very special needs of the disadvantaged gifted. These are children who, for a variety of reasons such as age, sex, economic and social factors, race, language background, etc., do not receive special recognition of their potential and consequently fail to develop these abilities.

Section 404 permits application of research to the identification and provision of services to such special target populations and dissemination of documentation of successful practices.

Plans for the NIE supported research program, as mandated in this law, are expected to be prepared in cooperation with USOE's Office of the Gifted and Talented.

Career Education — Career education as "the total effort

of public education and the community to help all individuals become familiar with the values of a work-oriented society, to integrate those values into their personal value systems, and to implement those values in their lives in such a way that work becomes possible, meaningful, and satisfying to each individual" is particularly significant in consideration of the gifted and talented. These young people are faced with a multiplicity of possible directions for development of life purpose — and require understanding, guidance, and development far beyond that of their peers if they are to realize their potential contribution to self and society.

Projects from local school districts (with state review) as well as projects under the 15% set aside provisions for special target programs will be funded with career education as one priority area.

Private Sector Cooperation — The Office for Gifted and Talented has been successful in working cooperatively with non-public resources to support projects initiated jointly by the Office of Education and private agencies. This is an area in which the Office for Gifted and Talented was given broad authority to enter into cooperative relationships. Some examples of products and activities include: the Exploration Scholarships program (a national competition to identify and place outstanding young people in career exploration opportunities with some of the world's leading scientists); a conference on educational needs of the disadvantaged gifted; support by a foundation directly to the technical assistance program of a state education agency; development of a national gifted student conference and resource directory; mentorships in the arts; and partial support to conference and other activities in which there is cooperative public-private investment.

These activities represent an important and complementary contribution to the national federal education program for the gifted and talented and cooperative private-public sector programs will be encouraged in conjunction with the implementation of programs now legislated.

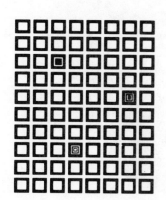

Office of Human Development Services, Department of Health, Education and Welfare.

Program Curriculum and Materials: Methodology

In a society dedicated to the ideal that each person should attain the heights of his capability, it is ironic that those individuals capable of the greatest intellectual attainments frequently have not been properly directed. The academically gifted child in this country is often the victim of inappropriate educational planning. The widespread underachievement of these students is most pronounced when looked at from the viewpoint of a longitudinal examination, which reveals the fact that the underachievement of the gifted child becomes more pronounced as they progress through school. The educational setting is the one agency in our society which has the greatest opportunity to correct this waste of intellect.

Educational experiences are frequently geared to the average child. When, in fact, alterations are made in the existing curriculum, often these are designed for the below average or slow learner. As the dilemma of the gifted child strapped into an educational setting that does not sufficiently meet his needs, continues to emerge into public awareness, a call for curriculum modification and program planning is heard universally. Successful programs for the gifted must be carefully and thoughtfully established. The sole claim of worth cannot be the mere fact that they are new. Time is an important ingredient in the process of developing new curriculums. Careful, time-consuming evaluation procedures must be carried out to assess the validity of the program.

The key to formulating a program for the gifted child lies in the acceptance of the fact that the purpose of a total program for these children should encompass a variety of learnings, extending from knowledge mastery, to development of skills, interests, and attitudes. Although an educational system should aim to provide a variety of activities for its entire population, those students who stand out intellectually have the abilities to roam and learn over a greater area. In establishing a program for the gifted population, striving to create a stimulating environment is crucial, one which places special emphasis on creature thought and social responsibility.

on education

CHARLES B. FOWLER

At Harrisburg's Riverside Center, a play written and directed by students

Special treatment for the gifted

SCHOOL SYSTEMS are learning how to develop diversified programs to meet the special interests and needs of their students. Some cities, like New Orleans, Philadelphia, and Houston, have developed "magnet" schools with curricula focused on the arts and programs specifically designed for students who show exceptional artistic ability. New York City's High School of the Performing Arts is a prominent example. These schools are open to all qualified city students.

There is evidence that this trend is spreading to smaller cities and school systems. In 1971 the Harrisburg School System in Pennsylvania set up the Riverside Center for the Arts, a public school for the arts that at first catered to talented students in grades five and six and is now concentrating on the seventh to twelfth grades.

Encouraging artistic experience

With the help of federal funds the Riverside School provides an environment and staff that encourages exploratory and in-depth experiences in art, dance, drama, music, photography, and television.

The Harrisburg story grew out of the ferment that typifies many school systems today. In the midst of redeveloping the school district in 1971, the Riverside Elementary School was abandoned. It was situated away from the mainstream and, with its nine rooms, was considered too small.

The building represented a resource that might be used in some new way. It was Benjamin F. Turner, now Superintendent of Schools and then Deputy Superintendent for Program Planning, who had the vision to establish an arts center for city students. The school board gave approval, and the plan was underway.

Harrisburg is an urban school district with students from many diverse cultural, racial, and economic backgrounds. The 26.6 percent of the school population that is white consists of students of German, English, Jewish, Italian, Greek, and Slavic extraction, while 69.4 percent of the population is black and 4 percent are non-English speaking. The arts center was developed to bring together

"On Education," Charles B. Fowler, *High Fidelity and Musical America*, Vol. 27 No. 4, April 1977. ©1977 ABC Leisure Magazines, Inc.

these groups in a way that encourages understanding, appreciation, and celebration of their differences.

Spotting talent

Identifying the talented, particularly when students come from such diverse ethnic backgrounds and vastly different home environments, is not simple. In 1970 the U.S. Commissioner of Education, Sidney P. Marland, Jr., together with an advisory panel, defined gifted and talented children as "those identified by professionally qualified persons who by virtue of outstanding abilities are capable of high performance. These are children who require differentiated educational programs and/or services beyond those normally provided by the regular school program in order to realize their contribution to self and society."

At first students were identified through an application form which could be submitted by a teacher, principal, counselor, parent, friend, or by themselves. Later, after the Center had been operating, the staff devised a list of characteristics of successful participants which became the basis of a new form to be filled out at each student's school. Among the desired characteristics sought are these: imagination and a sense of humor, self-control, the ability to deal with abstract ideas and to formulate original and divergent ideas.

Teachers, guidance counselors, and principals rate students on a scale of one to five on each characteristic. A test for creativity is also administered to all applicants. Students who rate high are then interviewed and asked to participate in specialized activities in the various arts. A student's art products or performances, interest and motivation, awards, and indications of leadership ability are also taken into account. Final selection is made on the basis of all the identification methods with a policy of inclusion wherever there is doubt about a student.

These procedures are still being refined, particularly to assure the discovery of the creative student from minority or disadvantaged groups. For many of these students, opportunities to explore their talents must be made available through the school or they will not be made available at all.

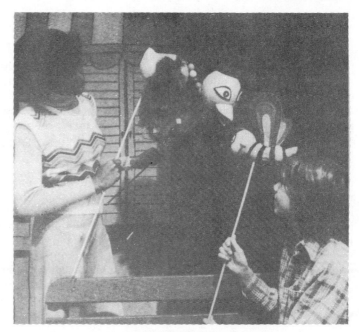

Students with puppets
they made for a
Little Red Riding Hood
production

Teacher and students
at work in Riverside's
electro piano lab

2. PROGRAM CURRICULUM

Ties with the community

While discovering students with potential in the arts is one of the primary aims of the program, there are other important objectives. The Center is determined to create an exciting program and environment conducive to exploration and learning through the arts. The faculty introduces students to the arts process in all its aspects and provides them with across-the-arts experiences. The Center has also developed ties with community arts organizations including the William Penn Memorial Museum and the Harrisburg Symphony Association.

Barbara McGeary, project director, says, "Our community has a rich offering of people and resources that can be used to help broaden student exposure to all the arts. Community artists act as supplemental teachers at the Arts Center. Community resources such as museums, galleries, theaters, playhouses, orchestras, and dance studios serve as out-of-school classrooms."

One evidence of this bond between talented young students and their community counterparts is the soap opera the students are developing for the local television station with the help of professionals from the community. Called "Fond Memories," the show is written, directed, acted, and filmed by the students.

A resident string quintet provides opportunities for students to work directly with professional musicians. The Center houses a piano laboratory and students have the use of a synthesizer for the creation of electronic music. Up to 150 students spend half of every day studying the arts at the Center. They take their other subjects elsewhere.

The Project is financed in part by local school funds, in part by funds from Title IV of the Elementary and Secondary Education Act. With the Center the Harrisburg School System has taken concrete action toward meeting the specialized needs of its students.

Fostering Creativity in the Gifted Child

A. HARRY PASSOW

D URING the decade of the 1960's, a vast amount of research was conducted on the psychological nature and measurement of creativity and problem solving and on curriculum and instruction in the nurturing of creativity. Almost every professional program and professional organization had programs dealing with creativity and its nurture. No teachers' meeting was respectable unless it had at least one symposium on the teaching of creativity. Is the current loss of interest in fostering creativity in the gifted child a reality or has the concern become a more integral aspect of nurturing talent? Have educators accepted the notion that creativity is an integral component of gifted behavior—that giftedness is only manifested when it includes an element of creativity?

Research of the 1960's

In the early 1960's the enthusiasts saw a whole new area opening up with challenges to identify and nurture creative potential and productive behavior at all stages of individual development. Many concurred with MacKinnon (1959), who wrote that the task of educators was not to label creative talent after it had manifested itself "either through our insight or through the use of validated predictors, [but] to discover talent when it is still potential and to provide the educational climate and environment that will facilitate its development and expression" (p. 29). There were those who were confident that research findings concerning the nature of human abilities required drastic reappraisal of all aspects of the educational process— teaching and learning, instructional materials, testing procedures, classroom and school organization, and staff use. School staffs, teacher training personnel, and others went to work on teaching creativity and creative teaching.

On the other hand, there were the cynics who saw nothing especially new in these developments, observing that *creativity, creative process,* and *creative thinking* were well worn terms in any teacher's lexicon and that few curriculum guides or instructional bulletins ever omitted some reference to the importance of nurturing original thinking and of providing opportunities for creative expression. Asked to assess their efforts, many teachers and administrators assert that such goals are standard. The belief that teachers have always taught for creativity has and continues to block an understanding of the meaning of the research for educational practice. Educators seemed to have latched on to the term *creativity* as still another fashionable expression. The absence of the mention of creativity at a 1974 conference on education of gifted and talented suggests what Taba (1963) called a "premature conversion of an idea into programs" (p. 248) or the lack of a conceptual base for such a program.

There are, of course, accounts of efforts to develop creativity long before Getzels and Jackson (1961) applied Guilford's (1959) notions of the structure of intellect to education. For instance, in 1929 Mearns wrote of his work aimed at stimulating creative expression, using a language not too different from today's. Other efforts, some dating back to the 1890's, were aimed specifically at nurturing creativity but most of them were isolated and shortlived.

Disturbing Undertones

Granted that the development of independent and original thinkers has long been a prime purpose of education, there are disturbing undertones to studies of creative adults whose unusual achievements have been recognized and rewarded. Looking back at their schooling, they seldom credit classroom learning with contributing to their personal development, although they often can cite one or two teachers as having been especially influential in shaping their lives. Roe's *The Making of a Scientist* (1953) reflects this. Some adult model is remembered as having affected the individual significantly but such recollections are usually of a personal style or of interpersonal relationships rather than of school curriculum or classroom experiences.

Similarly, the reported responses by a large number of high school students to an assignment to describe "the most creative work or activity ever engaged in" can only be disturbing to educators. Analysis of responses indicated that some 90% of the incidents reported were activities or work that had occurred outside of the school itself or in some extracurricular situation. It is clear that many a youngster does a good deal of his creative work or productive thinking outside the classroom or the school. This has serious implications for the kinds of arrangements educators make for student learning.

Even such studies as the classic *Genetic Studies of Genius* (Terman et al., 1925; Terman & Oden, 1947) or Ghiselin's *The Creative Process* (1955) seldom deal with the kind of educational experiences that might have made a difference in the development of individual creativity. Although the Terman studies revealed that many gifted subjects were accelerated one or more years and were graduated from high school or college early, it is impossible to discern any kind of picture of the educational environment from which these gifted men and women came, the courses they pursued or the curriculum content, the extent to which the individuals were encouraged to learn and use skills for independent work, or the emphasis on novelty or innovation that was provided and rewarded. Many educators have argued that the specific courses children take are less important than the teachers with whom they have contact. While accepting this generalization, the educational planner is obligated nevertheless to arrange conditions so that the teacher can stimulate the development of the potentially productive youngster and the student can operate in an environment that encourages personal growth in creative areas.

Development of Productive Thinking

Research and experimentation that focus more specifically on education and training support the concept that productive thinking can be developed and that certain teaching-learning practices will nurture creative behavior while others may stifle its emergence or divert its direction. The growing research literature, while just beginning to be translated into operational practicalities, does have implications for testing and assessment of children for identification purposes; arrangement of scope, sequence, and organization of curriculum content; selection of methods and instructional emphases; production of materials and resources for students and teachers; and use and deployment of staff. Furthermore, educational opportunities can be arranged for students both inside and outside of school. This is important because educators have come to recognize that there are many institutions and agencies that educate and schools must understand how to capitalize on and complement learnings that may be more significant than what goes on in a standard classroom.

The literature admonishes that children are not encouraged—often not permitted—to explore new ways of thinking, to try novel approaches to problem solving, to use divergent ways of dealing with traditional course topics, or to play with ideas and materials. Every teaching methods textbook includes a chapter on creativity in teaching and learning or, at the very least, several paragraphs exhorting teachers to nurture independent and original thinking in children. Yet, the practices give cause to wonder whether or not the textbooks are dealing with the same concepts and processes as the researchers and theorists. The loose application of terms such as *creativity, divergent thinking, ingenuity-originality,* or *productive thinking* and the poor understanding of the basic processes involved may have diffused educational practice and complicated the planning of sound educational programs.

Definitions

Ghiselin (1955) defined creativity as "the process of change, of development, of evolution in the organization of subjective life" (p. 2). Fliegler (1959) observed that during the creative act, man "manipulates external symbols or objects to produce an unusual event uncommon to himself and/or his environment" (p. 115). Kneller (1965) has pointed out that most definitions of creativity tend to fall into four categories. Creativity may be considered from the standpoint of the person who creates, in terms of his physiology and temperament and his personal attitudes, habits, and values. Creativity may also be considered in terms of mental processes—motivation, perception, learning, thinking, and communicating—which the act of creating calls into play. Another definition of creativity focuses on environmental and cultural influences. Finally, creativity may be understood in terms of its products, such as

theories, inventions, paintings, carvings, and poems. Kneller has pointed out that, for the most part, it is this last conception that has traditionally guided the study of creativity, since products are more easily assessed than personalities. Any definition of creativity, Kneller observed, must include the essential element of novelty: individuals create when they discover and express an idea, artifact, or form of behavior that is new to them.

In *What Is Creative Thinking*, Patrick (1955) described the creative process as having four recognizable phases, known generally as preparation, incubation, illumination, and verification. Such studies provide educators with significant leads to understanding the nature and meaning of creative potential and performance at different developmental stages, in various kinds of activities, and under diverse circumstances.

Development of Assessment Techniques

It is probably fair to say that Guilford's (1959) factor analytic studies of the structure of the intellect provided a major impetus for the development of assessment techniques aimed at measuring abilities other than those appraised by conventional tests of intelligence. Despite the cautions of the test developers, the possibilities of batteries of tests of creativity may have been too intriguing for the practitioners who have used and misused such tests since they have become available.

While pointing to the development of tests of creativity as "an exciting and promising field of investigation," Thorndike (1963) questioned whether the various batteries of tests of creativity share the instrumentation for measuring creativity, and whether the low correlations among subtests result in different children being identified as creative depending upon which combination of items is used. Educators certainly are not at a point where they can or should trade tests of general verbal intelligence for batteries of creative thinking abilities, but they are at a point where they can use such assessment procedures as supplements to other available techniques. Practitioners need to understand what the test batteries purport to measure, what the subtests attempt to assess, and what the relationships are that unite the various batteries and their component parts.

While there are variations in what intelligence tests measure, there are even greater differences in the tests of divergent thinking and creativity. The instruments do differentiate among children, revealing aptitudes and potential that do have significance for program planning and individual guidance. The studies thus far stress the need, though not the direction, of programs that will nurture original, productive behavior. The task is not to focus on refining assessment techniques and procedures but rather to develop the right kinds of education that will nurture talent development—the right kinds because there is no single, simple formula.

There is little question that one of the most justifiable charges leveled against the educational system is that it has too often neglected and more often suppressed the natural creativity of the young. The past decade has begun to reverse this situation but much needs to be done.

Introducing Creativity

There are essentially two approaches to introducing creativity into formal education. One approach is to teach it as a new subject or skill and the other is to modify curriculum—to teach creativity in its own right or draw upon the creative potential in all subject areas that are taught. DeMille (1963) explained it this way:

> Creativity can be thought of as a new sort of subject matter or skill that is imparted by means of language, numbers, graphic and musical activities, dramatics, etc. Or, the existing curriculum can be thought of as the essential core, and an effort can be made to teach it in a better way by bringing out the creativity implicit in it. The curriculum can be a vehicle for creativity or creativity can enhance the curriculum. (p. 199)

Those who support the latter course argue that as yet too little is known about creativity to teach it effectively on its own, there is no definitive theory about it, and it is not known precisely what kinds of information are best learned authoritatively and which are best learned creatively. Further, they view creativity not as an isolated process but as a component of many kinds of activities. Others have made a strong case for creativity being taught, at least in some aspects, as a subject matter or skill.

In examining the educational implications of his model of the structure of the intellect, Guilford (1968) has suggested that curriculum content and methodology be analyzed systematically to develop previously ignored aspects of thinking. With his associates, he

has taken different subject areas at various grade levels and examined possibilities for nurturing creativity within such frameworks. Other curriculum developers have given attention to the content (i.e., the scope, sequence, and structure) of the curriculum, particularly to the role of intuition in learning.

Much of the work dealing with productive thinking in the curriculum has been done in the image of mathematicians and scientists. Although it is not yet clear, studies are being made as to whether the models are equally appropriate and applicable to other areas such as language arts, humanities, or social sciences. Only as educators examine some of the less elegant disciplines where the structure is more hazy and the analysis more meager, will they be able to test content for its contribution to what Anderson (1961) calls "an open system of education"—one that contributes to the development of creative, imaginative individuals who are increasingly able to respond to new requirements and change in the light of new knowledge.

Whether some content areas have greater possibilities for contributing to the nurturing of creative abilities, whether the creative process can be considered apart from or unrelated to content areas, and whether a particular level of competence must be developed before productive thinking can be developed are issues that confront curriculum planners. Curriculum planning for developing creativity must deal with both questions of organization of content around significant ideas, as well as determination of the sequence and articulation of learning experiences.

Techniques for Classroom Settings

Aside from the curriculum content, many educational applications of creativity are centered on methods of teaching or techniques that can be used in classroom settings. Analyses of the teaching process indicate that most teachers do at least 70% of the talking in a class and that a large fraction of this teacher talk involves questioning students. The teacher plays a crucial role as the initiator and determiner of the kinds of thought processes expressed in the classroom, with the teacher's questioning determining the focus of the classroom operations and the kinds of thought operations the student is asked to perform.

Foshay (1961) has noted that as educators

became concerned with creativeness of children and examined their work in school, it became obvious that most children, most of the time, simply imitate what others have done. He observed that this in itself is neither good nor bad: "Imitation has served the children well before they came to school—the basic lessons of infancy are learned through imitation . . . . We continue to ask children to imitate in most of what we attempt to do in school, since we continue to teach in the main by precept and example ('this is the way you do it')" (p. 22). When children are asked to be imaginative (as in painting or sculpture), they continue to imitate, running through their existing repertoire of responses. Only if they can be led to be dissatisfied with the existing style of imitativeness are they likely to change it.

Foshay suggested that there are four major aspects of the creative process that, taken together, account for it, and that these four aspects have implications for teaching and learning. They are an individual's openness to his own experiencing, focusing of that experience, disciplining of one's actions to work out the focus, and bringing the work to an end. Kneller (1965) has made four suggestions for nurturing creativity:

1. Encourage students to have original ideas.
2. Encourage students to examine new ideas on their merits and not dismiss them as fanciful.
3. Encourage spontaneous expression, especially in younger children.
4. Whet the students' curiosity about their studies as they relate to the world about them: Constantly probe and unsettle their minds by asking provocative questions and presenting challenges.

The implication that seems clear from efforts to foster creativity in the classroom is that the teacher's approach must be more than a bag of tricks brought out at infrequent intervals for a change of instructional pace. There is some evidence that the specific intellectual skills of productive thinking can be taught if the teacher has a model of these processes at hand and plans activities accordingly. To simply encourage children to express themselves freely is not enough. To exercise creativity, the individual must have a base upon which to build knowledge. An openness to experience; an ability to play with ideas, elements, concepts, and relationships; the potential for evaluating internally are all qualities that must have a sound knowledge base. This is only to suggest that creativity is not fostered in children simply by permitting them to do their own thing in all aspects of learning.

There are many things that the teacher does that help create an environment and a climate that encourage growth of creativity. Describing the results of a number of his studies, Torrance (1965) concluded that the key concept that emerges is "respect for the questions and ideas of the child, respect for his right to initiate his own learning effort, and respect for his right to reject, after serious consideration, the adult's ideas in favor of his own" (p.252).

Importance of the Teacher

Clearly, it is the teacher—the parent, the professional, persons from the community, the peer—who creates the conditions for nurturing or inhibiting the development of creativity. Schools are often described as pressure chambers for conformity with teachers lacking the sensitivity to value the original and novel performance of their students. There are too many requirements, coupled with a reward system that inhibits novelty and originality—tests, grades, selection processes, syllabi, single texts, and so forth. What is needed is a reassessment of values, the ends of the educational process, and the goals of educational programs.

There is a message for educators in the United States in the fact that large numbers of children and youth are opting for alternative programs and schools, for so called free schools, and for other arrangements, which indicates rejection of conventional learning paths. Many are choosing to design their own independent study programs and pursuing original paths for problem solving, for creative expression, and for the challenge and satisfaction of the task rather than for the traditional rewards of schooling. Many of these activities are carried on in nonschool, out of classroom settings. Many are fostering creative growth but many are also incomplete. To free children to do their own thing is not sufficient; they must have a sound base on which to build their creative efforts. This calls for new approaches to teaching traditional disciplines and skills in ways that will nurture, not inhibit, creative growth. While schools must help youngsters develop such strategies, at the same time, they must give attention to the myriad of conditions and restrictions that contribute to repression of creativity in the first place.

Significance of Every Component

Every component of education and schooling affects the fostering of creativity. Educators are not yet clear how educational technology, media, and instructional systems influence creative expression. Taylor's (1962) suggestion for more experimentation to determine how the creativeness of learner response is modified by the message of the media—single versus complex stimuli, structured versus unstructured stimuli, single versus multi-channel sensory input (simultaneously or successively), fleeting (as in radio or television) versus stable stimuli (as in book or still pictures)—has had little response. Teachers have little insight into how their instructional resources help develop or stifle innovative capacities of learners, except that they can be sure that the use of a single text and workbook probably contributes little to such development.

Little information is known about the effects of organizational procedures, such as streaming and grouping, on the nurturing of creativity. It is known that different kinds of scheduling, grouping arrangements, and program flexibility are needed, even to the reconceptualizing of administrative and organizational provisions. Some kinds of creative endeavors are best nurtured by independent activity while others benefit from the interaction of individuals in various kinds of group activities. Independent study is not a panacea for fostering creativity but only one means.

Wide Spectrum of Endeavors

Creativity is manifested in a wide spectrum of human endeavors, not just in science, the arts, or in the obvious activities. It takes different forms with different developmental levels. Divergent thinking can contribute to the acquisition of knowledge, insights, and skills, and even more traditional subject matter can be taught in ways that promote novel, fresh thinking and underscore the need to reexamine the conditions for learning engagements currently provided in home, community, and school.

If gifted children are to become gifted adults—and surely the school's concern is not to raise the IQ or the standardized test scores or the rate of university attendance of students but rather to provide them with the stimulation, motivation, and competence to behave creatively in life situations—then their creativity must be fostered by all those who influence their development.

If educators are to comprehend the educational implications of research and development on creativity, they must reexamine educational purposes in general and the understanding of what the school must do to nurture diverse aptitudes and abilities. No healthier prospect could confront educators if a climate for creativity is the true goal. In doing this, fostering creativity among gifted children—and indeed among all children—will become an integral and meaningful activity among educators and parents, rather than another educational fad to be forgotten or ignored a decade from now.

References

Anderson, H. H. Creativity and education. *College and University Bulletin*, 1961, *13*, 1-4.

DeMille, R. The creativity boom. *Teachers College Record*, 1963, *65*, 199-209.

Fleigler, L. A. Levels of creativity. *Educational Theory*, April 1959, *9*, 115.

Foshay, A. W. The creative process described. In A. Miel (Ed.), *Creativity in teaching*. Belmont CA: Wadsworth Publishing Co., 1961.

Getzels, J. W., & Jackson, P. W. *Creativity and intelligence*. New York: John Wiley & Sons, 1962.

Ghiselin, B. (Ed.) *The creative process*. New York: The New American Library, 1955.

Guilford, J. P. Three faces of intellect. *The American Psychologist*, 1959, *14*, 469-479.

Guilford, J. P. *Intelligence, creativity and their educational implications*. San Diego CA: Robert R. Knapp, 1968.

Kneller, G. F. *The art and science of creativity*. New York: Holt, Rinehart, & Winston, 1965.

MacKinnon, D. W. What do we mean by talent and how do we test for it? In *Search for talent*. New York: College Entrance Examination Board, 1959.

MacKinnon, D. W. Creativity: A multi-faceted phenomenon. In *Creativity: A discussion at the Nobel conference*. Amsterdam: North-Holland Publishing Co., 1970.

Mearns, H. *Creative power: The education of youth in the creative arts*. New York: Dover Publications, 1929.

Patrick, C. *What is creative thinking?* New York: Philosophical Library, 1955.

Roe, A. *Making of a Scientist*. New York: Dodd, Mead & Co., 1953.

Taba, H. Opportunities for creativity in education for exceptional children. *Exceptional Children*, 1963, *29*, 247-256.

Taylor, C. W. Effects of instructional media on creativity: A look at possible positive and negative

ROOM 13, RONI HOWARD'S OASIS FOR KIDS

An intimate look
at a teacher/friend
who opens up
the world for
urban students.

BY DIANE DIVOKY

If the windows of Room 13 at Jose Ortega School in San Francisco weren't covered with boards and wire grating, the view would be spectacular. The school sits high on a bluff that overlooks, on the west, the Pacific Ocean and, on the south, the San Bruno hills. The quiet neighborhood at the foot of the school—described as "black middle class"—is vintage San Francisco: rows of attached, neatly kept boxy houses lining steep streets.

The appearance of the school is considerably less spectacular. The school itself is flat, modern pink-gray, badly kept in the urban manner. The lawn in front of the school is balding. The playgrounds have borders of paper/can trash. The driveway at the far right of the school climbs past a metal gate askew on its hinges, past one wing of classrooms, past a small fenced playground, past clumps of pink and yellow wildflowers and sprays of broken glass on the hard pavement. The road leads to another wing—scarred con-

2. PROGRAM CURRICULUM

crete walls relieved by orange classroom doors. All the wing's classrooms are empty of children, except for Room 13, Roni Howard's room.

Howard chooses to work in this wing; she likes the distance from the hurly-burly of the rest of the school. Inside the classroom, for some six hours each day, she teaches 27 fifth graders. The educationese labels for the class are easy: gifted, multiracial, a self-contained classroom in a financially strapped and troubled urban system. They say almost nothing about the daily happenings in Room 13.

The day begins officially at 8:27 a.m., when the bell rings and the kids come barreling into the school off the playground, where they'd been assembling since eight o'clock, after bus rides and trolley rides from homes about the city. Physically, they could not be more varied: tall and stubby; poised and bumbling; freckle-faced pale, rosy, tawny, black; slant-eyed and owl-eyed and almond-eyed; in sweatshirts and jeans, jumpsuits and smocks, sweaters and skirts; all-American and exotic; TV handsome and lovable homely. The official ethnic breakdown says that six are Chinese; six, black; two, Filipino; one, Korean. The 12 white children include two Greeks (mirror-image twin boys), a

Jew, and combinations of Irish and German and Scandinavian that reflect the makeup of San Francisco neighborhoods. "Last year's class was much more balanced," Howard notes. "I had two or more of everything. This year there are no Japanese, no Italians, and only one half-Spanish."

In spite of their diversity, the children share qualities that make them enormously attractive. For one thing, they are—at 9 and 10 and 11—on the shiny and innocent side of the stormy complications of adolescence. And almost all have a personal ease and confidence that speaks of good treatment. But perhaps most important, they radiate an awareness, an interest in the world, that shows intelligence.

Once in the room, Howard and the children come together in an area that looks a bit like a ramshackle living room, furnished with an ancient white vinyl-covered sofa and chair, an equally ugly beige corner sofa sec-

tion, a tattered yellow rug, bookcases and other homey touches. Howard, a big woman in her early 30s, sits majestically in a chair; the students settle on furniture and on the floor. They begin with the bureaucratic transactions that are inevitable in a large public system.

"Good morning. Let's take the roll first; then I'll collect the junk. I think I need a note from you, Terry. . . . Carla, your hair looks cute. Did your grandmother do it? . . . I'm impressed with the two of you. First day of the new semester, and you're here on time. . . . First of all, the ship trip notes and money." The verbal shorthand and the passing of pieces of papers goes easily. "Any book orders? Now the green things. Anybody else? I have contract meetings today with five of you. Do you know who you are? I have a math meeting with Lynn. I have math due from you and you. There's the thank-you note to Mrs. Gold. Who's working on that? Anybody else

Howard is an intelligent adult
with the enthusiasm of a ten-year-old—a nice combination
for someone teaching smart fifth graders.

need a contract meeting? A propaganda meeting? Remember there's speech this morning, Craig and Ricardo. We'll do a PE because we missed one yesterday, but not a double one." A student suggests making a game book for a classmate in the hospital; another asks that students bring in potting soil for the classroom plants. Howard files notes in envelopes and writes appointments with students into her plan book. The day gets ordered. Within 15 minutes the meeting is over; the class will not come together again except for PE at the end of the morning and "circle" during the last hour of the afternoon.

The format that takes over at this point looks effortless. Without a word of direction the students disperse—in ones and twos—about the room. During a class meeting, 27 seems like a big group, but it somehow grows smaller and entirely manageable as students move into corners, spread out in the loft, settle at tables or carrels. The room is not pretty—visual aesthetics is not Howard's forte—but it is functional, making excellent use of each square foot of space.

Quickly, everyone is at work in an atmosphere of relaxed seriousness. Heather brings her folder to Howard's desk in one corner of the room and begins a contract meeting. Two boys who are spread flat out on a rug read together a book called *Search for a Living Fossil*. They discuss it between chapters. Reading from an encyclopedia, Kendra researches whales.

Three students at one table make posters that are parodies of food commercials, an assignment that is part of the ongoing propaganda unit. At the next table, two others play a commercial game of fractions. Anne and Heather play a decimal game created by students in one of Howard's former classes; Craig works on a lesson on measurements in a programmed math workbook; Karen works in a Kottmeyer spelling workbook; Sharon and Roberta quiz each other on multiplication tables with homemade flash cards; Brad draws a ship for a special project; Marlene cleans the rats' cage. Damien and Ricardo read stories from the SRA Reading Laboratory. Matt designs the thank-you note for Mrs. Gold. In the loft, which runs along

more than half of one wall, four students are reading, legs propped on large throw pillows. The selections include *The Prince and the Pauper, Torpedo Run, Twenty Thousand Leagues Under the Sea* and *Sounder*.

This seemingly spontaneous enterprise runs on a tightly organized contract system. Howard and each student negotiate individual assignments (covering a specific period of time) in the areas of math, reading and spelling. The assignments that make up a contract can be as mundane as "Read 150 pages of *These Happy Golden Years*" or "Play Fraction Football twice and Frio once" or "Complete eight SRA reading cards"—or as broad as independent research on one specific topic.

Students begin the year with one-week contracts; as they gain independence, some move up to two-week or longer contracts. At the end of each contract, the student has a contract meeting with Howard to determine what work has been completed successfully and what areas need more work. Before long, students can pretty much write their own contracts, with approval from Howard.

The paperwork for the contracts is kept in individual student folders that are the students' private property. Twice a year—at parent conferences —parents review them. Contracts cover only basic skills, but the folders also contain records on the other areas in which the students are working. A typical folder includes a sheet showing the progressive math skills the student has mastered, a list of all the books read during the year, a record of the student's accomplishment in the first-aid course and the propaganda unit, diagnostic test and final examination papers, and selected writings and accomplishments the student chooses to include. The students use their folders often for reference, and they understand the function of each piece of paper in the file. "This shows you that I understand division of various bases," one student explained. "This is the math test that I took to see what I needed help in. Here's where Roni suggested that I do more in the Singer math. This shows that I'm finished with fifth grade spelling." The folders help as much in

ordering the students' sense of where they are as they do in keeping Howard abreast.

Reading—for its own sake—is a staple of each contract and of the general program. At any moment during the day, at least a half-dozen students have their noses in books. Some 500 books—mainly worn paperbacks that usually have been purchased or scrounged by Howard herself—are filed alphabetically by author in two sets of cheap bookcases in a corner of the room. A recipe file case serves nicely as a card catalog for the books, from Adams' *We Dare You To Solve This: No. 2* and Alcott's *Little Women* to Zim's *The Great Whales*. Another rack holds dog-eared magazines— *Time, Newsweek, Ebony*, even *Movie Mirror*. On shelves near the floor are stacked sets of heavy, little-used reading texts with pretentious titles like *Dimensions* and *Counterpoint in Literature*.

Books circulate rapidly, with students making their own choices. "Sometimes I'll make a deal," Howard says. "If somebody is reading horse stories endlessly, I'll say that every other book should be a Newbery winner or a classic. And I try to get girls into books that aren't girly books, and boys into books that aren't thought of as boy books—move a boy along from James Fenimore Cooper to *Little Women*, say. Sometimes so many kids have read a particular book that it becomes an assignment. Poe was one of those, and the O. Henry stories. Some of the kids took off on O. Henry and started writing their own stories nearly every night. That happened too with the book *J.T.*, and then we talked about it. Of course, by the time 27 of them have read a single copy of a book, you have a rag."

When a student finishes a book he's especially liked or disliked, he has the opportunity to write his comments for a special file of reviews that students use in selecting books. "But there are no book reports," Howard explains. "I don't need a synopsis of the book. I know how many pages they have and what they're about. I've read them."

To teach basic reading skills, Howard uses a SRA Reading Laboratory geared to somewhat older students. "If I lectured, three out of four would miss it. With SRA they can get the basics individually. Besides, they really enjoy SRA." As with all materials, the students are meticulous in their use of the SRA kit. They understand that one card ripped or lost affects all of them, and when a card is missing, a student calls out: "Attention, attention. One-purple in the SRA is missing." Everyone stops what he's doing to check lockers and notebooks for the missing card.

Kottmeyer workbooks are used in a similar fashion for spelling skills, and word games help build vocabulary. "I can never find enough good games," Howard says. She uses games to build and reinforce skills, to diagnose, and to set a tone for the class. With the help of a friend who knew more about football than she did, Howard created Fraction Football, a complicated game involving dice, a chalkboard and paper. "Sometimes kids will be using a game in a new way, and I ask them to write their rules, and we get a new game that way," she explains.

Last fall Howard came back to school on crutches, six weeks late, as the result of serious complications and a bout in intensive care resulting from a multiple-fractured ankle. "The parents were waiting for me to take over from the substitute and get down to business. The first day we played games all day. The second day we played games. The third day we played games. By the fourth day I could almost hear the parents screaming, 'What's going on in there?' Then I called a parents' meeting and explained the purpose the games had served. I'd gotten to know the kids, found out where they were, established a rapport."

Although reading comes easily for Howard's students, many are not particularly "gifted" in math, an area she considers extremely important and devotes much of her time to teaching. Once the day's round of contract meetings is over, she is available for special math meetings. She is strong in math and teaches it well. In a math meeting with Maureen, Howard looks over her work and asks: "Now, what if I said, 'What is the percent?' First of all, what do you have to do? What does percent tell you? How many is in a hundredth? What does 100 percent mean? Could you make that a fraction for me? Write it for me as a fraction. Now, reduce it to its lowest terms. You already know what your denominator is. Can that be reduced? What number will go into both of those? OK, do it."

Howard's head is on her arms on her desk, watching Maureen's face as she stumbles through the procedure. Something tells Howard all isn't clear and she takes another tack: "What's the matter with dividing both by 100? It's perfectly legal to do that, you know." Maureen works through the problem again and checks with Howard. "Good. So tell me something: What did you just learn about 100 percent? Based on what you understand about percent, can you show me what that would look like as a percent? . . . That's absolutely correct. Now, wait. I'm going to try to trick you." Howard turns the problem around and makes it a bit more complicated. She and Maureen continue to work for a half hour.

The system—the contracts, the meetings, the time left for Howard to move around the room or play games with students—works almost all of the time. There seems to be a computer in her head that knows at any given moment that Damien is a week behind in his work, that Roberta needs drill in math, that Nancy could use enrichment work in science. Once in a while, the system breaks down. Late one afternoon, when many of the students are away from the room on a special project, Howard gets to the math corner, where Lynn is working on her math contract. Howard looks at a page of problems, with most of the answers wrong. She asks Lynn to work one through for her, and the student sits silently. "Why are you doing that, Lynn?" Lynn mumbles: "To get the answer." For a minute, they both are silent—Lynn, sullen; Howard, fuming. "I don't think you understand that," Howard says finally. "And it's OK that you don't understand that. But it's not OK that you don't come and ask me for help. That bothers me. Don't sit here and do your big pout act. I don't expect you to know everything. If you did, you wouldn't have to be in here. But let's not waste time with you spending hours on things you don't understand and getting every one wrong. You understand equivalents but you don't understand how to use them. Tomorrow I'd like you to play a little Fraction Frolic. Now let's see. What number goes into both of those?" On another day a couple of weeks later, Howard watches Lynn as she attacks a kind of problem she's never done before, gets it right, and looks up smiling. "I got it because I understand what I'm doing now," she says.

The contracts and the packages and homemade materials are the bones of the program, but no more than that. Although the children work alone or in small groups for much of the day, they are very much a group. If someone needs a partner for a game or help with a problem, there are volunteers. Voices stay low, so as not to interfere with others. There are jokes and laughter, but none of the petty meanness or ridicule that can come into play among children at this age. They really seem to like and respect one another, and they show a surprisingly mature concern and consideration for each other. "Some people are more nice than others, even in here," Marlene explains. "But they're all nice."

This spirit is very much a reflection of Howard. Trained as a psychologist with a credential in counseling, she backed into teaching six years ago when she began working in a federally funded pilot drug-abuse-prevention program in San Francisco elementary schools. She often didn't like the way children were being taught or treated, but what hooked her was teaching itself.

When the two-year project was over, she got accepted for a position as a teacher of the gifted. She taught for one year in another school, picked up her teaching credential at San Francisco State, and was sent in 1974 to Ortega, where she taught one class for two years, a situation she considers ideal because of the continuity. She'll also keep her current class for two years.

During these years, Roni's philosophy of teaching and classroom practices were developing. She spent the summer of 1974 observing and teaching in open classrooms in England, then taught workshops in affective education and the open classroom. She began to learn the way she wanted to work with children—not as a psychologist but as a teacher. "She teaches children how to learn," a colleague says. "She doesn't tell them, 'I think that was good.' She says, 'You did it.' She doesn't direct. And I like what she does with children's heads. She works with the child and takes his problems seriously. She's a friend and counselor, and she's always on the phone to homes. Yet she can be pretty tough when they're out of line. She's way beyond the clichés about independent learning or affective education."

Howard is an intelligent adult with the enthusiasms of a ten-year-old—a nice combination for someone teaching smart fifth graders. At home she collects animals like some people collect records or stamps. She has seven cats, all with names like Sojourner Truth and Leon Trotsky. Her interest in animals is reflected in her classroom. Two years ago a stray kitten became Morris (after Ortega's principal, Walter Morris), the classroom cat, who learned to live in peaceful coexistence with the guinea pigs (Sammy and Cocoa) and the rats (Inky and Rajah). This year's class includes a student allergic to cats, so Morris is at home with Howard and the rest of her menagerie. For Howard's most recent birthday, her class gave her another guinea pig. "I didn't need an eleventh animal," she says, "but he's really lovable."

The classroom animals are more than just cuddly pets. Morris became the takeoff for a study of cats that involved a field trip to the zoo to interview the handler of the big cats and a classroom visit from a National Cat Fanciers' Association representative who brought in champions of various breeds. "We learned everything from anatomy to genetics," Howard says. The project culminated in the entire class going to the veterinarian's to observe Morris' castration operation. Howard explains: "The vet had loaned us a book and the kids had boned up in advance on exactly what was going to happen and why. He closed down his office for the morning, and was really impressed with the questions the students asked. Even the kids who thought they might be queasy got so involved with what was going on that there was no problem. Of course, I was fascinated watching the vet's staff watch my kids watch him operate. They were mesmerized." (The vet has been a boon to the class in other ways. He volunteers his services for the class animals, charging Howard only for lab fees and drugs that he must purchase.)

Although Howard looks like a big, comforting mother—someone the kids do grab onto in moments of pleasure or pain—that is not her role with students. She is more a friend who opens up the world for them in as many ways as possible. This year her class went to the symphony, ballet and opera; toured Chinatown, guided by a Chinese classmate, and had a meal of dim sum; visited Berkeley's Lawrence Hall of Science, San Francisco's Exploratorium, and the natural history exhibit at the Oakland Museum; and enjoyed the city's Christmas decorations from the rooftop of the Emporium, a department store. A weekend camping trip concludes each school year. "There are some places that I think are important enough to visit every year, and

there are some spontaneous trips," Howard says. "For example, I read in the paper that the Magna Carta would be here on display for just four weeks. So we immediately started to study it, relating it to the Constitution, and went to see it before it was gone." Always budget conscious, Howard looks for low-cost or free events, uses parent volunteer drivers or public transportation, and only grudgingly will finance trips out of the $300 she gets each year in "gifted" funds.

On Howard's desk is a chart—half-facetious, half-serious—that establishes a point system for the kinds of work students do. Some of the grades are silly: "whippy dip wit" and "ding-a-ling." But the highest grade is quite serious: "clear thinker." Howard never lets her students forget that the point of school is not simply getting work done or getting good reports but thinking well.

This semester's special study of propaganda is typical of Howard's efforts to let her students understand how people think and believe as they do. In a corner of the room are the basic reference books for the unit and a card file filled with laminated cards detailing the required and optional assignments. Categories include: The Sales Pitch, Getting Your Way, Searching an Article, The Writer's Meaning, Persuasive Propaganda, Attitudes and You, Knowing Why You Like What You Like, Your Politicians. One task card asks the student to be an advertising agency writer for two companies selling the same product, and to produce two very different advertising campaigns. Another asks the student to watch TV for a week, choose commercials they particularly like or dislike, and write about those spots and the reasons for their response. The assignments—both creative and demanding—reflect an enormous amount of work on the teacher's part. "The unit wasn't something I put together over Christmas vacation," Howard concedes.

Howard's students also know that she has strong values, that she will not abide—inside the classroom or out—racism or sexism or comparable prejudices. She helps students see and understand these attitudes in the world around them. Three years ago, in the heated climate of San Francisco's busing program, two students —one black, one Jewish—arrived at school one morning in tears over a pamphlet that had been passed out at their bus stop. It was a tract of the American Nazi party (National Socialist White Workers' Party), urging that

Jews and "niggers" be deported. Roni spent a good deal of time talking to the two girls about why people feel that way and what it means, and that afternoon the entire class shared their outrage and dismay. The group asked what they could do to counteract such attitudes, and came up with the idea of using the free speech spots on radio and TV. They wrote a statement explaining how well integration was working in their class. A number of the radio stations let them give the message and two radio stations did special talk shows with groups of the students. The TV stations were less responsive, explaining that the students were too young to read something on TV, that they'd be too nervous. " 'How can they be too young to read it?' I asked one station director," Howard recalls. " 'They wrote it!' But the TV stations wouldn't take them seriously because of their age. Which taught them a lesson about another kind of discrimination."

Just recently, a student reported that a vulgar sexist comment—comparing women to monkeys—had been a source of laughter on "The Hollywood Squares." Now she is writing a letter to the show, asking why women are demeaned on a program aired during family-hour time.

Late in the morning, a boy reminds Howard it's PE time and the students hurry outside to a playground to begin a touch football game of their own invention. The rules, posted in the classroom, include such dicta as: "The team captain organizes the team but he/she can't hog the ball!" And: "Only one blitz per set of downs."

The class breaks into four teams, two students are appointed referees, and for the next 40 minutes the kids pass and run and huddle, with lots of whooping and yelling. With no monitoring by Howard, they call plays, keep score, kibitz, and settle disputes. They've set up the league so that all four teams will make it either to their own super bowl or a runners-up bowl.

Central to the class's unique rapport is the circle, a technique Howard has refined through years in teaching. Anytime during the day students can sign up to talk in the circle. At the last hour of the day they come together, and as the room becomes quiet, a student who's chosen to speak begins to present a problem, an incident that happened in school or out, or some other matter he wants discussed. In an orderly way, others respond. No names are used.

2. PROGRAM CURRICULUM

Often the children know which classmate was making trouble on the playground or which teacher was mistreating kids in the cafeteria, but the phrase is "a certain person."

Room 13 is not utopia. There are enormous limits put on the class by the urban condition itself. Scarcity is a continuing theme. All paper gets used on both sides, and paper not totally filled up goes into a scrap pile for double duty. Basic materials often must be begged or borrowed. Encyclopedias have been donated, but the class still lacks an "E" volume. Parents who work in labs or libraries are dunned for throwaways. Howard still is praying for a microscope. The large metal cabinet that houses the class's extensive set of games was found by a janitor who saw it was going to be thrown out because the door was broken. "I'm known as the junk lady," Howard notes. "Everyone knows where to send their castaways." Even the children's individual folders are discarded central school office folders, turned inside out. The loft was built by Howard and students,

with the expert help of a student teacher. "When he applied and said he was a carpenter, I knew I wanted him," Howard says.

At one time, the class used a corridor for work space and bulletin boards. But the bulletin boards continually were defaced and ripped up, and materials were stolen. Students grew gardens in small plots outside their room. But the planting projects came to an abrupt end one day a year ago when a student noticed a man spraying their lettuce patch and all the rest of the ground. "He was defoliating the ground, just like in Vietnam," Howard recalls. "It was a way of killing all the weeds, so the district wouldn't have to take care of the grounds, but of course it meant nothing will grow in that ground anymore."

By working late at school, Howard has tried to develop friendly relations with neighborhood people, and she thinks that's responsible for her room getting broken into less frequently than others. "The first time it happened, they took the bookcase but

left the books all neatly stacked," she says.

Last December, the class arrived in the morning to find the floor covered with a mix of paint and glue and windows broken open. Luckily, the class animals had not been harmed, as had happened in other rooms, but the cold night air meant a number were ill for some time.

Even during the day the doors now stay locked, because when they aren't, items disappear from the student lockers near the door. The children clearly have a sense they live in a tight oasis in the midst of unfriendly forces. They put curtains over their lockers and post notices saying: "Important: Anyone Entering This Locker Is Violating a Rule of Room 13." Or more simply: "Please Stay Out." Every time they must get a key from Howard to go to the bathroom or to the office, they are reminded of their confinement. "It's simply a fact of life," Howard says. "They know that what we do must happen here in this room. That's just the way it is."

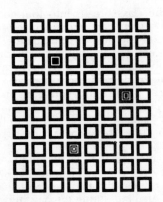

THE EDITH PROJECT

Jack McClintock

ON AUGUST 16, 1952, Aaron Stern called a press conference in a Brooklyn hospital. Stern, a survivor of Nazi cattle cars, Gestapo assaults, and midnight escapes into the black, snowy woods of Poland and Germany, showed the reporters a baby girl. He gazed raptly into her crib and said: "Meet my daughter, Edith. She is going to be a genius. I shall make her into the perfect human being."

With that Frankensteinian pronouncement, Stern devoted himself to what he calls "an idea that became an obsession"—the Edith Project. For the past twenty-five years, his life has had a benign sort of mad-scientist motif that has brought him into conflict with the educational establishment, his wife, and with Edith herself. Stern never swerved from his goal. The beloved daughter, weighing six pounds, seven ounces; nineteen inches long; three weeks premature, conceived in defiance of a doctor's warning to Bella Stern against having children with a man whose wartime experiences had left him with a medical dictionary full of physical and emotional maladies—this daughter, Stern vowed, would not be ordinary.

Twenty-one years later Stern was again talking to reporters. He was making the Philippine government the following proposal: he would study the Tasaday tribe, a group of cave-dwellers found living in Stone Age isolation, bring back two children, and rear them

to become geniuses (he was eventually turned down). It had worked with Edith, he said, and it would work with them.

"I have done what I promised the world," Stern says. "I have created a superior being."

Dr. Benjamin Fine, onetime education editor of the *New York Times* and a friend of the Sterns', said: "I've watched Edith develop through her teens. Her IQ might possibly be in excess of 200. She is certainly on the level of Einstein."

Edith, now twenty-four, consistently scores about 200 on an IQ scale on which 150 represents "genius"—whatever that may be. She entered school at the customary age of six, already reading two books and the *New York Times* every day. She skipped alternate grades through junior high, and skipped high school entirely to enroll in college at twelve. At fifteen she was teaching higher mathematics at Michigan State and working on her Ph.D.

But Stern's claims, even his accomplishments, have not always gone uncensured. He was warned that he might be creating a monster. Critics called him cruel and self-indulgent, accusing him of stealing Edith's childhood for his own aggrandizement. They suggested he was building a top-heavy structure—all brain and no wit or warmth. They say IQ tests mean little or nothing (a proposition with which Stern agrees: "I have subjected her to the indignities of IQ only to disarm my critics."). Dr. John Freeman, Edith's

department chairman at Florida Atlantic University, has said: "Time will tell if her development was too fast. I'm concerned at all the attention she received, apparently at the urging of her father. This may not prove good for her in the long run. I also question Aaron Stern's claim that he molded her mind. But, yes, she is very bright."

No one disputes that.

STERN HIMSELF cannot say where he got the idea. When asked, he launches into a long and complex tale, obviously told many times before. During the war years Stern lived for two years in a hole he scooped out in the muddy woods of Europe, eating wolf and bulldog meat when he was lucky and nothing when he was not. He was captured by the Germans twice and escaped twice. Once his jaw was crushed by a Gestapo agent's boot. After the war, in a refugee camp at Bad Reichenhall, he organized a school for orphaned street children.

Arriving in the U.S. in 1949, he and Bella, who were married in the Warsaw ghetto only to be separated by the war and later reunited, descended into what amounted to another ghetto: poverty and chronic illness in a Brooklyn tenement. Stern has never been well since. "I became," he says, "a notorious patient, a professional patient." He has had heart disease, hyperthyroidism, and cancer of the jaw, and has been hospitalized 170 times (he keeps

"The Edith Project," Jack McClintock, *Harper's*, Vol. 254 No. 1522, March 1977. ©1977 The Minneapolis Star and Tribune Company, Inc.

track). It was after one of those times that a vocational rehabilitation worker tested him and concluded that, although Stern spoke six languages (now ten), his intelligence was low. She recommended training as a welder. Instead he enrolled in Brooklyn College and finished in thirteen months.

While Bella worked, Stern, virtually unemployable, spent years writing a book documenting Nazi atrocities, the manuscript of which—1,600 handwritten pages in six languages—disappeared from his car one day while he was detained by Miami police on a traffic charge. In 1971 he wrote another book. This one was about Edith, his real vocation, and it was called *The Making of a Genius*. Stern himself published it, and has sold 3,500 copies.

The Sterns live in a small green-and-white house near the railroad tracks in North Miami Beach. There is a chartreuse living-dining room furnished inexpensively ("I am somewhat of an ascetic," says Stern), and stacked in the sun porch are cardboard cartons filled with unsold copies of *The Making of a Genius*. Shelves there were filled with folders of clippings and testimonials to his work. "I have always welcomed publicity," Stern said, "even though Edith has come to think of it as an invasion of her privacy."

Edith had recently taken her first job, with IBM, and moved to the small city of Boca Raton, about forty miles north of Miami, driving down to visit her parents on weekends. Her title was assistant programmer in the development laboratory, but no one could tell me exactly what she did. IBM spokesmen said only, "It's confidential." Edith said, "It's interesting."

Stern and I talked before Edith arrived. He dumped sheaves and folders of papers on the couch between us, speaking all the while of his critics, the "harassment," the difficulty of persuading others that he was not an ogre. He was at the center, he seemed to say, of a hostile universe—a man beset. I asked how he responded to charges that he had sacrificed his daughter's childhood to his own ego.

"Sublimation, I know," he sighed. "Every parent has the desire to fulfill himself through his child. It's not unusual." He paused. "Ask Edith if she missed anything. Those who say I stole my daughter's infancy are wrong. I didn't restrict her; I *added* to her life."

There had been early disappointments. As a youngster Edith was sometimes "excessively arrogant." She occasionally broke windows and furniture. Once she locked her father in the basement for half a day (she maintains it was an accident). He was not pleased, he said, by her excess weight. In college, Edith changed her major from pre-med, which she had selected as a child because she wanted to cure her father's many ailments when she grew up, to mathematics; Stern was certain it was "to cut the string, to leave me out. In mathematics I cannot follow her progress."

We inspected Edith's library, some 3,000 books and magazines obviously collected by a lover of science fiction and fantasy. There were books by Robert Heinlein, Harlan Ellison, Isaac Asimov, Theodore Sturgeon. There were also Camus, Steinbeck, the Durants. There were novelistic spin-offs from *Star Trek*, a book of B.C. cartoons, and *M*A*S*H Goes to Maine*.

"If she read that many books in the medical field," Stern said, "she'd be transplanting hearts by now."

T HE SCULPTING OF Galateas seems an arcane enterprise, but there was nothing mysterious in Aaron Stern's method. He calls it "total educational immersion" which, he says, "assumes that intellectual growth begins at birth and ends at death. It invites the utilization of all resources. When Edith wanted to go to the park, we passed by a construction site and she learned about physics. If we passed by a picket line, she learned about civics." Since he was unemployed, Stern gave Edith more attention, starting earlier, than most children get. And he demanded more back. All this may not be especially rare, but Stern's intensity and unwavering persistence over a period of many years surely are, and they may be unique.

The Edith Project began immediately after the infant was brought home and established in her crib, a blanket-draped bureau drawer. Stern announced that the family's cheap radio would be tuned to WQXR twenty-four hours a day. "Classical music," he swore, "shall beautify her soul." Except for repairs, the radio played for years.

Baby talk was forbidden. Stern, then himself perfecting his English, read

and talked incessantly, repeating words and holding bright magazine pictures before Edith's scarcely focused eyes. He gave her flash cards with numbers and animal pictures on them, reading off the name of each. As she grew he plastered old travel posters around the family's single room and spun tales for her of castles in Bavaria, pyramids in Egypt, and airliners over Manhattan. He filled her crib with multiracial dolls from the U.N. gift shop. He talked. For weeks little happened, and then he noticed that Edith would cry if the radio were tuned to jazz or popular music. Then she began to recognize the dolls.

Edith was five months old and being breast-fed by her mother when the conflict between the two parents first came out in the open. "This period is conducive to learning," Stern said, and announced that from then on *he* would feed the baby.

"Please don't deny me this pleasure," Bella pleaded. But from then on Edith got her sustenance from Aaron.

When she was eleven months old, Stern asked her how old she was. She rummaged in her crib, picked up the "10" flash card and held it up. Stern waited. Then Edith raised a chubby forefinger beside it. Stern kissed her many times (he used kisses and candy as rewards for good performance), and she counted aloud, "One, two, three, four, five. . . ." When she did not learn well later on, he would forbid her to read.

From Stern's diary, April 1, 1953: "Like the spring sunshine which melts the dreary, all-encompassing icy landscape, so does Edith's intellect emerge in all its splendor."

At one year she spoke simple sentences and identified letters on flash cards, at two she knew the alphabet. When she was one-and-a-half, someone gave the family an ancient set of the *Encyclopaedia Britannica*. "When I can read," announced Edith, "I will read the whole set." And Stern placed volume one into her crib. Today he says she had read it straight through by age four-and-a-half; Edith cannot remember, but believes she must have skipped around a little.

When she was two, portraits of Gandhi, Tolstoy, Schweitzer, and Einstein were hung on the walls, and there were lectures on humanitarianism. Then there was arithmetic which Stern taught using an abacus, and walks through the neighborhood, during which they would read aloud in unison: "Mermaid Avenue," "Barber," "Motorola."

Father and daughter were inseparable, shutting Bella out. She went to work; they studied and played. "You have stolen my child from me. You stole her childhood," Bella said. He scarcely heard.

When Edith was two-and-a-half, her father took her to visit Albert Einstein, who, several years before, had helped Stern get admitted to the Mayo Clinic for surgery that cured his cancer of the jaw. Edith read from the newspaper for Einstein, who confessed that he had not learned to read until he was seven.

Edith would visit her father in the hospital. She learned to read his EKG, found a stethoscope and listened to his heart, pestered physicians for definitions of words she found in medical books, and finally—inevitably—disputed their diagnoses. She announced that she would become a doctor. Stern kissed her many times.

When the neighborhood children began to talk about storks, Stern held a brief debate with himself and then disrobed to teach Edith about male anatomy and human reproduction. Edith, then five, relayed the facts of life to her friends on the block, an enlightenment which occasioned angry parental visits. It reminded everyone of the visits of years before, when Edith had dispatched Santa Claus and the Easter Bunny.

Edith horrified the neighbors, what with telling playmates their *epidermis* was showing, or that they displayed *narcissistic* tendencies. But Stern appalled them. The apartment was crowded with documents, transcripts, and boxes of grisly photos as Stern labored on his book of Nazi atrocities. Edith chose the photos. The neighbors tsk-ed. And Stern would say: "You allow your child to watch television, which glorifies crime and violence, while I am teaching Edith the irrationality of violence and hate."

When Edith went to school after the family moved to Miami, Stern quickly earned a reputation as a bore and a nuisance. He was the lone and embattled innovator striving against the forces of darkness and barbarism. His unscheduled classroom visits struck terror into teachers' hearts. "Her father drove us crazy," recalls a school official. "He avalanched us with letters,

pestered us on the telephone, interrupted school-board meetings. But how could we change the entire system just to suit one person?"

The Sterns' son, David, was born when Edith was seven, and Bella drew the line. "I want one child, just one, to grow up normal." So David's training was less intense, though he is very bright. His ambitions, unlike Edith's, are modest. When he was nine a reporter asked David whether he wanted to be a genius. He reflected a moment and then said simply: "No."

Everyone thought Stern was pushing too hard. Edith would be mediocre in spite of it, they said, or smart as new leather but socially retarded, loony, weird, goofy, lonely, mad, marooned in her own uniqueness. In school she cared more for her books than for her looks. Her popularity, never very high, would increase just before exams, when classmates would call and ask for help. She was perennially interviewed and written about, and received bagsful of letters from advertising agencies, religious nuts, educators, quiz shows. There were even proposals for Stern as well as Edith. Not long ago a thirty-year-old California woman asked if he would father her next child so that her offspring would be favored with his marvelous genes. Her husband wouldn't mind, she said. But Stern, who has always claimed that genes have little to do with intelligence, declined.

And is Stern content with the result of the Edith Project? "I will confess something to you," he said carefully. "I am not very impressed with Edith. She could have been much more given what the input has been. I don't believe she has reached the plateau of Einstein or that she is a genius." He paused again. "She will be a genius when she makes a contribution."

BEFORE I MET EDITH, I had thought of Mr. Spock, the superior being played by Leonard Nimoy on Edith's favorite TV show, *Star Trek*. She did not resemble him. She wore a gray sleeveless dress, a bit too tight and short. She was, she said, about twenty pounds overweight, and she looked five years older than she was. Her face was pale and a bit puffy, with a slightly receding chin. But her eyes, behind the lenses of wire-rimmed glasses, were

very pretty—large and dark with good strong brows. She reminded me of the solemn, competitive, bright kids I'd known in school, those who would strain forward in their seats to answer every question.

Edith was curt, almost sullen, and I learned later that her father had made the appointment without consulting her. Now he said severely, "I expect you to talk to him straightforwardly and in a civil manner." Edith squirmed. I was halfway through saying she was not obliged to talk at all when Bella said, glaring at Stern, "You have no call to make a speech like that. Edith, like me, is just home from work, and she is tired."

Stern said, "She looks mad to me."

"She is tired," Bella said flatly.

Edith said nothing.

Stern put the papers away, and we went in to a dinner of excellent borscht with carrots and apples, Kentucky Fried Chicken, and blackberry Manischewitz. Bella, toiling in the kitchen, said good-naturedly, "I'm the only person in this house who works." Stern alone did not laugh. "I am not such a liability," he said, and whispered to me later, "We are a closely knit family, though you see there is a certain conflict with my wife."

There was also a conflict with Edith; it erupted once again during dinner. Stern was chatting amusingly about how "she" denied enjoying publicity but was invariably the first to send off for reprints. Edith put a hand to her throat and gasped, "I do *not*!" and bolted to her room.

"I was talking about Bella. *Bella*, not you!" he shouted after her.

Edith later returned to the table, in a better mood. Passing the platter of chicken too fast, she dropped a thigh and a breast. Everyone laughed, and when Bella said, "Why are you so klutzy?" Edith laughed, too.

Edith willingly admits to her clumsiness. She had given up the violin years before partly because her fingers had grown too fat, and had been plagued by the same problem in her year of pre-med training. ("My fingers wouldn't work. I'd try to cut up the worms and I'd always mess it up.") She does not, however, admit to being bothered by it. "I don't care for my body," Edith says flatly, "I'd be happy to leave it home in the morning."

Such certainty is present in Edith's

reply to nearly every question, as if she never thinks out loud because she already knows the answers. All her life she has performed—for her father, for teachers, for Albert Einstein, for the neighbors and the reporters. She learned as a child of eight that she could pontificate and have her words duly set down in print to read the next day. She was tagged very early as a whiz kid, a girl genius, and it would be surprising if she did not become a practiced know-it-all, probably without knowing it.

Still, though Edith seldom laughs spontaneously, she manages to have a sense of humor about herself. The day after the chicken dinner, she and her father sat side by side at a sticky Formica table in the employee's cafeteria at Sears, where Bella works as a saleswoman. Edith badly wanted a cigarette. She had been smoking since she was twelve and the week before had quit for the third time. As we spoke, she nervously fondled a lighter. I asked Stern:

"Have you created the perfect human being?"

"Perfection is utopian. But she is destined for greatness."

"Edith?"

She replaced the lighter in her purse, pushing aside a paperback book called *The Weird Ones*, and said with a glance at her father: "How can imperfection create perfection? But I'm—you're asking me if I'm a perfect human being. I'm going to feel silly if I say yes."

I was startled. "Are you tempted to?"

Her answer, as always, was ready:

"I'm sitting here overweight, having withdrawal symptoms from something as silly as cigarettes, and wishing I had something sweet to stick in my mouth, and you're asking me if I'm perfect?

"But I'm delighted with the outcome of his experiments on my mind," she added. If she had children of her own, she said, she would rear them in the same way.

That was shortly after she had moved away from her parents' home. When we talked later, Edith was still working for IBM, was "immersed in real life in the business world," and doing relatively well.

"I'm independent now," she asserted. "I have no more problems than others who have strong parents. They are somewhat loath to realize I no longer accept the house rules, but I've broken my father of bad habits like committing me to be somewhere and then being angry when I don't show up."

Wilfrid Sheed has written about having been "a brutal case of precocity, a disease which can make both childhood and adulthood wretched, with just a few good years in between." When I read the quotation to Edith, she was startled and said that it made no sense.

"It was *not* a wretched childhood," she protested, "and I'm *not* having a wretched life. Of course, being a former child prodigy is like yesterday's newspaper when you're grown up. It's no longer as impressive as it was. When you're fifteen and just graduated, it's one thing, but when you're twenty-four and have graduated at fifteen, it's lost some of its immediacy."

Sooner or later, what she calls "the horrid truth" comes out, and people realize that she is *that* Edith Stern ("I have a problem with friends who are overproud, shall we say"), but it doesn't bother her.

If Edith and Aaron Stern are telling the truth, and they seem to be, his critics were mistaken. She is not a perfect human being. She has a few neurotic tics, but she functions perfectly well. She has her own car, she dates occasionally, though not seriously. She has lost weight; she still battles her addiction to tobacco.

She has thrown herself into so many pursuits that the uncharitable might assume she protests her well-roundedness too much. When I asked if I could reach her by telephone with a few further questions, she said, "If you can find me. I'm leaving on vacation soon, and—let's see. Monday is bowling, Tuesday is karate practice, Thursday is volleyball...." She is taking tennis lessons, was recently certified as a scuba diver, and is interested in underwater photography.

She is having fun.

And the great contribution for which she has been so carefully prepared? Does she feel the world watching, waiting for the fulfillment of her father's promise? No, she said, which struck me as quite a healthy reply for a girl of twenty-four. "I refuse to admit it or see it. I'll be disappointed only if I don't do what I choose to do, and I haven't chosen yet." Her future plans? She said, "I'll do what amuses me. That's the only plan I've ever had."

IDENTIFICATION OF THE GIFTED AND TALENTED

One of the foremost concerns in programming for the gifted and talented is identification. This process actually serves two purposes. It enables a Planning and Placement Team to determine which students possess exceptional abilities such that their needs are not met in the regular program. Further, it becomes prescriptive to the extent that the assessment process provides teachers with information used to individualize program planning.

No single identification scheme is without its shortcomings, nor is any one design appropriate for the identification of every type of gift or talent. What is needed is a variety of measures, both objective and subjective, which will support and supplement one another.

Connecticut legislation and administrative guidelines are based on a broadened concept of giftedness, one which views traditional academic ability as only one criteria within a wide spectrum of intellectual aptitudes and abilities, including creativity and talent in the graphic or performing arts.

As spelled out in Section 10-76 of the Connecticut General Statutes, "extraordinary learning ability" is deemed to be the power to learn possessed by the top five per cent of the students in a school district as chosen by the special education Planning and Placement Team on the basis of (1) performance on relevant and standardized measuring instruments or (2) demonstrated or potential academic achievement or intellectual creativity.

"Outstanding talent in the creative arts" is deemed to be that talent possessed by the top five per cent of the students in a school district who have been chosen by the special education Planning and Placement Team on the basis of demonstrated or potential achievement in music, visual arts or the performing arts.

Thus we see that children capable of high performance include those with demonstrated achievement and/ or potential ability in any of the following areas, singly or in combination:

1) general intellectual ability
2) specific academic aptitude
3) creative or productive thinking
4) leadership ability
5) visual and performing arts
6) psychomotor ability
7) disadvantaged potential

Using these as criteria for gifted and talented may result in the identification of three to five per cent of the total school population, depending on how many students the program can accommodate.

The responsibility for the identification of eligible pupils rests with the superintendent of schools or an employee of the school district to whom he may delegate this responsibility. Such identification should be based on a study of all available evidence as to the pupil's ability and potential made by personnel qualified to administer and interpret appropriate standardized tests, judge demonstrated ability and potential, and recognize outstanding talent in the creative arts.

Evidence as to a pupil's extraordinary learning ability and/ or outstanding talent in the creative arts must be satisfactory to the Secretary of the State Board of Education.

Evidence of giftedness and unusual talent may be determined in a multiplicity of ways. These screening and identification procedures should include objective measures as well as subjective evaluations by qualified professionals. These professionals are responsible for providing an integrated design which combines objective and subjective measures to cover such areas as:

1) Consistently very superior scores on a number of appropriate standardized tests.
2) Judgement of teachers, pupil personnel specialists, administrators, and supervisors who are familiar with the demonstrated and/or potential abilities of the individual
3) Evidence of advanced skills, imaginative insight and intense interest and involvement
4) Judgements of specialized teachers (i.e., art and music), pupil personnel specialists and experts in the arts who are qualified to evaluate the pupils' demonstrated and/ or potential talent.

As noted, systematic assessment practices vary according to the definition of giftedness used. In every case, however, the procedures should be designed to avoid arbitrary cut-off points or limitations. The identification process should identify a small percentage of pupils with extraordinary ability and outstanding talent whose needs are such that they cannot be met in the regular school program.

PROJECT IMPROVE
System for Identifying Gifted and Talented Students
By Joseph S. Ranzulli

The purpose of this system is to provide persons who are involved in the identification of gifted students with a comprehensive plan that will assist them in both the screening and the selection process. The system is designed

1) to take account of a variety of identification criteria,
2) to minimize the amount of individual testing required, and
3) to show a relationship between the objectives of the program and the criteria upon which selection is based.

The steps involved in identification should take place in the spring of the year before students are placed in the program. For students who are continuing in the program, the same procedure should be followed; however, test data should be updated and information should be obtained from special program teachers who have worked with the students during the preceding year. Screening and selection should be carried out by a committee consisting of teachers, adminis-

2. PROGRAM CURRICULUM

trators, and pupil personnel specialists.

Before the screening and selection system can be implemented the following three decisions should be made:

1) How many students will be involved in the program?

2) What area or areas will the program focus upon? (Language Arts, Science, etc.)

3) From what grade levels will the students be selected?

Once these basic program decisions have been made, the following steps should be followed:

PART I: SCREENING

Step A: Intelligence Test Information

Section A of the Screening and Selection Form should be completed for all students who are in the grade(s) below the grade(s) from which students will be selected for the program. In the very early stage of the screening process, all youngsters in these grades should be considered eligible for the program. This approach will minimize the chances of overlooking youngsters who do not earn a high evaluation on any one criterion, but who may be good candidates for the program when several criteria are looked at collectively. Each step in this identification system will be directed toward reducing the number of students who are eligible for the program.

If the program deals mainly with one or more of the traditional academic areas, a minimum group intelligence test score should be established. Any student who has scored at or above this cut-off point on any of his group intelligence tests should be continued in the screening process.

Because of errors in measurement that are inherent in group measures, and because some youngsters simply do not demonstrate their best performance in group testing situations, an individual intelligence test should be administered to all students who score five or less points below the group test cut-off score. Because of the cultural inequalities in intelligence tests, minority group students and students coming from low socioeconomic backgrounds who score 15 or less points below the cut-off score also should be given an individual test. Since individual intelligence tests are also culture bound, the subjective judgment of the psychologist should be used in interpreting test performance for minority group and low socio-economic youngsters.

Scores from intelligence tests should rarely, if ever, be used as the only criteria for admission to a program for the gifted. This is especially true if the program focuses upon the development of non-academic talents such as art, music, leadership, drama, and creativity. If the program does focus on one or more of the traditional academic areas, students with unusually high scores can usually be recommended for the program without further consideration of additional information. With the exception of students who are unusually low in intelligence, a good rule to follow is THAT NO CHILD SHOULD BE EXCLUDED FROM THE PROGRAM SOLELY ON THE BASIS OF INTELLIGENCE TEST RESULTS.

If the program deals with developing the creative potential which is present in all youngsters, or with special aptitudes and talents such as music, mechanics, drama, etc., Steps A and B should be skipped and screening and selection should focus on Steps C, D, and E.

Action based on Step A

After all intelligence information has been gathered for students who are eligible for a program that deals with one or more of the traditional academic areas and cut-off points have been established, the following decisions can be made:

1) Students who score ten or more points above the cut-off score should be recommended for placement in the program.

2) Students who score ten or more points below the cut-off score should not be recommended for placement in the program.

3) All other students should be continued in the screening process.

Step B: Achievement Information

If the program deals with one or more of the traditional academic areas, Section B of the Screening and Selection Form should be completed for all eligible students who have been continued in the identification process. Section B points out each student's best area(s) of performance, and this information should be carefully considered when the program focuses on a particular academic area. For example, if the program is designed to develop advanced levels of proficiency in science, then special consideration should be given to students who have demonstrated high performance in this area. If a variety of special program offerings are available, but space or scheduling problems prohibit enrollment in more than one area, student interest should be respected, and, if necessary, interviews with a guidance counselor should be arranged to help students clarify their interests.

At this point, the screening and selection committee should have a fairly good idea about which students are the best achievers, but whenever there is some doubt about a student's past performance, the information required in Step C should be gathered.

Special consideration should be given to students who score unusually high on intelligence tests, but who display poor performance on achievement tests and/or course grades. These youngsters may be bored by a curriculum which has failed to challenge their superior abilities, and this lack of challenge sometimes causes them to be discipline problems in the regular classroom. A special program may be the best way to renew these students' interest in learning.

Action Based on Step B

Because of variations in student motivation, different standards in grading practices, and the frequent lack of relationship between course content and standardized achievement tests, decisions based on Step 2 should be approached with great caution. Whenever there is any doubt about a student's motivation and ability to accomplish work in the special program the additional information suggested in Step C should be gathered. With these cautions in mind, the following action might be based on Step B:

1) Students who have unusually high achievement in the area(s) with which the special program will deal should be recommended for placement.

2) Students with unusually low achievement should not be recommended for placement (note above caution about students who have high intelligence scores but low achievement test scores and/or course grades). Students who are eliminated at this step may be nominated later as a special recommendation.

3) All other students should be continued in the screening process.

Step C: Teacher Judgment

A Scale for Rating the Behavioral Characteristics of Superior Students (SRBCSS) should be completed for all students who have not yet been selected for the program. This

cale was designed to serve as a guide for teacher judgment
n the areas of learning, motivation, creativity, and leader-
hip. The scores from this scale should be recorded in Sec-
ion C of the Screening and Selection Form. The mean
cores of the four separate scales of the SRBCSS should be
omputed and the comments of teachers should be carefully
onsidered.

ction Based on Step C

1) Students with the highest scores on the SRBCSS or
ther rating scales should be considered for placement in the
pecial program.

2) Remaining students should not be recommended for
lacement unless they are nominated in Section D.

tep D: Special Nominations

After a final list has been compiled, the list should be
rculated to teachers from the sending classes and they
hould be allowed to make special nominations for any stu-
ents who are not on the list but who they feel should be
iven further consideration. Teachers should meet with the
creening and placement committee and be given an oppor-
unity to make a case for their special nominations. When-
ver a child is not placed in the special program, a brief
tatement which summarizes the reasons for not being placed
hould be sent to the teacher who nominated the child.

tep E: Special Aptitudes and Talents

Whenever a program deals with the development of spe-
ial aptitudes and talents, the screening and selection process
hould show a close relationship between the ability being
eveloped and the criteria which are used for identification.
n other words, if the program is mainly directed toward the
evelopment of general creativity, then tests of this aptitude
hould be given primary consideration in the identification
rocess. If the program deals with the development of talents
uch as art, drama, or music, then persons who are qualified
o make judgments in these areas should conduct auditions
nd/or review samples of students' work. Because of the
mited number of objective instruments for measuring
arious kinds of talents in the fine arts, a good deal of the
riteria for selection in these areas will have to depend on the
ubjective judgment of experts. Some instruments are avail-
ble for measuring specific abilities such as mechanical
ptitude, judgment for design, physical dexterity, etc., and
urrent listings of instruments in these areas should be re-
ewed as a possible source of identification criteria.

PART II: SELECTION

At the conclusion of Step D (or Step E if the program
eals with special aptitudes or talents), the Summary box on
he first page of the Screening and Selection Form should be
ompleted and all students who have been recommended in
ne of the screening steps should be reviewed by the screen-
ng and selection committee. In most cases, the list of stu-
ents recommended for the program will exceed the number
f students that the program can accommodate, and the
ajor task in selection will be to trim the list down to the
esired number. In addition to certain practical considera-

tions such as balance between boys and girls, geographic
locations of students, scheduling, etc., some general guidelines can be used to assist in making the final decisions.

The most important consideration is to achieve a balance
among the various types of students who have been recommended. A good idea is to arrange the groups in such a way
that they contain some high IQ students, some high achievers, and some students who have received high ratings in
motivation, creativity, and leadership. This approach may
cause the committee to eliminate some high IQ or high
achievement students in favor of students who are lower in
these abilities but high in characteristics that will be important to the overall functioning of the group. The result will
be a more heterogeneous group that can profit from each
other and that can engage in activities that require a cooperative blend of various abilities.

A second guideline in making the final selection is to
consider which students might suffer adverse effects from
participating in a program that requires high performance.
Some students do not adjust well to the heightened competition that is almost always present in programs that bring
together highly able youngsters, and for this reason, it may
be wise to eliminate students whose participation in the program will place them under undue pressure.

The development of the Scale for Rating Behavioral
Characteristics of Superior Students (SRBCSS) represents
an attempt to provide a more objective and systematic
instrument that can be used as an aide in guiding teacher
judgement in the identification process. It is not intended to
replace existing identification procedures such as measures
of intelligence, achievement and creativity; rather, it is offered as a supplementary means that can be used in conjunction with other forms of identification.

A guiding principle in using the SRBCSS emphasizes the
relationship between the student's subscore and the types
of curricular experiences that will be offered in a special
program. Every effort should be made to capitalize on an
individual's strengths by developing learning experiences
that take account of the area or areas in which the student
has received high ratings. For example, a student who earns
high ratings on the Motivational Characteristics Scale will
probably profit most from a program that emphasizes self-
initiated pursuits and an independent study approach to
learning. A student with high scores on the Leadership
Characteristics Scale should be given opportunities to organize activities and to assist the teacher and his classmates in
developing plans of action for carrying out projects.

In addition to looking at a student's profile of subscores
for identification purposes, teachers can derive several useful hints for programming by analyzing student ratings on
individual scale items. These items call attention to differences in behavioral characteristics and in most cases suggest
the kinds of educational experiences that are most likely to
represent the youngster's preferred method or style of learning. Thus, a careful analysis of scale items can assist the
teacher in her efforts to develop an individualized program
of study for each student.

FOCUS...

Table 1

Three Levels of Program Models in Special
Programs for Gifted and Talented

INITIATORY MODELS	*DEVELOPMENTAL MODELS*	*INTEGRATED MODELS*
Models are vague, intuitive in effects to be achieved. Objectives are stated as general outcomes and social goods to be achieved. There is much concern with theory, the debates on alternatives are theoretical rather than operational or data based. Justification of the program may be drawn from analogous programs in other contexts or be based on philosophical assumptions. Details for operationalizing the proposal are sketchy.	Models, where a mixture of objectives prevails. Macro objectives give general guidance and some micro objectives are defined. Objectives still seem to be shifting and the model still takes different forms in individual staffs' descriptions. There is more concern with operational alternatives than a given alternative. While the program is operating there are many unknowns and frequently considerable improvisation.	Models have specific objectives to be achieved. There is monitoring of procedures for consistency of operation. Relationships of treatment (what is done educally) and effects (outcome are specified, and reproducibility is enhanced by elaborated descriptions of the model in operation. Logical relationships are explicated, and empirical data are being collecte. The outcomes are being assessed and the range of effects are capable of being attributed to the program treatment.
Precis of a Program A special program for gifted and talented children is drawn up. Decisions on the form it will take; special classes, enrichment, independent tutorials or the mix of these are still open. There is lack of agreement on definition of clients. Who is a gifted or talented student? How should he be educated? Should he be identified? At what grade? By whom? Will there be extra monies allocated to the education of these students? Will there be a need to establish a separate administrative unit for this program? What type of research will be conducted on a program? When will parents be involved? A committee has been set up to resolve some of these issues. Administrative responsibilities and a sum of money for planning have been allocated. The committee has been meeting for one year, a set of minutes, a list of consultants and a description of the field trips to visit programs for gifted children exists.	*Precis of a Program* One special program for gifted and talented children has been underway two years. Fifty children are involved. In some cases teachers nominate students for the program, in others they are selected on the basis of test scores. The first year students spend four hours per week in the program, the second year this has been extended to six. The program has focused on scientific interests though there is concern about including more humanities. One teacher made arrangements for 25 of the students to see the Old Vic perform at the local college. Some data, mostly of a descriptive nature has been collected on the students, their achievements and the program. Teachers do not have fixed style for instruction, the instruction reflects personal teaching style.	*Precis of a Program* A program for gifted and talented students has been in operation for f years. Open-ended instruction is featured with teachers and students co operatively planning the curriculum for three months at a time. The Dir tor of Research for the school distri monitors the program through teac records, student interviews and regu classroom visitations. Program outcomes are investigated through thei effect on student's achievement and interest. A contrast group of studen not in a special program, in a neighboring school district with a similar student body is supplying compara data on achievement and interest. further dimension of the study supplies data on special programs' influence on the regular program. At th end of the five years a summer wor shop composed of teachers and pup in the program in conjunction with administrators and university consu tants will draw up the program description for the next three year Decisions will be rendered on the p gram organization, the selection an retention of students and the resea to be conducted.

Table 2

Differential Evaluation in Three Program Models

...ATORY MODEL	DEVELOPMENTAL MODEL	INTEGRATED MODEL
	EFFORT	
What have been the main direc- of the committee's efforts? What has been the level of par- tion among the committee ...ers? Has the committee broadened ...nstituency and recognized the ...political aspects of its efforts? How much time has been spent ...rtain phases of the program?	1) What have been the main thrusts of the program's efforts? 2) What objectives have received the major attention? 3) Who has been involved in the program, to what extent, voluntary or mandated, volunteer or paid? 4) Where has the support for the program emanated; what has been the total developmental costs - financial and psychic? 5) How much total time has been spent? What parts of the program are consuming the bulk of time?	1) What are the major goals the pro- gram is trying to attain? Who is in- volved in the effort? 2) What percentage of staff and student time is committed to the pro- gram? Total time? 3) What data are available that per- mit building a history of the effort and projecting a scenario for future thrusts? 4) What areas of effort are per- ceived as worth while by the different role participants?
	EFFECT	
What is the level of knowledge ...ested in the committee on spec- ...ograms for the gifted and tal- ...? Are the committee members con- ...t with issues, trends and pro- ...? What is the present stage of the ...are they near operationalizing? What are the main impediments ...mulating a developmental model ...m?	1) What data on functioning of the program have been collected or can be collected? 2) What have the effects been on program students, other students, teach- ers, parents and adminstrators? 3) Has the data on effects been used to modify or shape the program, explore alternatives? 4) Can the effects on students be attributable to the program? 5) Have there been any unanti- cipated effects?	1) What are the programs short range effects on students to the pro- gram, students not in the program, teachers, parents and administrators? Are data available to study both pro- cess and product effects? 2) Is any provision made for study- ing long range effects? 3) Can the desired effects stated in the original goals be attributed to the program? 4) Have there been any unanti- cipated effects?
	EFFICIENCY	
Does the committee have an ...zed plan for carrying out its ...with deadlines and completion ...les for phases of activities? Is the committee clear on its re- ...bility to the Board of Education ...perintendent? Given the amount of time and ...y invested has a useful product ...ed? How far are they from an ...ing program?	1) Are there records or other evi- dence that program problems are being systematically encountered and re- solved? 2) How does the cost on this pro- gram compare with costs on other programs in the district and in other districts? 3) What goals seem within attain- ment? What goals have not been at- tained? 4) Given the program's experience, what will be the approximate cost of an integrated program model?	1) Are problems systematically studied? Are the participants conver- sant with the decision making process? Has it been scrutinized? 2) What is the cost of this program compared with other programs in the district and similar programs? 3) How do these costs project out for the future now that developmental costs are large-met? 4) What has been the cost of attain- ing certain effects, what tradeoffs were made in the interest of cost?

Some New Thoughts on the Development of Creativity

JOHN CURTIS GOWAN

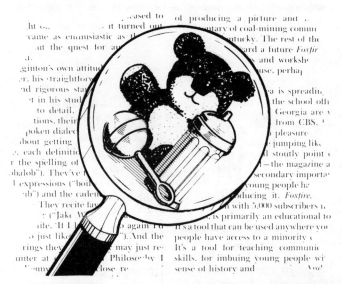

One of the most curious characteristics of creativity, and one that generally appears to have escaped critical attention, is the fact that its variability in individuals far exceeds the limits of variability characteristic of other traits and abilities. Wechsler (1974), for example, has conclusively demonstrated that the interpersonal variability of such psychological and physiological measures as height, weight, cranial capacity, grip strength, blood pressure, respiration rate, reaction time, pitch, Snellen acuity, intelligence, mental age, and memory span has a limit of 3/1, where $e = 2.818$, the basis of the natural logarithm system, and in most cases has a mean of 2.3 or less. Yet comparing the creative productions of a genius such as Einstein, Mozart, or Picasso with those of more ordinary mortals, one finds a ratio of 100/1 or over. Obviously the trait and factor theory of creativity cannot account for all the variance.

It is the thesis of this paper that the remaining variance can best be accounted for by the concept of "psychological openness" akin to the mental health concept of Maslow (1954). Certainly this trait is consonant with Maslow's concepts of high mental health, since it was one of the characteristics he identified in self-actualizing persons.

Both J. P. Guilford (1967) and Alex Osborn (1953) believed that creativity was an outcome of certain problem-solving aspects of intellect; that it could therefore be taught or stimulated; and that it was rational and semantic, consisting essentially of what Hallman has called "connectedness"—that is, the ability, through the use of verbal analogy, to connect (by common ratios or otherwise) elements that heretofore had been viewed as incommensurable or disparate.

If this view is correct, then the obvious way to stimulate creativity in the classroom is to facilitate the child's ability to make such connections via the Williams Cube material, the Meeker method, or by similar curriculum procedures. But while the Structure-of-Intellect and the creative problem-solving methods are certainly useful, it is perhaps time to ask whether we are putting all of our educational eggs in one basket. This is especially pertinent since two other theories as to the genesis of creative ability have gained currency, and each has important educational applications.

The first of these new theories is, of course, Maslow's view that creativity results from mental health. To the extent that this theory is true, we ought to be strengthening the mental health of children, primarily through developmental guidance procedures along lines set down in Blocher (1966) and Bower and Hollister (1968). When the author was director of a summer workshop in creativity for gifted children, this aspect proved to be so important that a full-time counselor accompanied the children to every class (at a 1/25 ratio).

A second theory, in some minds even more important, is that creativity is nothing but psychological openness to preconscious sources. A careful perusal of Ghiselin (1952) will certainly do much to make this theory palatable, and there is considerable other evidence for it besides—in particular, the above-mentioned fact that creative production does not obey the Wechsler law of interpersonal variance less than e. If this is true, then we need to learn how to rub Aladdin's lamp to get the genie to come, and it appears that meditation, reverie, fantasy, and the like are the most promising methods. Outside the Khatena and Torrance *Sounds and Images,* however, there are few facilitations in this area.

But if psychologists are in doubt about which theory of creativity contributes the most variance to the whole, let us turn to an even better set of witnesses—namely, the creative geniuses themselves, in the rare moments when they reveal the workings of the creative process. Consider Mozart:

> The whole, though it be long, stands almost complete and finished in my mind, so that I can survey it . . . at a glance. Nor do I hear in my imagination the parts successively, but I hear them, as it were, all at once. . . . What delight this is I cannot tell! (Vernon, 1970).

And Tchaikowsky:

> The only music capable of moving and touching us is that which flows from the depth of a composer's soul when he is stirred by imagination . . . it takes root with extraordinary force and rapidity, shoots up through the earth, puts forth branches, leaves and finally blossoms. I cannot define the creative process in any other way than by this simile (Vernon, 1970).

And finally Poincaré on his discovery of Fuchsian functions (among the most complicated in higher mathematics). Having labored a long time in vain, he had the following revelation:

> At the moment when I put my foot on the step, the

"Some New Thoughts on the Development of Creativity," John Curtis Gowan, *The Journal of Creative Behavior,* Vol. 11 No. 2, Second Quarter 1977. ©1976 John Curtis Gowan.

idea came to me, without anything in my former thoughts seeming to have paved the way for it that the transformations I had used to define the Fuchsian functions were identical with those of non-Euclidean geometry. . . . Most striking at first is this appearance of sudden illumination, a manifest sign of long, unconscious prior work . . . it is only fruitful if it is on one hand preceded and on the other hand followed by a period of conscious work . . . (Vernon, 1970).

What each of these geniuses is doing is confirming the correctness of the Wallas paradigm, which states that preparation and incubation must precede illumination and that verification must follow it. But what is the exact mechanism by which such creative ideas may be induced to occur? It is obvious by the sudden uprush of new ideas which seem to break into consciousness with a shock of recognition that we are here dealing with material that has somehow accumulated at subconscious levels of the mind. Since such ideas are generally not accessible to the ego, but appear to be so under the creative impetus, it is evident that they belong to the preconscious, which has been defined as consisting of just such occasionally accessible material. Moreover, there is a *collective* aspect about the knowledge, as if we were all drilling into a common underground aquifer for well water. Indeed, many great scientific discoveries have had more than one discoverer—Leibnet and Newton in the case of the calculus, and Darwin and Wallace for the theory of evolution.

We theorize that the collective preconscious is best compared to the terminal of a giant computer which is in another realm, outside time and space, and contains an infinity of potentialities; all are real in that realm but only one will eventuate in our dimension. Under conditions of relaxation, meditation, incubation, and the like, messages in the form of images manifest in the printout of that cosmic computer and collator. But with all that random dissociated infinity in the machine, why is it only the creative ideas that are brought through to consciousness?

Poincaré explains the subliminal self's activities as follows:

All the combinations would be formed in consequence of the automatism of the subliminal self, but only the interesting ones would break into consciousness. . . . Is it only chance which confers this privilege? . . . The privileged unconscious phenomena . . . are those which affect most profoundly our emotional sensibility. . . . The useful combinations are precisely the most beautiful . . . (Ghiselin, 1952).

As the recovery process proceeds from the germ of a creative idea down deep and rises like an expanding bubble through successive layers of consciousness, various individuals become cognizant of the nascent creativity in different modes. Some feel it first prototaxically, like Houseman:

Experience has taught me, when I am shaving of a morning, to keep watch over my thoughts, because, if a line of poetry strays into my memory, my skin bristles so that the razor ceases to act. This particular symptom is accompanied by a shiver down the spine; there is another which consists in a constriction of the throat and a precipitation of water to the eyes; and there is a third which I can only describe by borrowing a phrase from one of Keat's last letters, where he says, speaking of Fanny Brawne, 'everything that reminds me of her goes through me like a spear.' The seat of this sensation is the pit of the stomach (Ghiselin, 1952).

Others feel it parataxically through images and emotions; for example, Einstein:

Words or language do not seem to play any role in my mechanism of thought. The psychical entities which seem to serve as elements in thought are certain signs and more or less clear images . . . (Ghiselin, 1952).

Wordsworth:

Poetry is the spontaneous overflow of powerful feelings: it takes its origin from emotion recollected in tranquility (Ghiselin, 1952).

Coleridge, speaking of himself in the third person:

All the images rose up before him as *things*, with a parallel production of the corresponding expressions, without any sensation of conscious effort (Ghiselin, 1952).

The major question is how to transfer these images/emotions to the alphanumeric syntaxic level, and this analysis is the source of considerable testimony. But the prime secret is relaxation of the conscious mind. Says Kipling:

When your daemon is in charge, do not try to think consciously. Drift, wait, obey (Ghiselin, 1952).

The reason why it takes higher ability to be verbally creative is that the crossing of the successive discontinuity of psychic layers during the bubble's trip upward to full consciousness requires a complex level of verbal analogy fitting each stage; for one must both see that a proportionate ratio exists below, and also intuit the same ratio in the higher elements which may be semantically very different. This correspondence of a ratio across a semantic chasm from the known to the unknown is the secret of transferring creative affective images to full verbal creativity at the syntaxic level. Amy Lowell says of the poet:

He must be born with a subconscious factory always working for him or he can never be a poet at all, and he must have knowledge and talent enough to "putty" up his holes. . . . Here is where the conscious training of the poet comes in, for he must fill up what the subconscious has left, and fill it in as much in the key of the rest as possible. Every long poem is sprinkled with these *lacunae*. Let no one undervalue this process of puttying; it is a condition of good poetry (Ghiselin, 1952).

Indeed, Gerard tells us plainly:

Imagination is more than bringing images into consciousness; this is imagery or at most hallucination. Imagination . . . is an action of the mind that produces a new idea or insight. "Out of chaos the imagination frames a thing of beauty. . . ." The thing comes unheralded, as a flash, fully formed. . . .

Imagination, not reason, creates the novel. It is to social inheritance what mutation is to biological inheritance; it accounts for the arrival of the fittest. Reason or logic applied when judgment indicates that the new is promising acts like natural selection to pan the gold grains from the sand and insure the survival of the fittest.

Imagination supplies the premises and asks questions from which reason grinds out the conclusions . . . (Ghiselin, 1952).

Gerard then quotes Dryden as naming "fancy moving the sleeping images of things toward the light . . . then chosen or rejected by the judgment," and recalls Coleridge's phrase: "the streamy nature of association, which thinking curbs and rudders." It would be hard to paraphrase the symbiotic relationship between the conscious and preconscious minds in more trenchant manner.

Figure 1 indicates the symbiotic relationship between the conscious mind and the collective preconscious, which produces creative products. On the left the conscious mind has taken over completely, and only convergent production ensues. The part played by the preconscious then, gradually increases and that of the conscious decreases until in the middle of the figure they are both equally present. This represents the acme of creativity. As we move toward the extreme right the preconscious assumes a larger and larger share until eventually it becomes all, and the product is analogous to automatic writing. In the middle of the diagram creative products would be distinguished from one another by the amount of each which they contain. Mathematical and physical discoveries might be toward the left of center, and abstract artistic productions such as "Kubla Khan" or surrealistic paintings would be toward the right.

Because all this "psychological openness" is so much more bizarre and less "respectable" than, say, the Structure-of-Intellect theory with its solid dependence on statistics, it is desirable to reinforce this testimony with other, even more credible witnesses describing even more incredible processes and events.

Recognizing the importance of preconscious inspiration, many creative persons have intuitively derived individual mechanisms for throwing themselves into this mode of knowledge.

FIGURE 1

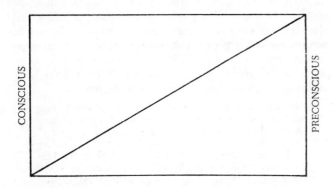

Gerald Heard says:

> To have truly original thought the mind must throw off its critical guard, its filtering censor. It must put itself in a state of depersonalization. . . . The best researchers when confronting problems and riddles which have defied all solution by ordinary methods, did employ their minds in an unusual way, did put themselves into a state of egoless creativity, which permitted them to have insights so remarkable that by means of these they were able to make their greatest and most original discoveries (Weil, Metsner & Leary, 1971).

Lord Tennyson was accustomed to pass into "an ecstatic state" and had a formula for inducing it. Tennyson says in a letter written in 1794:

> I have had . . . a kind of walking trance . . . when I have been all alone. This has often come upon me through repeating my own name to myself silently, till, all at once out of the intensity and conscious of the individuality, the individuality itself seems to dissolve and fade away into boundless being . . . (Prince, 1963).

Prince (1963) similarly describes the inception of *Uncle Tom's Cabin*, quoting from the biography of Harriet Beecher Stowe:

> Mrs. Stowe was seated in her pew in the college church at Brunswick, during the communion service. . . . Suddenly like the unrolling of a picture scroll, the scene of the death of Uncle Tom seemed to pass before her. . . . She was so affected she could scarcely keep from weeping. . . . That Sunday afternoon she went to her room, locked the door and wrote out, substantially as it appears . . . the chapter called "The Death of Uncle Tom."

But no matter how eminent or noteworthy are writers and authors, creative persons in the sciences carry the most weight of evidence. We are indebted to Krippner (1972) for the following:

> One can cite as well creative dreams of scientists and inventors that gave the solution of a problem analogically or symbolically.

The chemist, Friedrich August Kekule (cited by Koestler, 1964), had a tendency to make theoretical discoveries in hypnagogic reverie states. Kekule wrote:

> I turned my chair to the fire and dozed. Again the atoms were gambolling before my eyes. The smaller groups kept modestly in the background. My mental eye, rendered more acute by visions of this kind, could now distinguish larger structures, of minifold conformations; long rows, sometimes more closely fitted together,
>
> all twining and twisting in snakelike motion. But look! What was that? One of the snakes had seized hold of its own tail, and the form whirled mockingly before my eyes. As if by a flash of lightning I awoke.

At this juncture, it is instructive to break into the narrative to ask a searching question: "What did Kekule see?" While you are thinking of the answer, it may be helpful to tell a baseball joke.

Three umpires were arguing about calling balls and strikes. The first said: "I calls 'em as they are."

The second said: "I calls 'em as I sees 'em."

The third said: "They ain't nothin' 'till I calls 'em."

Kekule said that what he saw was a ring. In Krippner's words:

> The dream image of a snake holding its tail in its mouth led Kekule by analogy to his discovery that Benzene has a ringlike structure (usually represented by a hexagon) and to his "closed-chain" or "ring" theory which showed the importance of molecular structure in organic chemistry. The imagery granted Kekule a glimpse into a non-ordinary reality of molecular structure.

Despite what Kekule *concluded* (which was a concept), let us persist in analyzing what Kekule *described*. To do so, please reread his description. In the light of what we know now about molecular structure, the "long rows, sometimes more closely fitted together, all twining and twisting" clearly describes the DNA molecule. Kekule was in the presence of a noncategorical numinous archetype in a nonordinary state of reality—in other words, in the cave of Aladdin. He went in looking for a dollar, and he came out with a dollar. Had he been prepared by prior discipline to look for a thousand dollars he could have found that also. An orchestra can play only the symphonies for which it has the men and instruments. One is reminded of George Kelly's phrase: "One is constrained to experience events in the way one anticipates them."

The numinous archetype presented in hypnagogic dreams and creative reveries is a noncategorical image, and is hence as capable of as many interpretations as there are percipients (e.g., the smile on the *Mona Lisa*). Each participant will interpret the numinous archetype idiosyncratically, in accordance with his level of development (like the seven blind Indians who went to see the elephant). The archetype hence acts as a generating entity, which may produce a number of art forms or alphanumeric scientific statements. Since this nonordinary experience may occur in many persons, the key concept of creativity is to possess the previously prepared matrix of verbal or mathematical analogy which will catch the ephemeral vision and preserve it in concrete form.

In 1969, D. I. Mendeleev went to bed exhausted after struggling to conceptualize a way to categorize the elements based upon their atomic weights (cited by Kedrov, 1957). He reported, "I saw in a dream a table where all the elements fell into place as required. Awakening, I immediately wrote it down on a piece of paper. Only in one place did a correction later seem necessary." In this manner, Mendeleev's Periodic Table of the Elements was created (Krippner, 1972).

We have stated earlier that the collective preconscious seems to be in a realm of nonordinary reality, outside time and space, which of course gives it access to the future. In curious reinforcement of this hypothesis, many creative discoveries have an element of precognition about them. When Kekule saw the whirling forms, he may have glimpsed the DNA molecular structure. When Mendeleev dreamed the atomic order of the elements, he left a hole, where later helium was discovered, and still later his open-ended model had places for all the radioactive and transuranium elements such as plutonium. Again we quote from Krippner (1972):

When Igor Sikorsky was ten years of age, he dreamed of coursing the skies in the softly lit, walnut-paneled cabin of an enormous flying machine. Sikorsky later became an eminent aircraft designer and inventor of the helicopter. Three decades after the dream, he went aboard one of his own four-engine clippers to inspect a job of interior decorating done by Pan American Airways. With a start, he recognized the cabin as identical to the one in his boyhood dream.

Max Planck, the physicist, first spoke of his "constant" when he was twenty-three years of age; however, he did not understand its implications for wave theory until much later. Indeed, he had to convince himself of its correctness; it varied so greatly from the logic of his time that he could not comprehend it when the idea first came to him.

The case of Jonathan Swift (cited by Haefele, 1962), the writer of *Gulliver's Travels* and other novels, combines artistic and scientific creativity. When Gulliver reaches Laputa, the astronomers state that the planet Mars has two moons quite close to the planet. One completed its orbit every ten hours, the other every 21.5 hours. It took astronomers in ordinary reality 150 years to discover that Mars did, indeed, have two moons which completed their orbits around the planet every eight and every 30 hours.

A final instance of the possible association between ESP and creativity concerns *Futility*, a popular novel written by Morgan Robertson in 1898. It described the wreck of a giant ship called the Titan. This ship was considered "unsinkable" by the characters in the novel; it displaced 70,000 tons, was 800 feet long, had 24 lifeboats, and carried 3,000 passengers. Its engines were equipped with three propellers. One night in April, while proceeding at 25 knots, the Titan encountered an iceberg in the fog and sank with great loss of life.

On April 15, 1912, the Titanic was wrecked in a disaster which echoed the events portrayed in the novel 14 years previously. The Titanic displaced 66,000 tons and was 828 feet long. It had three propellers and was proceeding at 23 knots on its maiden voyage, carrying nearly 3,000 passengers. There was great loss of life because the Titanic was equipped with only 20 lifeboats.

If all this sounds wild to you, listen to the most famous aviator of our day, Charles Lindbergh (1969):

. . . I think the great adventures of the future lie—in voyages inconceivable by our 20th century rationality—beyond the solar system, through distant galaxies, possibly through peripheries untouched by time and space.

I believe early entrance to this era can be attained by the application of our scientific knowledge not to life's mechanical vehicles but to the essence of life itself: to the infinite and infinitely evolving qualities that have resulted in the awareness, shape and character of man. I believe this application is necessary to the very survival of mankind . . . will we discover that only *without* spaceships can we reach the galaxies . . . I believe it is through sensing and thinking about such concepts that great adventures of the future will be found.

To conclude this amazing testimony of men of science, we again return to Krippner (1972):

It can be seen that creative persons in their dreams sometimes appear to experience non-ordinary reality, and at the same time make different types of consolidations. Finding a new reality in a creative dream gives the person a novel slant or direction for consolidating his information, and the consolidation enables him to see the details and structure of the new reality more clearly. In some cases, finding a new reality not only gives the person a new direction for consolidating his information, but even involves finding additional information to be included in the consolidation.

Perhaps we have labored the point too long, but these concepts are so new and unusual that it is very important to impress them firmly on minds unused to such views. We have long thought of man's brain as a problem-solver; perhaps an even better model would be that of a radio receiver. When the set has been properly assembled through preparation and discipline, the static in the locality has been cleared through relaxation and incubation, and the power is on, then we may hear the faint calls of distant stations—signals which are always in the air, but are only received with the best equipment under the best and clearest operating conditions. Such a simile tells us why high giftedness enhances the creative range and why the easy production of verbal analogies (like the proportion between radio frequency and audio frequency) facilitates high-fidelity reception.

These ideas are so new that all we can do in turning from theory to practice is to sketch some ways in which such views may affect the classroom in the future. It would be a grave error to conclude that we should abandon all that has gone before and delve into divination and the occult; indeed, such a procedure would be disastrous. The Wallas paradigm still holds true and useful. Mental discipline and scholarship are still required for the preparation phase. What we are talking about is more conscious attention to the incubation phase.

Moreover, to look at the end product in highly creative geniuses at their best hardly tells us much about how to induce creativity consciously through educational procedures. What they gained in flashes of creative intuition may come to lesser lights through longer and more painstaking efforts. Inducing creativity in the classroom may not be the same as observing it in the field.

There are, however, some procedures we can begin to make use of. I should like to list a few for you now:

1. We should study creativity directly in high school and university classes. Almost no schools at the present time have courses on this subject. The 21st century will find this lack incomprehensible.

2. We can help young children learn techniques of relaxation and incubation. This does not mean that we should teach them any particular form of meditation, but it might be useful for all children to know what meditation, relaxation, and other types of unstressing are.

3. We should help children practice imagination and imagery during such relaxed periods. The Torrance and Khatena record, *Sounds and Images*, is only one of several devices on the market for this purpose. As a consequence of such periods we should encourage the production of poetry, art, music, etc.

4. As long as the child is in the concrete operations phase, the images will tend to be static and not particularly creative; but when he enters the formal operations phase one can expect and should push for more finished artistic creations, especially in poetic form. Children at this stage should be strongly encouraged to keep a journal and put their poetry and other thoughts into it. The development of the easy ability at this level helps the child to become truly creative in the next stage, and this is where (in upper high school and in lower division college) most gifted children do not make the transition to creative production. I think the most important facilitation which can take place at this time is a seminar type home room where the adolescent can be with others of the same persuasion, for (because of the strong gregarious needs at this stage) nothing does more to inhibit creativity than group sanctions against it in other adolescents.

It might be prudent of us to listen to the last testament of a prophet and sage on educational objectives in a utopia:

> How does he do his thinking, perceiving, and remembering? Is he a visualizer or a non-visualizer? Does his mind work with images or with words, with both at once or with neither? How close to the surface is his story-telling faculty? Does he see the world as Wordsworth and Traherne saw it when they were children? And if so, what can be done to prevent the glory and freshness from fading into the light of common day? Or in more general terms, can we educate children on the conceptual level without killing their capacity for intense non-verbal experience? How can we reconcile analysis with vision? (Huxley, 1962).

Few orthodox teachers will agree with Huxley's tripartite prescription for accomplishing this educational miracle, which consisted of *maithuna* for the psychomotor level, *moksha*-medicine (drugs) for the affective level, and meditation for the cognitive level. But let us remember that Huxley was a visionary, and that many of the predictions in *Brave New World* have come true. Certainly his ideas are worth thinking about, if only to trigger our own.

About 9,000 years ago, prehistoric man was suddenly catapulted into history as the result of an astonishing social discovery. Previous to this, small bands of nomadic tribes had roamed a large hunting area looking for game and gathering live fruits and vegetables wild. Then someone found out that if one domesticated animals and plants, one could have a ready supply of food always at hand in a confined space. Thus was agriculture and civilization born, and man escalated into history, and to the possibility of a far greater population on a given land mass. We are still reaping the benefits of that change, but our continuing ecological crises show us that we are nearing the end of that period. Fortunately we are on the brink of another momentous discovery which will have even greater impact on cultural and personal escalation.

Heretofore we have harvested creativity wild. We have used as creative only those persons who stubbornly remained so despite all efforts of the family, religion, education, and politics to grind it out of them. In the prosecution of this campaign, men and women have been punished, flogged, silenced, imprisoned, tortured, ostracized, and killed. Jesus, Socrates, Huss, Lavosier, Lincoln, Gandhi, Kennedy, and King are good examples. As a result of these misguided efforts, our society produces only a small percentage of its potential of creative individuals (the ones with the most uncooperative dispositions).

If we learn to domesticate creativity—that is, to enhance rather than deny it in our culture—we can increase the number of creative persons in our midst by about fourfold. That would put the number and percent of such individuals over the "critical mass" point. When this level is reached in a culture, as it was in Periclean Athens, the Renaissance, the Aufklarung, the Court of the Sun King, Elizabethan England, and our own Federalist period, there is an escalation of creativity resulting and civilization makes a great leap forward. We can have a golden age of this type such as the world has never seen, and I am convinced that it will occur early in the 21st century. But we must make preparations now, and the society we save will be our own. The alternative is either nuclear war or learning to speak Arabic and bow down four times a day toward Mecca.

In conclusion, if we may be permitted a peep at the future, we see an integrated science of human development and talent. The gestalt we are talking about there is at present at best a shore dimly seen, but it is the coming science of man of the 21st century. A genius is always a forerunner; and the best minds of this age foresee the dawn of that one. All of these branches of humanistic psychology will be welded together in a *structure d'ensemble*, greater than interest in the gifted, greater than interest in creativity, greater, in fact, than anything except the potential of man himself. We may come from dust, but our destiny is in the stars. Thoreau, that rustic seer, prophesized in the last sentence of *Walden*: "That day is yet to dawn, for the sun is only a morning star."

Toynbee tells us that each civilization leaves its monument and its religion. Our monument is on the moon, and the "religion" our culture will bequeath is the coming science of man and his infinite potential. This potential is truly infinite because man may be part animal but he is also part of the noumenon. And as Schroedinger correctly observed in *What is Life*, "The 'I' that observes the universe is the same 'I' that created it." The present powers of genius are merely the earnest of greater powers to be unfolded. You need not take my word for this. Listen instead to the words of the greatest genius of our age— Albert Einstein:

> A human being is a part of the whole, called by us "Universe"; a part limited in time and space. He experiences himself, his thoughts and feelings as something separated from the rest—a kind of optical delusion of his consciousness. This delusion is a kind of prison for us, restricting us to our personal desires and to affection for a few persons nearest us. Our task must be to free ourselves from this prison by widening our circle of compassion to embrace all living creatures and the whole nature in its beauty. Nobody is able to achieve this completely, but the striving for such achievement is, in itself, a part of the liberation and a foundation for inner security (cited in Gowan, 1975).

Centering as a process for children's imaging

Robert B. Kent

Robert B. Kent is Associate Professor of Art,
the University of Georgia, Athens, Georgia.
Photographs by Butch Hulett.

It is an overstated truism in education
that we must teach the whole child.
Without fear of contradiction, it can be
said that the main thrust of American
education is and has been cognitively
oriented. Recent research on the
human brain suggests that cognitive
processing is a general function of the
left hemisphere. Broadly speaking, researchers believe that each cerebral
hemisphere is specialized for particular modes of information processing.
The following modes of thinking and
processing are attributed to the left
hemisphere which also controls the
right side of the body: speech and
verbal centers; logical and mathematical processes; sequential and intellectual centers; and the origin of complex
motor sequences.

The right hemisphere, which controls the left side of the body, is responsible for the following modes of information processing: origins of spatial
and musical processes; artistic and
symbolic modes of apprehension. It is
also the origin of emotional, intuitive
and creative processes. It is gestalt in
perception and is responsible for the
recognition of complex figures.

Just a brief contemplation of these
concerns would indicate that the education of children directed mainly to
exploit left hemisphere processing
leaves a vast, untapped, potentially
creative source to wither and quite
possibly never mature to its potential.
Reflection of these concerns seems to
indicate that education must indeed
pay attention to what is now an old
cliche — that we must teach the whole
child. And, we must try for balance. In

2. PROGRAM CURRICULUM

so doing, we must develop a more sensitive program in the teaching of art which gives greater attention to intuitive processes of the mind.

We can see from the above brief discussion that the brain is not one total functioning structure. In reality, it is a dual structure, each hemisphere capable of unitary and independent functioning, quite different from one another.

The understanding of hemisphere functioning and processing, if implemented educationally, can have a profound affect on future educational planning. This understanding, if put into curriculum development, would develop educational concepts that could fairly balance the uneven treatment now afforded our students. We could more carefully develop learning situations and strategies that complement one another, rather than oppose. Knowing that the left hemisphere is concerned mainly with verbal and analytical processing and that the so-called "minor" right hemisphere is concerned with the nonverbal and image-metaphoric processing, could for the first time, aid in teaching the "whole child."

The question is, how can we in art education develop the appropriate insights and skills to implement the necessary strategies for young children, which will foster right hemisphere processing? For many of us, this may be a difficult task because we are mainly products of a verbal and analytical tradition which is the dominant mode of education of the western world. Can we shift gears, hang loose in our own thinking and permit the flowing of genuine intuition? Can we really trust our senses in an educational context? I believe we can if we are prepared to take chances, to dig deeper into our own being and to ask the basic questions of what, why and how of education. Let me propose some possibilities that may help us obtain this rather elusive insight into ourselves; or so to speak, how we must actively court the Muse.

We must be prepared to deal with modes of apprehension, i.e. images, dreams, daydreams and intuition which in our culture has traditionally received a bad press. As art educators, this would appear to be our natural environment. But a careful, objective analysis of our teaching methods may reveal that the intellect does indeed override the intuitive. Do we not inordinately stress, in our teaching methods, the "scientific" basis of art? Is the intuitive mode clouded by objectivity, such as in our concern for teaching one-and two-point perspective to our young students, for example. Do we

not too often stress the "logical" understanding of color? Is not our language of instruction in art geared mainly for left hemisphere processing? Are we really tapping the metaphoric, image-making world of our young students?

I am not suggesting that we resurrect the old, but yet controversial, argument of intervention vs. non-intervention, but rather to go beyond this point of debate to a clearer understanding of human potential. Art experiences without structure can lead to meaningless expression. Expression without structure can lead to sterile academic exercises. Obviously, we need both structure and expression, but in proper balance.

How can we approach this new awareness in the teaching of art? The following possibilities can be used in art instruction which relate to revealing self-awareness through strategies which deal with psychological integration, often called centering. This is a method which enables people to focus

in on psychological processes which in turn generates appropriate physical relaxation. Both work in tandem, each is necessary for optimum growth of the individual. To be centered is to have the cognitive-intellectual mode (left hemisphere). When we are integrated, our bodies and minds are in balance, and we respond more completely and sensitively to our environment. The raw material for the synthesis of the intellectual mode with the intuitive mode is in some cases, the stuff dreams are made of.

It is beyond the scope of this paper to greatly elaborate the many possibilities that art teachers can learn and present to their classes, therefore, I will just discuss briefly a few which I hopefully believe will be illuminating.

We can utilize known techniques for working with dreams. Dreams are powerful vehicles for image-making. Two prerequisites are very important. First, much dream-work involves finishing dreams in "the imagination." For this reason, teachers who lead ream groups must learn how to guide magery. Second, participants in ream groups must learn to remember heir dreams. Remembering a particular dream-image should quickly be followed by visually constructing the mage with appropriate materials of art. he following are some techniques hat can be utilized in helping children raphically explicate the dream-image:

If a child dreams of a design, he or he should be motivated by the teacher to draw or paint it and then share it with is or her classmates.

If an unusual object or possible invention is dreamed, the child should be ncouraged to build it, regardless of its resumed practicality.

If an unusual or dramatic image occurs, it can be the subject of a painting r drawing.

Children highly motivated in this process can turn almost any dream into an illustrated storybook.

Another important teaching process is guiding children's imagery. The ability to experience vivid imagery occurs very strongly in most children, but it usually wanes as one's age increases. One reason for this decrease in "imagibility" is that it receives very little support and encouragement in our educational process; another is that imagery is often disapproved outright by most adults. A sensitive teacher can help children move creatively through the image state. Basically, this is a non-thinking state, more of a phenomenological feeling, which is a direct and immediate experiencing of the image. This is achieved not by manipulating or controlling the image, but by sensitively redirecting children's attention to feeling and accepting immediate experience.

This redirecting process of the image can be dramatically enhanced by children, if in a relaxed state, they are motivated to illustrate or construct the image. Children well-grounded or centered in these techniques are less inhibited, more motivated, and therefore, more creative.

In summary, we as art educators have a particularly important role to play in this attempt to more fairly balance education. In the light of recent scientific findings, artists, art educators and young children involved in art no longer need feel the slightest inhibition in resisting the common myth that the cognitive process, particularly rationality, is superior to sensitivity, or in pointing out that this myth leads to a half-brained educational product.

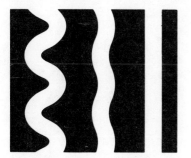

The Gifted Child With Learning Disabilities

JOEL ELKIND

Joel Elkind is Principal of the Grandview School,
Monsey, New York.

The topic of this paper seems like a contradiction, a dichotomy, but in reality individuals embodying this apparent paradox do exist and perform outstandingly. Leonardo da Vinci, Woodrow Wilson, Albert Einstein, Winston Churchill and Igor Sikorsky are but a few of the more eminent examples who have exhibited these supposedly antithetical qualities. The definition, identification and ameliorative procedures and programs for this group of children will be discussed in this paper.

The definition generally accepted of learning disability was adopted by the United States Office of Education in January, 1968; it states: "Children with special learning disabilities exhibit a disorder in one or more of the basic psychological processes. They include conditions which have been referred to as perceptual handicaps, brain injury, minimal brain dysfunction, dyslexia and developmental aphasia." The disabilities included above range from mild to severe and present themselves as difficulties in language, memory, perception and conceptualization. The child may also exhibit difficulty in attention span and motor coordination.

The above-mentioned manifestations of learning disabilities make the identification of a gifted child doubly difficult. The "normal" gifted child is frequently overlooked on group-administered tests; in fact Barbe has indicated that up to seventy per cent of gifted children may not be identified if only group tests are used. Gifted with learning disabilities perform extremely poorly on these group tests since their deficiency is generally in the area of visual perception and they cannot read with understanding. It is even more critical that these children be given individually administered tests than the "normal" gifted child. Not only will individual testing indicate their high intelligence, but it will also point out the area in which learning disabilities exist, such as perceptual or motor. With this indication the Illinois Test of Psycholinguistic Abilities can further pinpoint in its nine subtests the area of difficulty so that supportive efforts may be instituted. The Illinois Test of Psycholinguistic Abilities developed by Kirk and McCarthy in 1961 is still a most useful tool in identifying areas of learning disabilities in children between two and nine years old.

A battery of tests is also most useful in establishing a differential diagnosis of the gifted child with learning problems. Hanvik recommends that the Wechsler Intelligence Scale for Children, the Bender Gestalt and the Goodenough Draw-A-Man Test be administered. Assessments of these children should be done periodically for as Bateman has pointed out, "the level of performance and the manner of performance over a period of time are necessary for an accurate picture of test results."

Reprinted from *The Gifted Child Quarterly,* Vol. 17, No. 2, 1973. ©1973 National Association for Gifted Children

The educational program for a gifted child with learning disabilities must be so constructed that we capitalize on his strong modalities of learning while at the same time strengthening those modalities that are weak and need shoring up. This may mean providing auditory materials for the child if his weakness is in the visual perceptual modality. Letting the child get more of his input from records, tapes or other auditory means is an example of this. Conversely, if his deficiency lies in the auditory discrimination area, activities which are geared to the visual area should be employed such as film strips, pictures and soundless films. Children with coordination problems who have difficulty with their fine muscles in writing should be taught to type or use drawings to convey their ideas.

At the same time these adaptations and adjustments indicated above are being made, the child should be receiving supportive reinforcement and training to ameliorate his deficiencies. Word and number games can be used to sharpen and strengthen his auditory memory. If he is highly distractible, a sheltered learning place should be found in the room, possibly behind a screen, away from other children. Orientation skills can be improved through exercises adapted to strengthen the child's concepts of laterality, directionality and place in space. The use of walking beams, spatial relationship exercises, throwing and batting a ball will improve motor skills.

Classroom management techniques can also be developed to accommodate the gifted child with learning disabilities. For the child experiencing visual problems his assignment might be read to him by his parents or a classmate. Reports could be submitted in project form which could be constructed by the child. Examinations could be given orally to the child. Children with auditory problems should be given succinct directions one at a time in order to preclude the confusion which can result from a series of directions rapidly given.

With appropriate modifications and adaptations of programs and classroom management techniques, the gifted child with learning disabilities can function and flourish in any setting whether it be in the regular classroom, in enrichment groups, in special classes for the gifted children or in special schools for gifted children. The gifted child with learning disabilities can fulfill the potential that is within him and achieve the open-endedness of human ability as envisioned by Gowan. (Complete references are listed with the original article.)

CREATIVITY IN THE CURRICULUM

BY HERB KOHL

START FROM SCRATCH
This is a particularly good way to introduce new themes or to provide models against which existing institutions or theories can be compared.

Systems of Measurement
Last year, I showed my students a simple visual illusion (see illustration at right) and then asked whether the lines were the same or different sizes. When one student guessed they were the same, I asked for proof. She laid a piece of paper along both lines, marking the beginning and the end of each, and showed me that they matched.

At that point, I explained there were other ways to measure things and asked one of the boys to trace his hand a number of times. Then by cutting out and taping the hands together, I made a "Ben's-hand" ruler and with it we measured a table.

All the students wanted to create their own measuring systems, and so Toni's hands and Charlie's feet and Celine's shoes all became units of measure. Soon the class saw the need to standardize measures, and Carol's hand was chosen by lot to be the standard for our class system.

I raised the problem of how we could measure an object smaller than Carol's hand. We followed a suggestion to use the length of Carol's thumb from the tip of the nail to the first joint as a smaller measure and found that five such units made up one "Carol's-hand." We had the beginning of a system of measurement with simple relationships between its parts.

Before long we needed a larger measurement to determine the length of the room and decided to call 10 "Carol's-hands" a table. Later the students devised a 100-hand measure called a "room" and a two-room tape to measure the playground and ball field and the length of paper airplane flights.

Thus, our system finally evolved into the following form. The standard measure was Carol's hand. Its equivalents: 5 thumbs equal 1 hand; 10 hands equal 1 table; 10 tables, or 100 hands, equal 1 room.

Then I brought in some rulers containing both the metric and imperial systems. We talked about the two basic systems now used to measure length and how trade and communication make it more practical to use just one system.

My first-grade students had no trouble using and thinking in both systems. And because of their own experiences could imagine how other people could devise a variety of systems. They could also see that such systems were the creative acts of real people, not abstract universal and unquestioned principles.

Other Mathematical Systems
It is possible to build all kinds of math systems from scratch. For example, you can invent numerical symbols. Try adding and subtracting using only two or three symbols, without mentioning the notion of different base systems. Ideas flow more freely and understanding develops more easily when invention precedes exposure to already developed systems.

Inventing games, developing a notation to describe them and then trying to explore these games in an abstract sense, asking such questions as "Does the first or second player have an advantage?" or "Is there a way to play so that a win is guaranteed?" provides a good introduction to mathematical systems and proof theory. (Ed.'s note: For an elaboration on the use of games, consult Kohl's *Math, Writing and Games,* N.Y. Review, 1974.)

Other Curriculum Areas
Starting from scratch can be equally effective in studying society or culture or the individual psyche. The design of a city, the creation of an imaginary history, or the development of a theory to explain behavior offer the insights and understanding that memorization or parroting others' ideas cannot.

In the case of the city, for example, one can prepare the students by laying out the terrain, describing the number and type of settlers and the resources and wealth available. Then students can try to develop a city. With such open-ended problems, students are limited only by their own imaginations and ability to share ideas and by their teacher's patience, time and willingness to innovate.

In the reading curriculum create writing systems that transcribe the way your students speak, develop a gesture language or construct a musical notation that includes noises made by machines as well as a variety of secret codes and languages.

Very young children can understand the relation between activities (such as speaking) and abstract systems that are used to transcribe them (such as our alphabet), if they are given a chance to develop some such systems themselves and in that process to see the problems that creation brings. Reading is too often mysterious to young children because they don't know what written symbols are or how they were created.

STAND THINGS ON THEIR HEADS
This technique is especially useful for getting out of a rut and breaking a pattern of repeating mistakes. When faced with students who couldn't grasp a crucial idea, I often responded by repeating the same thing until I became frustrated and hostile. Recently I learned to instead stand things on their heads.

In the Curriculum
Often starting with an answer helps. Instead of asking someone to read a

"Creativity in the Curriculum," Herb Kohl, *Teacher,* Vol. 92 No. 7, March 1975. ©1975 MacMillan Professional Publications, Inc.

word, "frog" for example, tell the class that the word is "frog" and ask them to puzzle out why that particular word says frog. Instead of asking what five and six equal, ask the students to think of all the different ways that two numbers can make up 11.

I have one student who used to throw temper tantrums when asked to read. At first I tried to stop him by lecturing him on how smart he was and on how he shouldn't be afraid of reading. Recently I instead asked him to cry louder and informed him that when he ran out of tears he'd be able to see the page better and read. It worked. I simply refuse to reward him with my anger for behavior that cripples him.

In Human Relations

In cases of group conflict, it often helps to stand things on their heads by acting out an event with all the roles reversed. I have also found this technique useful when preparing for confrontations. If my students want to confront another teacher or principal or school board, I have them role play the meeting, insisting that the students role play the different "adversaries" at least the first few times they act out the situation. People who dare to confront and change things must understand as much as they can how the other people involved feel and anticipate their responses to pressure.

RECOMBINE THE ELEMENTS

Significant artistic and scientific works are never wholly new. Rather, they consist of bold recombinations of what has gone before—forged into new ways of perceiving the world.

Arts and Sciences

In the elementary school there are many materials that provide some exposure to this strategy—tangrams, puzzles, visual illusions, discovery units in science or math. Often, however, other materials can be used in new ways. With sequence stories, for example, let students put the pictures in random order and make up a story to fit any sequence.

The same is true for words. I do an exercise with my first-graders that seems to enable them to think more freely and creatively. Each student in turn says a word (any word each wants), which I write on the chalkboard. An abbreviated list might read: *red, mommy, first, sleep, stop, car, day, lunch, Hot Wheels.*

After we complete the list, we consider some combinations and give the words some sense no matter how disconnected they seem. We start down the list two words at a time. Thus, we would read and talk about *red-mommy, first-sleep, stop-car, etc.* Then we take three words at a time.

The students don't find it difficult to fuse the images the words represent, and after a few weeks of doing this, I suggest that this fusion of images can be part of their writing just as it is part of much contemporary (and classical) poetry.

Social Sciences

In dealing with economics and politics, recombining the elements is not only a good mind exercise but also a practical necessity if we are to solve and to help our children solve with us the problems of society.

One way to do this is to present students with an analysis of an actual situation—a city or community or nation in a state of crisis. Then the students can recombine the elements present to create a humane solution to the problem of people living and growing together.

For example, a ghettoized city in the United States can be studied in terms of total resources available to the community. Or, study a developing nation struggling for political and economic independence.

Of course, the honesty and effectiveness of this kind of study will depend on the teacher's willingness to entertain bold redistributions of power and wealth. Students may also consider ideas that are more rigid than your own. Their mental development and freedom to grow, to uncover and explore their own values and to express their thoughts in an atmosphere of trust, without fear of censorship, will also free them to imagine and create.

Teaching: Mainstreaming vs. Separate Programming

the broadest sense, high ability makes it necessary to set high standards including problems which contain enough difficulty so as to make the problem an educational challenge and not the difficulty itself . . . This is the challenge for those who teach the gifted student.

Presently, the majority of schools place gifted students within the regular classroom with others in their own age group. Theoretically this allows them to work with students of varying ability levels, with accelerated studies and special grouping being eliminated for the gifted . . . in other words, traditional heterogeneous grouping. In this setting the teacher must design her class so that each student has the opportunity to learn at his own level of achievement.

However, age standards and common assignments decrease markedly in value as intellectual increments come about for the gifted student who has the ability to interpret and integrate knowledge with an intensity beyond their peers. Therefore, individualization and differential assignments make a laboratory type assignment necessary.

Some programs advocate a broadening of experience for the truly gifted student, while others of a more cautios vein preclude objectives which might narrow and completely ignore aspects of natural and environmental learning, thus making academic learning the ultimate discipline. This form of limited experience gives rise to ethical questions of responsibility which

surly further narrows avenues of experience, thus producing an extremely bright person who is well informed, but socially unprepared, worldly unwise and in a personal sense, extremely unhappy.

The gifted child should have the opportunity to actively engage in school activities, expressing himself fully in debating, art, poetry, or the school newspaper. Their high level of intelligence offers them an equally wide-ranging enthusiasm for language, reading, games, music, painting, and all other social activities which develop their accuracy of knowledge and further positive development of their sense of responsibility.

In order to achieve this, the atmosphere around the gifted child should be one that will be philosophically and creatively condusive to individual thought. It should offer encouragement coupled with a flexible and emotionally secure format. This climate should further include creativity and variation encompassed with precise knowledge of just punishment and free of external evaluations which might inhibit or slow his understanding.

The student should be allowed to self-evaluate his efforts in order that he might begin a knowledge of his own sense of worth in enrichment activities, along with goal setting and recognition of that which he already knows. With these fundamentals in check, the teacher can then guide the gifted student toward full achievement commensurate with his abilities.

A BETTER BREAK IN SCHOOLS FOR GIFTED CHILDREN

LONG PHOTOGRAPHY

Students at the Brentwood School in Los Angeles play game designed to sharpen their skills with numbers. Such programs intend to make learning more fun.

For many of the nation's brightest youngsters, school means boredom, alienation—and often, poor grades and misbehavior. Now a push is developing to remedy that situation.

After a lapse of nearly two decades, attention is being paid again to yet another neglected group in the U.S. school population: 2.5 million unusually gifted children.

Federal and State lawmakers are showing more inclination to provide money for special education of the gifted and talented. Court decisions, too, reflect growing pressure by such youngsters and their parents for recognition of their needs.

Concern for the gifted reached a peak following the first Russian space launch in the 1950s, then declined during the 1960s when emphasis shifted to help for the disadvantaged: the poor, the national minorities, the physically and mentally handicapped.

In the 1970s, concern for the special needs of the gifted is being reawakened in large measure by evidence that many of these youngsters are bored by the lock step of mass education and are turning into chronic underachievers and dropouts.

In one State, for example, it was found that a significant percentage of school dropouts had I.Q.'s of 120 or higher.

What's being done. A special office for the gifted and talented was established at the U.S. Office of Education in 1972. In 1974, Congress specifically approved aid for the gifted and talented—the first such legislation since the National Defense Education Act, which was passed in 1958.

A report prepared by the Office of Education defines gifted children as those who consistently achieve very superior scores on standardized tests or demonstrate advanced skills, imaginative insight and intense interest. In some school districts that use I.Q. tests to help identify the gifted, that term is applied to all youngsters with a score of 120 or better. Others set the cutoff point at 140 or higher.

In the present fiscal year, federal funds in the modest amount of 2.56 million dollars became available, mostly for comprehensive State programs.

The goal of the Office of Education is to double the number of gifted and talented youngsters served by special school programs from 80,000 in 1971 to 160,000 by mid-1977. The office reports receiving 30 to 40 letters a day from parents, educators and other concerned citizens.

The courts, too, are getting into the act. In order to avoid a lawsuit, the Pennsylvania State board of education has ruled that, starting next July 1, parents of gifted children can compel the school authorities to provide them with a special education.

Twelve institutions of higher learning in the country are now training teachers for the gifted.

Eighteen States have a full-time employe at their department of education to work with the gifted, compared with only 10 States in 1971. An additional 23 States have a person working 50 per cent of the time on behalf of the gifted.

Increasingly—though admittedly still to a limited degree—those youngsters identified as gifted by tests, or by their teachers and principals, parents, and sometimes even their fellow students, are offered accelerated or enriched instruction in regular or special classrooms and schools.

Local action. Some of the important efforts on behalf of the gifted across the country are these:

New York City's program reaches

LONG PHOTOGRAPHY

Pupil creates map of a country from her imagination in this special gifted class.

from kindergarten through high school. Two hundred gifted children aged 4 to 6 attend special classes at four schools, learning at their own pace. Most grade schools start accelerated separate classes in grades four through six.

Gifted junior-high-school students can compress three years of work into two, or else spend the same three years but go into greater depth in each subject. Also, there is a special junior high school for gifted pupils.

Some 13,000 New York high-school students attend four special schools, of which three stress science and math and a fourth stresses the arts.

In Los Angeles, some 32,000 pupils, or 5 per cent of the public-school population, have been identified as gifted, and get a little over three hours a week of special instruction. The State contributes about $65 per student annually for such programs.

In the San Francisco area, 1,400 gifted children aged 4½ to 16 attend late afternoon and Saturday classes at the College of Marin to study a variety of subjects such as computers, speed-reading, electronics and marine biology. The children learn at their own pace, and no grades are given.

Chicago's schools let seventh and eighth graders commute part time to museums and the zoo for study. The State of Illinois is spending 2 million dollars this year on programs for gifted children.

Accelerated learning. Houston has special programs at the kindergarten through high-school levels. Its high school of engineering, which offers accelerated instruction with graduation at the end of the eleventh grade, has received $25,000 from private engineering companies.

In Georgia, a State law requires that all school systems have special programs by 1977. Out of a million students, some 21,000 have been identified as gifted. The State pays 80 per cent of the salaries of 303 special teachers allocated to local systems for these students.

In the Atlanta area, 80 gifted children in grades one through six are brought to the campus of Georgia State University each Saturday for discussions and classes in such subjects as flying an airplane, operating a computer, African studies and photography.

At the Governor's School of North Carolina, which is supported by the state legislature, 400 academically talented high-school upperclassmen get an opportunity each year to engage in a six-week residential program of concentrated studies at the Salem College campus in Winston-Salem.

A project to study mathematically precocious children at Johns Hopkins

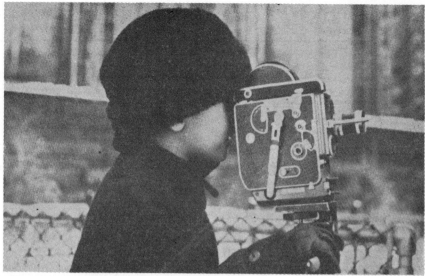

New York City's program for gifted and talented children ranges from kindergarten through high school. One project is the making of a movie called "Fun at the Zoo."

University in Baltimore, Md., has led to the publication of a book, "Intellectual Talent: Research and Development," in which a number of authors offer suggestions for identifying and assisting the gifted.

Educators still regard themselves as waging an uphill struggle against public apathy or even resentment. Laments Harold C. Lyon, Jr., director of education for the gifted and talented, in the U.S. Office of Education:

"Unlike some of the other clients of education, the gifted and talented have never had a large lobby. Probably they never will, for they are a minority, not much more than 1 in 20. They are burdened with the seemingly antidemocratic stigma of elitism and hampered by false assumptions such as the inaccurate belief that brilliant people will make their own way and need no special encouragement."

Even among those who recognize the need for special programs, agreement on programs is not general.

Finding the gifted. How does one go about identifying the gifted child? Tests used for this purpose have their critics.

Nor are recommendations by teachers viewed as foolproof. In a recent survey by the U.S. Office of Education, 57.5 per cent of the schools reported that they could not find any gifted children among their pupils.

In some cases, educators who report difficulties in identifying gifted but inarticulate children from poor families, are bringing in consultants to help solve the problem.

Furthermore, school officials say, a child who is creative and gifted in a particular area may not necessarily be the best of scholars.

What to do about gifted youngsters? Again, educators disagree. Some let such children "skip" grades to join older children. Other school officials say it's better to keep them with students of the same age and give them more challenging work to do, to avoid undue emotional stress.

Should talented pupils be segregated from others? Some educators say "No." Harold Turner, director of special education for De Kalb County, Ga., makes this observation:

"The more you segregate them, the more you limit their socialization skills."

On the other hand, Virginia Z. Ehrlich, director of gifted-child studies in New York City, reports that more emotional problems occur among gifted children in regular high schools than in specialized schools. Her explanation: "For the very bright youngsters there's peer pressure to hide their ability."

Norman Mirman, who heads a private school for gifted children in Los Angeles, says that gifted students who always stand out in public schools "can get inflated ideas of their importance." He adds: "When they come here, it takes the hot air out of them. They see others just as bright. Coming here is more of a humbling experience."

Whatever approach is used, teachers and students who participate in special help for the gifted appear enthusiastic. This comment comes from a Houston elementary-school teacher, Henrietta Campbell:

"We learn just about as much as the kids do. It's almost a daily occurrence that a child comes to me with a question or problem that I can't help with. So we work out ways we can all learn together."

Gifted Children In A Bind

VERNA TOMASSON

CONTRARY to the belief that "genius will out" and that smart kids get by on their own, the Office of Education reported to Congress in 1971 that more than 2 million above-average minds are languishing from want of attention in the country's elementary and high schools. The study found that services for the gifted and talented enjoy very low priority at the federal, state, and most local levels of government and educational administration, that one-third or more of the known gifted receive no special instruction and that, as a result, these high-potential youngsters perform far below their capacity.

Although almost every child can be regarded as gifted at something, studies made for the 1971 report show that by conservative estimate 3 to 5 percent of our school children exhibit outstanding abilities at an early age. Such traits are found in individuals from all backgrounds and levels of society: rich and poor, urban and rural, black, white, yellow, and red.

Research done in the last 50 years indicates that the gifted have their own educational needs. State surveys show that more than half of the gifted children taught themselves to read before they entered school. They are more interested than other children of like age in social and ethical problems. They require less drill and can handle independent projects with less supervision.

Gifted youths do not necessarily have an easy or satisfying life. Bored by the slow pace and intellectual confinement of a standardized curriculum, they often become troublemakers in the classroom, or join the dropout population.

Children not fortunate enough to have parents who recognize their abilities and persist in finding them appropriate educational facilities often suffer tragically. Because of their extreme sensitivity, many of these youngsters, made to feel that they are "different," develop emotional problems. The girls, especially, divert their abundant energies into disguising their talents in order to be popular. Some, from disadvantaged environments, turn to drugs and other anti-social activities.

Teachers of the Gifted

Teachers of exceptionally bright children do not have to be unusually gifted themselves, but they must be able to respect those who are. Only 12 colleges throughout the United States offer graduate programs in Education of the Gifted. Untrained teachers cannot spot gifted students and would be unable to provide them with challenge and stimulation if they did.

The overwhelming majority of parents who testified at the 1970 regional hearings on the gifted and talented reported that most teachers were openly hostile to and fearful of outstanding pupils and set themselves up in power struggles with the gifted child.

Many schools feel that a program of generally high intellectual quality fulfills the needs of bright youngsters. But cognitive learning, Harold G. Lyons (director of the HEW Office of the Gifted and Talented) said, must be integrated with

"Gifted Children in a Bind," Verna Tomasson, *The Education Digest*, Vol. XXXIX No. 6, February 1974. ©1974 Prakken Publications, Inc.

emotional experience. Although to outsiders, many gifted children appear "haughty," their self-imposed standards often give them feelings of deep inferiority. They must learn to cope, too, with the open hostility of schoolmates and teachers. Career training for the gifted is also important, Dr. Lyons emphasized, because these many-faceted youngsters are often confused and discouraged by an excess of choices.

The Fleischmann Commission (New York State) report in 1972 recommended an early identification of gifted youngsters, so that they could be channeled into enriched programs. This has not yet been implemented. When asked by the U.S. Office of Education to give the number of gifted and talented children in their schools, more than half the schools reported *none*, a statistical impossibility. Nor are IQ tests reliable, since they do not identify the creative child or the disadvantaged child whose skills are nonverbal.

Paul Torrance at the University of Georgia is working on ways to identify gifted black youngsters. He finds that a sense of humor is a good indication of intelligence, and also that youngsters can usually identify the gifted among them.

After Russia sent up the first Sputnik in 1957, there was a flurry of interest in programs for the gifted, stimulated by Admiral Rickover who felt that our military superiority was at stake. Most of these programs were geared to the applied sciences, with the focus not on what the government could do for the gifted but what the gifted could do for the government. Then the civil rights battles of the 1960s changed our priorities, and the educational spotlight turned on the "disadvantaged."

Successful Patterns

Many people assume that education for the gifted means a return to a caste system, but experimental programs have proved this assumption unwarranted. Some of the patterns which were found successful in working with the gifted include: acceleration (grade skipping or early entrance to kindergarten or first grade); ability grouping (children spend most of the time with their age group, but are placed in some classes such as reading and math according to ability level); individualized instruction (study hall or recess is replaced by special tutoring); enrichment (field trips and extra cultural experiences); and acceleration of content (fourth graders given sixth-grade materials). The Talcott Mountain Science Center in Connecticut, and the workshops run by the Gifted Child Society of New Jersey, use an apprenticeship system, whereby outstanding children study with experts in their fields of interest.

America is a Scrooge when it comes to spending money on its future leaders and professionals. Twenty-one states have legislation on the books authorizing programs for the gifted and talented, but in only four states—California, Connecticut, Georgia, and Illinois—are programs in actual operation. The federal role is almost nonexistent. In one region, federal allocations for the gifted for fiscal 1974 are coming out of the budget for the handicapped!

Whenever the education budget is cut the first "frills" to go are music, art, drama, science—the very programs the gifted need to pursue their special interests. Private agencies have had difficulty raising money for this cause. There is, however, some evidence of a new interest. One big advance has been the establishment this year, under a grant from the Office of Education, of a National Clearinghouse for the Gifted and Talented as part of the Council for Exceptional Children. The Clearinghouse will respond to requests for information and will help to provide curriculum materials. It is preparing a list of existing programs and courses.

The newly created Office of the Gifted and Talented, which advocates but cannot allocate, recently sponsored a National State Leadership Training Institute at Squaw Valley, California. Educators met there with representatives of 18 states to encourage and direct the formation of programs.

Hearings were held last June in the Senate on a bill introduced by Sen. Jacob Javits (R-N.Y.) which would provide federal assistance in four areas: support for the National Clearinghouse; funding through state programs for the gifted and talented, in public schools from elementary through high school; training of teachers and personnel; and research and demonstration projects. Similar legislation has been introduced by Dominick Daniels (D-N.J.) in the House.

Educators are concerned that new programs for the gifted should not become just another educational fad, but rather an ongoing concept based on respect for the individual needs of every person in our society.

One major step toward appropriate education has been the introduction of open classroom teaching. When several activities are going on simultaneously in a classroom, children will choose what interests them, and good teachers can use the situation for individualized instruction. Good *teams* can make such instruction even better.

Hunter, Antioch, and other colleges are experimenting with independent study programs. High schools and primary schools may want to offer independent study to boys and girls who complete the required work swiftly. If it does not become synonymous with solitary confinement, but includes guidance and encouragement, independent study can be an important way to meet special educational needs within the comprehensive school system.

The question is not whether we should put the education of the gifted above and against others with severe needs. The mere fact that this suggestion arises shows how well Americans have adjusted to the divide-and-conquer psychology. The real question is: Shall we encourage every student, swift or slow, to reach full potential?

The Gifted, Talented Child

MARJ WIGHTMAN

TEXANS today are focusing much of their energy and some of their money on public school children who are both "gifted" and "talented."

In some districts, we have populated entire schools with the super bright; in others, we have set aside classrooms or isolated whole wings of buildings for the gifted. In all, we have injected the curriculum with more pizzazz than many students found in a whole school career barely five years ago.

According to the U.S. Office of Education, the gifted and talented total about 5 percent of the youth in our elementary and secondary schools. What we are doing for this 5 percent (or approximately 145,000 students) in Texas can best be examined through two sets of activities:

• Texas Education Agency (TEA) efforts to increase statewide awareness and development of new programs; and

• School district efforts to offer the best possible program to all talented students from every ethnic background.

Individual school districts had for many years shaped curriculums into new forms tailored to the needs of their students. Then in 1975 the idea of a state plan for the gifted drew legal support from the Texas legislature. Federal help in funding the program came from the U.S. Office of Education.

Texas is beginning with a meticulous cadence of staff development; pilot projects; and early program evaluation, revision, and rapid expansion. The State Board of Education set 1978 as the target date for implementing programs in 50 percent of its more than 1,100 school districts. It also helped form a precise state definition of "gifted and talented"—students who "exhibit superior academic achievement and ability, talent in any esthetic area, mechanical ability, potential for leadership, and qualities of creativity."

Now the challenge is to find these students—then to give each one the schooling that will help develop his potential.

Fortunately, we have many building blocks already formed into a strong base. One of these is the National/State Leadership Training Institute on the Gifted/Talented, organized in 1971 and designed to "upgrade supervisory personnel and program planning for the gifted at the state level." Its staff includes widely recognized program planners, researchers, and teachers.

Working with TEA, the Institute staff came to Austin for three intensive work sessions with specialists from the 20 regional education service centers, selected school districts within each region, and a cadre of Agency professionals to develop the nucleus of the state's program. The Phase I workshop, held in December 1976, began the development of program planning for the gifted; the Phase II session in March 1977 worked toward identifying students and refining and evaluating programs; the Phase III workshop held in May focused on additional improvement in the curriculums.

The proving of this development process will begin in September, when pilot schools in each region begin selecting and working with their own gifted and talented students.

"These prototype programs will vary considerably from region to region or school to school," explains Ann Shaw, TEA program director for gifted and talented. "One district may offer a highly specialized program for elementary-age children while another tests its best ideas in a more comprehensive effort for high-school students."

The state program is not a start-from-scratch effort, however. Many school districts have already developed their own local programs. The most visible examples include the specialized high schools, such as the High School for the Visual and Performing Arts in Houston.

Two Elementary Programs

Some of the most far-reaching efforts to serve the top 5 percent begin in the elementary grades. Houston's Vanguard Program and Corpus Christi's Athena Program are two well-known examples.

Vanguard draws its students from a base of children already working at 1.5 years above grade level. Combining tests for creativity with attendance, conduct, and recommendations from teachers, the district assigns children to the one high-school program, three junior high, or six elementary schools. Each Vanguard program is a school-within-a-school. At River Oaks Elementary, for instance, the 200 Vanguard children in grades 4-6 concentrate their academic study in a single wing of the building, mixing with the other pupils in art, music, and physical education classes for one-quarter of the school day. Lanier Junior High's 467 Vanguard students are less isolated, spending two-thirds of the day in their own academic classes and the remainder in physical education, art, music, or woodworking classes with the other 800 teenagers. Teachers are specially selected for each program position.

The district tries to identify youth who are creative and academically able for its elementary programs. In junior high the emphasis is on hard academics. In the high-school program, students must show considerable creative thinking and academic flair.

Houston administrators have used many recruiting devices to bring their most promising students into these special programs, trying everything from TV and radio spots to notes on the back of the weekly lunch menus sent home to parents. They also search school records, send letters home to parents, and ask principals to recommend students. This approach seems to work, for Vanguard, which matches its racial/ethnic mix with total district enrolment, is growing yearly.

The Corpus Christi Athena Program, now completing its first year, with 822 children in the first six grades, was also built on a local commitment to the top 5 percent. Parents have become deeply involved in the program, serving as advisors, resources of information of special interest to students, and volunteers in the library and media center.

During this first year, administrators used two approaches for serving the gifted. One group of 522 children, selected by lottery from 900 identified as gifted and talented, enrolled in the single concept school at Windsor Park Elementary. The remaining 378 youngsters were placed in individual programs at other elementary schools. All were chosen through tests and recommendations by teachers and parents.

The selected teachers were given three days of in-service training before school opened in the fall and 24 more hours during the year.

The program is regularly evaluated. Parents answer a questionnaire about effectiveness, teachers check lists of student progress comments, and the children take pre- and post-tests in reading and mathematics as well as check lists on the effectiveness of the program. Changes based on this evaluation will become a part of the 1977-78 Athena Program.

Next year all gifted and talented elementary students will attend the Windsor Park school. Teachers will emphasize creative and critical thinking, and much teaching will be highly individualized through learning packets and student contracts which map progress in language arts and mathematics.

Does this effort really benefit gifted children? Houston and Corpus Christi believe it does.

These two examples may be somewhat more than typical, but they represent the thinking and planning currently under way at the Texas Education Agency and throughout the state. Even now, some 24 districts are developing their own such programs using federal funds available under Title IV-C of the Elementary and Secondary Education Act.

Texans today aren't waiting. We know we have our share of gifted youth and we're working to make their school days better.

How the Arts Function as Basic Education

Keith P. Thompson

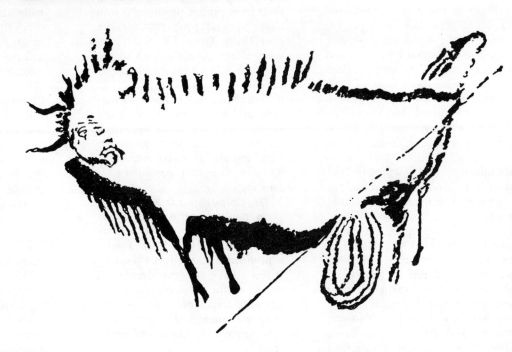

In response to the recent "back to basics" movement in education, numerous philosophers, psychologists, and educators have voiced the opinion that the arts should occupy a more dominant role within education curriculums. And yet an examination of practices in many classrooms reveals that teachers do not have a clear concept of how the arts are "basic" nor how they can function at the core of the curriculum. A little reflection should convince them that what students "basically" need—and parents and teachers as well—is as much knowledge as possible about themselves, other people, the environment, and the relationships among these. To gain this knowledge, they also need to be able to perceive sensitively, to interpret what they perceive, to understand its significance, and then to express it.

The attainment of knowledge and the skills for processing it is the basic goal of education. This goal is generally approached through the various subject areas that comprise the school

The author is associate professor of music education at The Pennsylvania State University, University Park.

The photograph at left was taken by Gail S. Rebhan at The Mountain Gap School near Leesburg, Virginia, a property of The National Trust for Historic Preservation.

The line art is taken from cave drawings in Lescaux, France.

curriculums. The more apparent the contribution of a given subject, the closer its place to the core of the curriculum. The sciences are considered "core subjects" because they obviously provide knowledge about the environment. Mathematics is considered "core" because it provides students with knowledge about numerical relationships and the ability to interpret and understand them. Similarly, social studies give students knowledge about other people and their relationships with one another and to the environment, and the language arts help students develop processing skills in verbal expression. The arts have remained on the periphery of the curriculum because their contribution to the basic goal of education is not as obvious as that of other subject areas. It is time, however, that educators go beyond the obvious to see whether or not the arts do make a significant contribution to the goal of education.

A knowledge of the self can be gained through experiences in the arts. When a student chooses an instrument to produce a sound, paints a line on a piece of paper, molds a form from a piece of clay, or dances across the room, he is learning a bit more about who he is. The knowledge so gained may be at the factual level—"I have arms, feet, and toes"—or, at a much deeper level, a knowledge of one's feelings—"I am afraid," "I like the feel-

"How The Arts Function as Basic Education," Keith P. Thompson, *Music Educators Journal*, Vol. 63 No. 8, April 1977. ©1977 The Music Educator's National Conference.

ings I get when I do this," or "I am in control of my body and my world." Knowledge of the self can also be obtained from the art work of others. The student can experience the feelings of others as he sings their songs, listens to their music, performs or observes their dances, reads their poetry, and views their paintings, and then can compare these feelings with his own. He can gain this knowledge of the commonalities and differences of feelings and move closer to self-identity.

Knowledge of others can be gained through shared experiences in creating art, which, again, can range from a surface knowledge of fact ("you use bright colors") to a knowledge of the other's feelings ("you feel sensitive to small details of the world around you"). Knowledge of others and their feelings can also be gained through the works of art of times past ("Michelangelo believed the Universe was created by God").

Learning through the arts can extend to the physical world as well. The cave man's drawings depict the world as he saw it, the objects of the world that were important to him, the shapes and colors that he knew. Similarly, as a student draws a flower, creates a composition utilizing the song of a bird, choreographs a dance using movements of the crawling lizard, or writes a poem about a rainbow, he becomes acutely aware of his feelings toward these objects in his world.

A work of art is a dynamic force and, as such, provides the student with a source of knowledge about relationships. Form, structure, balance, unity, and variety are essential elements in works of art. As a student performs in a music ensemble, he gains knowledge of the relationships between his part and the parts of other performers and with the total composition. A given melody may be symbolic of a particular feeling. As that melody is sounded with the timbre of different instruments and combinations of instruments, the feeling changes and the listener becomes aware of the relationships between the various feeling states. Likewise, as the melody is sounded with rhythmic, harmonic, and dynamic variations, new feeling relationships are established and communicated. The melodic material that precedes, follows, or is juxtaposed over the given melody also presents additional complexes of feelingful relationships.

The arts do make a contribution toward the acquisition of that knowledge that is basic to education. It is a significant contribution, not so much because of the amount of basic knowledge that students may gain from arts experiences, but rather because of the kind of knowledge gained. The knowledge a student obtains through a study of most curriculum subject areas is a factual knowledge. But factual knowledge is only partial knowledge. There is also a knowledge of feelings. Feelings are an intrinsic part of the human species. They are, in fact, the essence of humanness. If education is to provide the opportunity for the development of human potential, it must be concerned with enabling students to become knowledgeable about feelings that are a part of themselves and other people and that greatly affect the relationships that are established between people and with the environment.

In addition to the knowledge that is basic to education, there are also basic processing skills—perception, interpretation, understanding, and expression—that the arts help develop. An experience in the arts is first of all a sensuous experience. A music composition is sound and silence existing in time; a sculpture is shape and form existing in space. Both are presented for direct perception. Learning in the arts is learning to perceive. It is learning to be more aware of what is heard, seen, and felt.

The arts have remained on the periphery of the curriculum because their contribution to the basic goal of education is not as obvious as that of other subject areas. It is time, however, that educators go beyond the obvious to see whether or not the arts do make a significant contribution.

Interpretation may be defined as a "search for meaning." Each work of art provides a laboratory within which a student can work to develop this skill. In most instances, interpretation of a work of art is appropriate only in terms of the work itself. The red circle acquires its meaning from the other colors and shapes on the canvas; the meaning of the melodic fragment can be found by listening to the other sounds that are presented in the composition. Unlike events in life that are constantly changing, a work of art can be examined and often reexamined by students and teachers.

If interpretation is the search for meaning, understanding is the search for relevance. Understanding is the assimilation of the facts and feelings perceived and the interpretated meanings found in such data with the conglomerate of one's life experience; the end result is the realization that the composite data can provide a basis for present and future action. Most content areas of the school curriculum strive toward the development of understanding, but few have the potential for success that is to be found in the arts. Social studies, for example, attempt to develop skill in searching for relevance through examination of historical events, such as the Civil War. Certain facts about social conditions before, during, and after the war are presented. Meaning is sought as these facts are examined in relationship to one another and in relationship to events and social conditions of our time. Students are expected to develop an *understanding* of social conditions through the process of discovering the relevance of these facts to decisions they will make today or at some future time. There are several weaknesses in this. First, it is impossible for the student to directly experience the event itself. The perceptions of the event and in some instances the meanings of the event are presented to the student, usually in verbal form. Even if such materials are highly accurate, the very nature of verbal discourse necessitates the separating and stringing out of ideas and events when in reality they occur simultaneously. Verbal symbols may be an effective means for the communication of isolated facts but are most ineffective in the communication of feeling and relationships.

The arts, on the other hand, have several distinct advantages as vehicles for developing the skill of understanding. The facts and feelings contained in a work of art are presented directly to the student for his immediate and first-hand perception. In art the presentation of many ideas and events can occur simultaneously, as they do in real life, and each art work is a complete entity. The student can directly perceive the facts and feelings presented in the art work, interpret meanings in combination with other life experiences, and come to an understanding of the ways in which these meanings can influence future directions. It is through experiences in creating, in performing, in viewing, and in analyzing and discussing works of art that students can develop this skill of understanding—that they can learn how to search for relevance.

There is one additional skill that is essential for the processing of knowledge—the skill of *expressing*. Perceiving and interpreting provide input channels for knowledge from external sources. Understanding provides a source of internal knowledge—a knowledge of self as one comes to a realization of the relevance of external knowledge. Because of the uniqueness of each individual this internal knowledge is also unique. It is through this search for relevance in external data that new knowledge is created. As the relevance of two heretofore unrelated substances is understood, a new substance, a new fact, is created. As the relevance of two previously unrelated feelings is discovered, a new feeling is experienced.

Occasionally the new facts and feelings conceived and born through understanding are complete, refined, finished products. More often, however, they are rough gems in need of shaping and polishing. This can only be done by pushing them out of the self and recycling them through the processing stages. The new facts and feelings must be expressed so that they become part of the external world where they may be validated and tested through subsequent perceiving, interpreting, and understanding.

While the knowledge of feeling cannot be expressed through words, it is in as much need of validation and refinement as knowledge of facts. Feelings that have been perceived, interpreted, and understood need to be expressed; pushed out into the world where they can be compared with their source and with other feelings and reperceived and reinterpreted for a more complete understanding. The arts provide a means for such expression of feelings. By examining works of art, students can learn the techniques through which others have expressed feelings; by creating and performing works of art, students can learn how to express their own feelings. Through experiences in the arts, they can learn the skill of expressing that is essential for the processing of knowledge.

When education and the arts are each reduced to "basics," many commonalities become evident. The goal of education is the acquisition of knowledge of facts and feelings about ourselves, other people, the world, and relationships between and among these, and the development of skills for the processing of that knowledge. The basic content of art is knowledge of ourselves, other people, the world, and relationships. While some art does contain factual knowledge, an even more basic content of art is knowledge of feeling—a kind of knowledge that is not available through many of the other subject areas that comprise the typical school curriculum. The basic skills that are necessary for experiencing art, be it as a creator, performer, or consumer, are those skills that are necessary for the processing of knowledge—perceiving, interpreting, understanding, and expressing. When these skills are developed through artistic experiences, students are prepared to utilize them in the processing of not only factual knowledge but, more importantly, knowledge of feeling. The uniqueness of the arts is in their ability to symbolize and express human feeling. Knowledge of these feelings and skills in processing that knowledge are part of the basic goal of education.

Do you have to be gifted to teach the gifted?

Preliminary results of January 1977 questionnaire

DO you have to be gifted to teach the gifted? "Probably not—but it sure does help!" This comment appeared often on the replies to our January questionnaire on characteristics essential for teachers of gifted and talented children. In more than 1,500 responses, teachers indicated a real concern about how best to meet the unique educational needs of the gifted and talented. There is also much uncertainty —where to find out more about identifying these children, where to look for model programs, who can best teach them.

Most responses came from teachers and school administrators, but some were from students, parents, grandparents, college professors. Even one from an engineer. And they are still arriving.

At the right are results from a random sampling of 200 responses. Items have been arranged in order of importance, according to the average rating for each item. For example, the 5.713 rating of the first item indicates that almost everyone, on a 1 (unimportant) to 6 (very important) scale, gave it a 6. The second column indicates the average rating of respondents' self-image for each item.

Ten items on the questionnaire concern observable characteristics of gifted and talented individuals. Twelve items reflect specific teaching skills or components of courses for teachers of G/T children. Those items reflecting G/T characteristics were rated higher as a group than the group on specific skills or courses. This observation suggests that while you don't *have* to be gifted to teach the gifted, this ability should be strongly considered when selecting teachers for this group.

The backgrounds of those replying to the questionnaire were also interesting. Over 50% of the respondents have a bachelor's degree; 46% have achieved five years or more of college work. Thirty-one percent are identified as gifted and/or talented; 40% don't know if they are gifted; 29% are not gifted. While our results do not correlate with the general population (a sampling identifies only two to ten percent as gifted), we must remember that teachers represent that part of the population which is college educated, generally requiring above average ability to gain admittance and to successfully complete a college program.

Teachers of gifted/talented children should have:	(by rank order)	(self)
1. Flexibility and acceptance of differences.	5.713	5.384
2. Skill at developing independent activities.	5.611	4.740
3. Originality, imagination, curiosity.	5.610	4.968
4. Desire to teach G/T children.	5.595	5.058
5. Honesty.		5.500
Persistence, follow-through.	5.590	4.827
6. Independence and self-motivation.	5.485	5.121
7. Ability to study self and children, and use the results to improve teaching.	5.470	4.603
8. Self-assurance.	5.465	4.821
9. Knowledge of nature and needs of G/T children.	5.460	4.052
10. Skill with a wide variety of teaching methods.		3.978
Keen and versatile sense of humor.	5.390	4.915
11. Wide base of information, knowledge, resources, and a good memory.	5.335	4.568
12. Skill at organizing and implementing learning.	5.323	4.589
13. High degree of verbal communication skills.	5.305	4.671
14. Skill at wide-range questioning techniques.	5.290	4.291
15. Skill at bringing together the learnings from the cognitive and affective areas.	5.266	4.201
16. Leadership ability (an action originator).	5.110	4.700
17. Knowledge of current research and information about G/T children.	4.905	3.298
18. Skill in psychology and practice of working with groups (group dynamics).	4.736	4.000
19. Special coursework and preparation.	4.641	2.869
20. Skill at testing and evaluating G/T children.	4.410	3.439
21. Perception of self as G/T.	4.020	4.060
22. Supervised experience teaching G/T children.	3.930	2.553

Would you have wanted John in your class? Yes 88% 12% No

Have you ever taught a G/T child? Yes 84% 16% No

Have you ever taught a group of G/T children? Yes 32% 68% No

Would you like to teach G/T children? Yes 85% 15% No

Should G/T children have special programs? Yes 94% 6% No

G/T children should be grouped: 7% Separately 14% Mixed 79% Combination

Degrees held: 53% Bachelor's 29% Master's 14% M + 30 3% Doctorate

Average age of respondent: 33.75 yrs. Average years taught: 8.25 yrs.

"Do You Have To Be Gifted To Teach The Gifted?" *Instructor*, No. 9 Vol. LXXXVI, May 1977. ©1977 The Instructor Publications, Inc.

Education of the Gifted and Talented

HAROLD LYON

The gifted and talented are a new national priority and a broad definition of giftedness is being emphasized. The BEH staff of Gifted and Talented Education are as much concerned with leadership ability, creativity, and artistic talent as they are with academic prowess and high IQ's.

Our national effort had its beginning in 1970 when Congress asked the US Commissioner of Education to submit a report on what was happening educationally to gifted and talented youth throughout the country. The report revealed the following:

1. Fewer than 4% of the country's gifted and talented youth were receiving services commensurate with their needs.
2. Fifty-seven percent of the school administration said they had no gifted or talented in their classrooms.
3. Only 10 of the 50 states had employed a full time person to oversee the needs of the gifted and talented.
4. There was a prevailing myth that the gifted and talented came almost exclusively from upper middle class and wealthy families.
5. Also prevalent was the false notion that the gifted will easily achieve success on their own.
6. Considerable hostility was directed toward the gifted and talented.
7. Only 12 American universities were training teachers at the graduate level for the gifted and talented student.

Strengthening of State Leadership

In the face of these kinds of problems, the US Office of Education (USOE) began 4 years ago a national effort for the gifted, initially without any specific federal funding. Since that time, both legislative provisions and supporting appropriations have been forthcoming. Strengthening of state leadership became the highest priority, and the result was the creation of a National Leadership Training Institute (LTI) for the Gifted and Talented, with the mission of training teams of 5 leaders each from every state.

At annual training sessions starting in 1972, each team developed comprehensive state plans for the gifted and talented. With $1.1 million in funds provided under the Education Professions Development Act for a 3 year period, the LTI also held such activities as regional awareness conferences on the culturally different gifted and more localized discussions involving parents, administrators, and school board members.

In addition to the programs sponsored by LTI, 3 projects were funded under Title V of the Elementary and Secondary Education Act to enable consortia of 10 to 15 states in each project to undertake cooperative ventures focused on the gifted and talented. Such projects have reached about one-half of the states, with funding totaling $250,000 in 1974 and slightly below that level in 1975. Meanwhile, BEH had helped establish a national clearinghouse for the gifted and talented. Located in the ERIC Clearinghouse on Handicapped and Gifted Children at The Council for Exceptional Children in Reston, Virginia, the clearinghouse now disseminates information concerning research on the gifted and talented

and the best practices available for dealing with such youngsters. Progress over the last 4 years has been such that today 21 state departments of education employ a full time person to work with the gifted and 23 other states have a person working 50% of the time in their behalf.

Meanwhile, significant activities have been launched in certain fields of perhaps special interest to the gifted and talented. One such activity was the convening of an institute for career education for these youngsters, with a number of leading experts in this field invited to attend. An outgrowth of this activity was the 1974 publication of *Career Education for Gifted and Talented Students* edited by Kenneth B. Hoyt, Associate Commissioner of Education for Career Education, and Jean R. Hebeler, Professor in the Special Education Department, University of Maryland. Two more recent projects in this area involve the development of curriculum materials and teaching guides for career education for the gifted and talented and the establishment of three exemplary projects in Wisconsin, Rhode Island, and Washington.

In another special field, a program undertaken with assistance from the USOE regional offices and the National Endowments for the Arts and Humanities involves seeking to infuse the arts into all learning experiences of the gifted and talented. As part of this effort, a national conference on this subject was held last year under the joint sponsorship of USOE and the South Dakota State Department of Education.

Another program that the Gifted and Tal-

"Education of the Gifted and Talented," Harold Lyon, *Exceptional Children*, Vol. 43 No. 3, November 1976. ●1976 The Council for Exceptional Children.

nted Education staff coordinates is the Presidential Scholars Program, which brings 121 of the country's most outstanding high school seniors (a boy and girl from each state and outlying area plus 15 from the nation at large) to Washington, D.C., to receive a presidential medallion and to meet top level government officials.

Appropriations

Education of the gifted and talented gained its initial foothold in legislation under the Education Amendments of 1974 (P.L. 93-380). With the appropriation of $2.56 million for fiscal year 1975, regulations were drafted concerning the issuance of grants and contracts for projects focused on the gifted and talented.

The largest proportion of the initial allocations is going to states, with 26 states receiving 2 year grants the first year. Each such grant may contain three components: a state element, an inservice teacher training element, and a local element made up of one or more model projects with statewide implications. Also, mini-grants of from $1,000 to $20,000 were made to 18 local school districts.

A third category of allocations is devoted to training grants for professionals who will work in various capacities in educational programs for the gifted and talented. Included is a $190,000 grant to a consortium of academic institutions based at Teachers' College, Columbia University, to develop a graduate training program that will produce a cadre of 50 leaders over the next 3 years, a National Training Institute (NTI) funded at $165,000, and a National Intern Training Program at the George Washington University Institute for Educational Leadership funded at $70,000 to enable selected teachers or graduate students to spend one or two semesters working in an intern capacity with programs for the gifted and talented.

In addition to the grants, the program includes 2 categories of contracts. The first funds 6 national model projects for such target groups as members of minorities, talented youth with visual and performing arts, rural children, young children, and creative youth, in addition to a model community mentor program. This money will not be used to initiate new projects but to replicate and demonstrate already proven projects. The second category of contracts is for information clearinghouse projects for gifted and talented youth.

Goals

In these efforts and in all other activities under the Gifted and Talented Education program runs a humanistic theme: an awareness that a particular teacher or coach or other respected adult can impel young people in new and more constructive paths. That awareness also recognizes that the tendency in dealing with the gifted and talented is too often to force them down the purely cognitive track, with little or no attention paid to their feelings or affective development. Alfred North Whitehead said: "After you understand all about the sun, the stars, and the rotation of the earth, you may still miss the radiance of a sunset." Our goal is to stimulate the kind of educational environment for the gifted and talented that nourishes not only their skills but also their capacities for awareness, empathy, communication with their fellow human beings, and appreciation of a sunset.

In Search of the Potentially Gifted: Suggestions for the School Administrator

AARON D. GRESSON and DAVID G. CARTER, SR.

Dr. Gresson is a Research Associate, Department of Behavioral Science, College of Medicine at the Milton S. Hershey Medical Center of the Pennsylvania State University. Dr. Carter is an Associate Professor of Education, Department of Educational Administration, The Pennsylvania State University.

There is no doubt that the 1970s have been and will be remembered as the decade of egalitarianism in education, the ideal or principle that each individual should have educational opportunity commensurate with his needs and capabilities. This principle is based on the assumption that school officials are able to determine the students' particular needs. Since this in itself can be difficult, however, the purpose of this paper is to provide some suggestions which may assist the urban administrator in identifying the potentially gifted and talented child.

Like most other educational issues, the identification and education of the gifted is a political matter. As such, it presents the school administrator with a variety of specific problems. The recent redefinition of giftedness to include the *potentially* gifted or talented child represents one of the many problems.[1] It is, of course, admirable that educational leaders recognize that there are gifted persons who never reach their potential because they go unidentified; nonetheless, the problem of identifying these young people remains.

The difficulty centers around the use of culturally biased tests with minority group children,[2] and the inability or relative disinterest of school administrators in identifying the gifted minority child. For example, the early research of Witty and Jenkins[3] provided clear evidence of highly gifted black children in substantial numbers. Their work also indicated the need for active recruitment of these children. Yet, a recent study reported that the results of a national survey found that 57.7 percent of the elementary and secondary school principals interviewed reported that they had no gifted students in their schools.

No doubt, these figures do not tell the entire story. Several non-administrator generated factors contribute to the disinterest, including teacher attitudes toward both the gifted and minority child.[4] Nevertheless, recent court decisions concerning other forms of exceptionality and equal educational opportunity, coupled with continuing advocacy actions by parents and friends of the gifted, should serve to alert school administrators to the need for some action regarding the potentially gifted and talented child in their schools. The following represent some of the initial considerations necessary to identifying the potentially gifted and talented.

The Gifted Child: An Overview

Over the years, educators have vacillated continuously in their definitions of giftedness. At one time or another, the following criteria have been used:

- Capable of completing comprehensive assignments and assuming more responsibility
- Intelligence tests ratings
- Physical characteristics
- Scholastic achievement
- Reading comprehension
- Inferential statistics
- Capability of high performance in (a) a specific academic aptitude, (b) the visual or performing

"In Search of the Potentially Gifted Suggestions for the School Administrator," Aaron A. Gresson, David G. Carter, Sr., *The Clearing House*, Vol. 50 No. 8, April 1977. ©1977 Heldref Publications.

arts, (c) leadership ability, (d) psychomotor ability, and (e) creative or productive ability.

These criteria have their places in the formal assessment but are of little value to the administrator whose own involvement in the identification process must be both broader and less "rigorous." The chief requirement for the administrator is, perhaps, a "looseness of mind and method"—which is, incidentally, necessary for working with all gifted children. This is so, since the unusualness of the gift can be, in itself, a deterrent to easy identification. After all, what is one looking for? Extraordinary memory? quickness in learning? personal charisma? imaginativeness? The point is simply that what to look for is partially determined by what is desired. This is, moreover, why the so-called minority student (i. e., black, Chicano, female, etc.) can be even more of a problem in terms of identification. After all, given all the emphasis on minority difference, especially in the black child, it is often difficult for the administrator or even the classroom teacher to fathom a "potentially gifted" black student. It is in response to this legitimate difficulty that some educators have recently sought to provide some suggestions for guiding identification of the potentially gifted and talented child. Some of the more useful ideas contained in these guides have been adapted for the school administrator and appear in the following figure. Taken alone, however, each is insufficient to making a meaningful modification in the dominant trend in respect to the minority gifted child. Acceptance of several assumptions regarding the minority gifted also seems indicated.

Assumptions Regarding Minority Giftedness Which Facilitate Identification and Education

Even in this age of enlightenment, people retain negative attitudes toward the gifted and talented. Beliefs about physical abnormality and moral weakness still abound. In addition, there is a general fear of the inability to contain and guide the gifted or talented child. These children are not necessarily evil, unmanageable, or unapproachable. They are like any other child in many ways, and often they are "nicer" than the typical child.

While it is true that in certain school settings, these children will sometimes seem learning-disabled or socio-emotionally involved, they do not necessarily stand out socially or academically across all areas. Thus, it is not recommended that the urban school administrator should consider every child brought to the office for some behavior difficulty as a frustrated genius. It does suggest,

Figure 1.–A Developmental Framework for Possible Identification of the Gifted Black Child

FOCUS	ELEMENTS
A. Cognitive Superiority	1. General and Specific Knowledge 2. Comprehension 3. Application (use of abstraction) 4. Analysis (elements, relations, principles) 5. Unique facility for combining ideas 6. Extraordinary Judgment
B. Psycho-Social Superiority	1. Maturity 2. Responsibility 3. Leadership 4. _____ (Specify) 5. _____ (Specify)
C. Talent-Specific Superiority	1. Art 2. Dance 3. Music 4. Voice 5. Athletics 6. _____ (Specify) 7. _____ (Specify)

however, that a watchful eye be kept and that this possibility be considered when other supporting evidence is received.

Recently, it was suggested to one of the authors by a local district official that middle class white parents often feel embarrassed to acknowledge their feelings regarding the possible exceptionality of their child. While this is a harmless, perhaps valid, statement in itself, it may also indicate that parents who might otherwise be helpful in identifying a gifted child are negotiated into positions which prevent their proper involvement in the educative process. In this instance, the administrator was trying to explain why the district had no programs for the gifted, despite the large number of professionals and well-educated families in the community.

Similar claims of parental failure have been made regarding minority parents, despite considerable evidence to the contrary.[5] Parents are generally interested and will cooperate in the identification of a gifted or talented child. In the case of black parents, it should not be assumed that they do not want to deal with the special arrangements and discomfort such an identification might necessitate.

In conclusion, with respect to the black gifted or potentially gifted child, two other points bear stressing. It is not true that the ghetto home must lack the educationally relevant experiences which

supposedly facilitate academic achievement. Giftedness in the ghetto home is no aberration, anymore than it is in the middle class home. The concerned administrator must be convinced of this.
He should, therefore, become familiar with the
cultural world in which black children live, read
achievement-oriented publications published by
the black community, and learn about the middle-
aged black males and females who have successfully acted on the behalf of their communities,
even though they have not gained the recognition
of more publicized persons. The following questions could serve as a checklist for establishing a
community-based identification council:

- Have efforts been made to establish
  relations with the minority community?
- Have known and unknown community
  leaders been contacted and their cooperation enlisted?
- Do the persons contacted represent a
  broad sampling of the target community?
- Have objectives and priorities been
  established in terms acceptable to everyone?

- Has the role of the community group
  been clearly defined?
- Does the school or district keep in con-
  tinuous communication with the various
  group members?
- Is the council effective in its efforts to
  increase the number of children identified as gifted?

NOTES

1. James J. Gallagher, "The Psychology of Planned Change," in
   *Not All Little Wagons are Red: The Exceptional Child's Early
   Years* (Washington: The Council for Exceptional Children),
   pp. 180-191.
2. A. R. Sullivan, "The Identification of Gifted and Academically
   Talented Black Students: A Hidden Exceptionality," *The
   Journal of Special Education* 7 (1973): 373-379.
3. D. Meehan, "An Evaluation of Simulation as an Approach to
   Assisting Elementary Teachers to Identify Children with
   Learning Disabilities and to Utilize Ancillary Personnel in
   Initiating Remediation Programs within Their Classrooms,"
   D. A. I. 32 (1972): 4478-A.
4. P. J. Burke, "Simulation with General Education Administra-
   tion and Its Effect on Their Attitudes and General Information
   about Special Education," *D. A. I.* 32 (1972): 4478-A.
5. R. A. Martinson, "Children with Superior Cognitive Abilities,"
   in *Exceptional Children in the Schools*, ed. R. Dunn (New
   York: Holt, Rinehart and Winston, 1973).

EXECUTIVE HIGH SCHOOL INTERNSHIPS

A Boon for the Gifted and Talented

Sharlene P. Hirsch

Almost 2,500 gifted and talented juniors and seniors from 26 school districts in 17 states are learning about organizational leadership from the top—as Executive High School Interns to business executives and managers, government commissioners and administrators, newspaper editors, television producers and directors, hospital administrators, judges and attorneys, and directors of social service agencies and civic associations.

For a full semester, on sabbatical from regular classes, they are immersed in the world of organizations and administration, learning how decisions are made and earning a full range of academic credit in the process.

A UTOPIAN EXPERIENCE

"It's like utipia," says Vicki Cook (Hillsborough County, Florida), who has spent her Executive Internship semester with the president of Ensslin Advertising in Tampa. The week finds her variously meeting with clients, presenting storyboards, editing TV commercials (including those in which she has appeared), and spending time in areas such as accounting and production.

Another Hillsborough intern, Karl Miller, is equally delighted with the experience. "Since I've joined the program, I feel like one of the best informed citizens in Hillsborough," he reports.

Karl's placement with the executive director of the Hillsborough County Planning Commission involves law and city planning, areas he hopes to combine in a future career. His internship responsibilities include attending public hearings of the commission and updating research and analytical information on economic development in the county.

Both placements were arranged by coordinator JoAnn Hunter of the Hillsborough County Public Schools, which initiated the first Florida model in 1973. Ms. Hunter has been largely responsible for spreading word about the program to her colleagues in gifted and talented education throughout Florida.

One offshoot of the Hillsborough model is in the Orange County Public Schools, where coordinator Doris Prather has just completed her second year. Ms. Prather learned that Joe Finger, a Oak Ridge High School senior who ranks second in his class, was interested in a career in broadcasting, so she found him the perfect spot, with WKIS Radio in Orlando, where he has written

commercials and news stories and even broadcast sports reports. "The program has given me an opportunity to gain some exposure to the business world," he adds.

"I have a natural interest in making money," grins Kevin Hanks, (Pinellas County, Florida) in explaining his selection of an Executive Internship with the president of Raymond, James & Associates, where he has developed expertise in the stock market and in the management of a brokerage house with 12 offices throughout Florida.

His placement has brought Kevin into contact with other brokers, analysts, and "a multimillionaire oilman." A research report on nonferrous metals which he prepared was used in an analyst's speech.

Kevin, who is pursuing an accounting course through independent study, reports that he has offered his father some advice on investments. "I gave him a tip that wasn't so hot," he adds with a shrug.

The Pinellas County Public Schools coordinators are Jan Rouse and Stan LeBoss who, like their other Florida counterparts, are operating models of the program funded as gifted and talented education through a special state formula.

The strong interest in law found among many high school students is reflected in a Palm Beach placement with the counsel to the Florida State Commission. There, Executive Intern Patrick Healy can be found researching pretrial information on securities frauds and "an occasional murder."

One of the highlights of his semester was accompanying his sponsor to the state capitol, Tallahassee, where he met with the lieutenant governor and other officials. "Law used to be a remote interest, but now I'm very caught up in it," reports the Palm Beach intern. Winner of several scholastic awards and selected by the American Legion to attend Boys State, he has addressed both the Lions Club and a school board meeting about the program.

PROBLEM SOLVING CURRICULUM

Besides the excitement of their placements, which extend from Monday through Thursday during the entire business day, the interns also attend Friday seminars on management, administration, and decision making. Adapted from the Harvard

3. TEACHING

Business School case study approach, the curriculum emphasizes a problem solving focus in which interns learn to function, management consultation fashion, as analysts of organizational problems.

After the first few weeks of reading prepared cases, the interns take over and begin to develop their own. "I was hesitant at first about presenting a case study to the Palm Beach group," recalls Patrick Healy. "However, the other interns quickly got caught up in it."

ROLE OF THE COORDINATOR

The Palm Beach County Public Schools coordinator Harriet "Penny" Hogan considers her job ideal. Ms. Hogan and other coordinators throughout the country are responsible for identifying potential sponsors, developing the role of the high school student, briefing the teachers and additional school personnel, and recruiting students in the high schools. Coordinators speak to student groups; perform the necessary administrative tasks of distributing applications and program materials; and personally follow up with students who have displayed an initial interest in the internship program.

In addition, the coordinators orchestrate sponsor and student interviews, decide which students will be seen by what sponsors, and arrange final placements based on mutual preferences.

Students keep extensive records of their experiences through daily logs, which are reviewed by the coordinators.

A NATIONAL BASE

Like the other program managers, Coordinator Hogan wa initially prepared for her assignment through a week-lon National Coordinators Training Academy sponsored by th parent organization. Executive High School Internships America. Located in New York City, the national office provide training and ongoing technical assistance to participatin districts, along with program materials, coordinators' bulletin newsletters, and intern insurance. An annual National Sta Training Institute brings together all the Executive Internship coordinators from around the country, and the National Co ference of Executive High School Interns attracts studen delegates from each of the districts to Washington, D.C., for week.

The national office works with school systems that agree fund a full time coordinator position for the program; releas students full time for participation, without having to atten classes or keep up with schoolwork; provide optional indeper dent study opportunities; and award a full semester of academ credit for participation.

Founded in 1971 as a joint undertaking of the New York Cit Human Resources Administration and Board of Education, th program has been expanded around the country through th national office, which opened in 1973. Its support has come fror major foundations, including Ford and Rockefeller, the Nation Institute of Education (NIE), participating school systems, an corporations such as Exxon Company, 'USA. NIE is unde writing a two year evaluation of the program through the Cent for Vocational Education at Ohio State University.

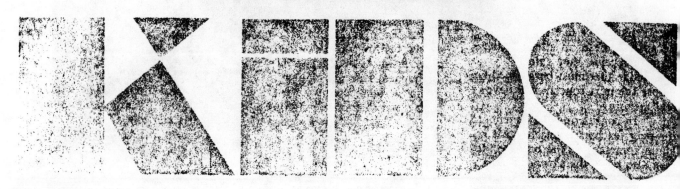

Drumright Elementary's
peer teaching program—
from small start
to big success

BY
DAVID HAUN

AT FIRST glance it looks like any other school during a rainy day recess. In one corner, two boys are working on a balance board. Some children are drawing pictures on the chalkboard. A few are sitting on the floor playing a game. Scattered around the room are children of different ages, quietly reading, drawing or listening together.

Although this scene at the Drumright (Oklahoma) Elementary School may not look unusual, there's a big difference. These students are taking part in a highly successful peer teaching program. Of the 40 to 45 children scattered through the reading center and halls, half are peer teachers.

Drumright Elementary is one of a growing number of schools across the nation that, recognizing how easily children learn from other youngsters, assigns classroom instructional tasks to specific children as their responsibility.

Twylah Haun, reading specialist and coordinator of the program, is enthusiastic about the benefits peer teaching has brought to all involved—the children teaching and being taught and the classroom teachers.

Of the help the program brings to Drumright's staff she says, "Teachers are constantly aware that some students in any class grasp certain new concepts quickly and are ready to move ahead, while others need to have some new material presented very slowly and with much repetition. Our program aims to take care of that repetition. The classroom teacher is thus freed

for other efforts. A child might not be able to handle a *group* of other children in an instructional setting. But on a one-to-one basis, we have found they make fine teachers. Because of the extra attention the learners receive, they gain knowledge that must be grasped before the next concept will have real meaning."

In considering the benefits to the peer teachers themselves Ms. Haun comments, "The practice they give also helps their own learning. But perhaps more important is the sense of personal satisfaction that peer teachers gain."

HOW IT ALL BEGAN
Drumright's program started two years ago on a small scale—during the last period of the day. The first peer teachers were two fifth-graders selected for their patience, perseverance and ability to communicate well with younger students. They were asked and agreed to help first-graders learn to recognize letters of the alphabet.

As the first effort succeeded, other programs and personnel were added. Additional fifth-graders were chosen to listen to younger students practice their reading. This second group included peer teachers who were themselves experiencing some difficulty in reading. It was hoped that their own self-image would improve with success.

A fifth-grader who reads a favorite story to a younger child can easily see the need for fluency and expression. The experience certainly

provides strong motivation for advance practice.

The initial success of the program was greater than anticipated. As a result, it has gradually been expanded to include more and more peer teachers. And the idea of being a peer teacher has become increasingly appealing. Right now the majority of the older children who are not involved in outside activities or who do not need a study period participate.

And there has been an unexpected benefit. Since it was decided that students would be allowed to teach only if their own classwork was up-to-date, children who once wasted time now tend to

work faster so they won't "miss their chance at teaching."

HOW PEER TEACHERS HELP
Peer teachers aid in the operation of machines. They also gather lesson materials, keep records of lessons completed, help with reading by making a record of errors (which Ms. Haun uses to make practice cards), direct reading games, help younger children develop comprehension skills by listening to them retell stories they have read together, help the children practice hand-eye coordination activities, read books aloud to them, lead in visual tracking exercises and help the younger ones learn the letters of the alphabet and how to write them.

Each younger child involved in the program has an individual folder containing a log sheet showing his or her learning accomplishments and needs. The peer teacher examines the log sheet to see what the child is to do. When the peer teacher and the student feel a specific area has been mastered, the learner reports to an adult for a final test before moving on.

A recent program expansion has peer teachers helping

GUIDELINES FOR PEER TEACHING PROGRAMS

1. Remember that peer teachers *are* children, and, while they provide significant help, adult supervision and guidance are required.

2. Peer teachers have bad days and get frustrated with the progress of their students just like any teacher, but youngsters need special help in handling such difficulties. An adult supervisor can change the situation.

3. It is most important to strive continually to help the peer teachers see the purpose of their teaching. They need help in understanding what the skills they are teaching do for their students.

4. Remember that student teachers are volunteers. From the very beginning we make it clear that our peer teachers are free to terminate their teaching at any time. We do ask them to give one week's notice.—*D.H.*

kindergarteners prepare for the first grade. Materials were assembled, and the older students were trained to work in several kindergarten readiness areas.

Today the program also includes younger children as peer teachers. Third-graders, for example, help others with such tasks as learning math facts.

One of the most exciting things happening at Drumright is that peer teachers constantly come

a "pretest" to give her students, so she could follow progress carefully.

The peer teachers are encouraged to experiment and improvise, Ms. Haun notes, and "students are really thrilled when their ideas work. Even unsuccessful attempts help the peer teacher's learning experience, and we make sure nothing is done to harm the younger student."

Ms. Haun attributes a great measure of the program's success to its modest start. "By involving only a few peer teachers in the beginning, we could rearrange and solve difficulties as they arose."

EVALUATION

The Drumright program is reevaluated by the involved faculty every six to eight weeks and redesigned as necessary. At times this means dropping some aspect of the program because it has accomplished its purpose. At other times it may involve reassigning peer teachers to give them new challenges. Or new activities may be designed to meet new needs.

Any changes that result from the evaluation indicate that needs have been met or new goals determined. The use of peer teachers has become an important and well-established part of the Drumright teaching program.

David Haun is a free-lance writer and doctoral candidate in education in Drumright, Ok.

up with new ideas and new methods to improve their teaching. In some areas, like motor coordination with kindergarteners, definite learning patterns are suggested. But in other areas, such as teaching the letters of the alphabet, reading, language development and math skills, the kids are freer to improvise.

HOW PEER TEACHERS INNOVATE

Some peer teachers have made booklets to indicate their students' progress. Others have devised "rewards," such as stars and certificates, to present when a problem area has been mastered. One student suggested and devised

IDENTIFYING KEY FEATURES
IN PROGRAMS FOR THE GIFTED

Joseph S. Renzulli

Abstract: A study was undertaken to determine which
features and characteristics of programs for the gifted are
considered by authorities in the field to be the most necessary and sufficient for comprehensive programing. The seven
features that were considered to be relatively more essential
than others have been designated as key features of differential programs for the gifted. Discussion includes a description
of the important dimensions of these key features.

In recent years renewed attention and effort have been
directed toward the development of special programs for
gifted and talented students. Evidence of heightened interest
in this area is found in the rapidly increasing number of states
which have taken legislative action dealing with special provisions for the gifted. In addition to increased support at the
state level, a number of communities have developed programs
through the use of resources available locally and available
under various titles of the Elementary and Secondary Education Act. In view of the renewed interest in this area, it
may be useful to call attention to those aspects of differential education fot the gifted which are considered to be the
keystones of a quality program. Concentration upon a relatively limited number of indispensable program characteristics provides the complicated task of program development with structure and focus, and such an approach may
be helpful in avoiding some of the hastily contrived adaptations that characterized the post-Sputnik era — adaptations
which, in many cases, suffered an equally hasty demise.

The study reported here was undertaken to identify
characteristics considered to be the most necessary for a successful program of differential education for the gifted. The
purpose of the study was to isolate through systematic procedures a basic core of key features that could be used for
program development and evaluation. The concept of key
features represents an essential part of the rationale upon
which the study was based. Reflections upon the entire span
of characteristics which any educational program might
possibly include, from the quality of the classroom teacher
to the adequacy of the supplies and materials that a teacher
has at her disposal, leads to the conclusion that certain program
features and characteristics are extremely more consequential
than others. With respect to the whole array of practices and
provisions that posses potential, although in varying degrees,
to further the objectives of differential education for the
gifted, the concept of key features holds that concentration
on a minimal number of highly significant features will facilitate both program development and evaluation. This concept
also holds that if the more essential features of a program are
found to be present and operating excellently, then the
probability of less critical features being similarly present is
high.

Procedure

The first step in carrying out the study consisted of searching the literature in order to identify the principal aspects of
the problem and to locate relevant information and ideas that
might prove useful in developing a comprehensive list of features and processes of programs for the gifted. This initial
step included a nationwide survey aimed at locating lists of
criteria used at state and local levels to evaluate special programs for the gifted.

The second step involved the selection of a panel of 21
expert judges. A larger group of persons who had made substantial contributions to the field of education for the
gifted was identified according to a number of specified
criteria; then this group was asked to nominate, from among
themselves, those persons whom they considered to be the
most qualified for judging the adequacy of educational experiences for superior and talented students.

The third procedure consisted of developing a relatively
comprehensive list of general features and processes which
represented various identifiable dimensions of programs for
the gifted. This list was based upon those aspects of differential education which have received considerable and continued
emphasis in both the general literature on the gifted and in
the literature dealing more specifically with programs and
program evaluation. The list was submitted to the panel of
judges with the requests that (a) they rank in order of importance those features which they consider to be the most
necessary for a worthy program, and (b) they stop ranking
when that number of features which would assure a program
of high quality had been reached. Thus, it can be seen that
isolating the key features of programs for the gifted was
based on the judgment of persons who were considered to
represent the very best thinking in the field of education for
the gifted.

The results of this inquiry were tabulated by means of a
pooled frequency rating technique that was based on the
popular method of assigning to the most frequently chosen
response the rank of number one. In order that the rank
numbers used in summing the data correspond to increasing
magnitudes of importance, each rank was assigned a rank
value. The rank values consisted of a series of numbers which
were in the exact reverse order of the ranks. Since the maximum number of program features ranked by any one member of the panel of judges equalled 16, this rank value was
assigned to rank one. Accordingly, rank two was assigned a
rank value of 15 and so on, down to rank 16 which was assigned a rank value of one. These results are presented in
Table 1. The pooled frequency rating of each program feature
was expressed in terms of its total rank value. In addition to
the 15 program features included in the original inquiry,
Table 1 also contains 7 write ins submitted by various members of the panel and the total rank value of each. The program features are listed in hierarchical order according to
total rank value.

It is readily apparent from Table 1 that the uppermost 7
features of differential programs emerged as a relatively
distinguishable group. It should be noted that the remaining
features were both good and desirable elements of special
programs; however, the ratings of the judges seemed to warrant the assignment of priorities to certain aspects of pro-

---

3. TEACHING

gram development and evaluation. For this reason, the 7 features which achieved the highest collective ratings by the panel of judges were designated as key features. In the sections that follow, brief attention will be given to these important aspects of differential programs.

Discussion

Key feature A: The teacher. Although there is little question that all students should have well qualified teachers, the relatively greater demands made upon teachers by vigorous and imaginative young minds require that special attention be given to the selection and training of teachers for gifted and talented students. A number of statements in the literature in the form of principles (Ward, 1961; Williams, 1958) call attention to this important dimension of special programing and Newland (1962) has provided us with a breakdown of essential qualifications that can serve as guides in teacher selection.

Key feature B: The curriculum. Experiences comprising the curriculum for gifted and talented students should be recognizably different from the general educational program that is geared toward the ability level of average learners. These experiences should be purposefully designed to evoke and develop superior behavioral potentialities in both academic areas and in the fine and performing arts. A systematic and comprehensive program of studies should reach all children identified as gifted at every grade level and in all areas of the curriculum where giftedness is educationally significant. The careful development of distinctive syllabi, methods, and materials will help guard against a fragmentary or "more of the same" conception of differential education. A number of Ward's (1961) theoretical principles of education for the gifted are particularly relevant to curriculum development and can provide valuable guidance in constructing truly differential experiences.

Key feature C: Student selection procedures. The literature on giftedness is replete with information relating to the identification and placement of superior students. This key feature acknowledges the existence of all reliably identifiable types of giftedness and calls for the appropriate and discriminating use of several identifying instruments and processes. Periodic screening to obviate overlooking talent of any kind should be followed by increasingly refined, exacting, and fair appraisal of specific abilities. Identification and placement procedures should be carried out at least once annually, and provisions for succeeding search beyond the initial screening and for transfer into and out of the program should also exist.

Key feature D: A statement of philosophy and objectives. The essential role played by statements of philosophy and objectives in guiding the developing of *all* educational enterprises is well known. Underlying statements of philosophy and objectives should take into account the arguments that support special programs, the broad and specific goals of the program, and the distinction between the objectives of general education and those that have particular relevance to differential education for the gifted. Although there is some possibility of well developed programs existing without written statement about the nature of philosophy and objectives, it seems highly improbable that school systems that have not taken the time to develop such documents will make serious inroads toward the implementation of comprehensive differential programing.

Key feature E: Staff orientation. In order to succeed, any educational venture needs the cooperation and support of those persons who are responsible for its implementation. A sympathetic attitude toward special provisions for the gifted and a basic understanding of the theory and operation of a special program on the part of all staff members are considered to be important elements in helping to realize a program's maximum effectiveness. In most instances, staff members not directly connected with the gifted student program usually participate indirectly by identifying and recommending students for placement. It is therefore necessary that they recognize the nature and needs of potential program participants, are knowledgeable about the available facilities, and are committed to the value of differential qualities of experience.

Key feature F: A plan of evaluation. Within the field of education for the gifted, the need for evidence of program effectiveness is well recognized. But the particularized objectives and relatively unique learning experiences that characterize truly differential programs require the use of objective evaluative schemes that take into account a variety of important program dimensions. One approach to program evaluation developed by Ward and Renzulli (1967) utilized each of the key features here reported as focal points around which a set of evaluative scales were developed. The instrument, entitled Diagnostic and Evaluative Scales for Differential Education for the Gifted, was designed to point out specific areas in which program improvement seems warranted.

Key feature G: Administrative responsibility. A clear designation of administrative responsibility is an essential condition for the most efficient operation of all school programs. Although size and resources of a school system will determine the amount of administrative time that can be allotted to the gifted student program, it is necessary that the person in charge of even the smallest program be given sufficient time and resources to carry out his administrative duties in this area. Already overburdened administrators, supervisors, and teachers who are given the responsibility of a special program as an extra assignment without a corresponding reduction in other duties are likely to approach the task with less than optimal enthusiasm.

Summary and Conclusions

The intent of this study was to isolate those features within programs for gifted that are considered by recognized authorities in the field to be the most essential for a worthy program. The effort was aimed at providing a sound rationale for decision making to persons who are involved in various aspects of programing for the exceptionally able. On the basis of the rankings by the panel of judges, there appears to be justification for designating certain program elements and characteristics as key features in programs for the gifted. Such a designation is considered to be useful in identifying areas in which concentration should be placed in the process of program development and evaluation. The key features isolated in the present study do not pertain to any given pattern or organization, but rather attempt to embrace excellent practices presently operating, either individually or in varying combinations, and practices that can and should be inaugurated in view of the behavioral potential of students who possess identifiably superior abilities.

TABLE 1

Matrix of Frequencies with Which Each of 15 Program Features Were
Ranked in Each of 16 Positions by 21 Selected Judges

Rank / Rank value (frequency; weighted value in parentheses).

Program features	1 (16)	2 (15)	3 (14)	4 (13)	5 (12)	6 (11)	7 (10)	8 (9)	9 (8)	10 (7)	11 (6)	12 (5)	13 (4)	14 (3)	15 (2)	16 (1)	Total rank value
The teacher: selection and training	7 (112)	4 (60)	4 (56)	1 (13)	1 (12)	1 (11)	1 (10)										274
The curriculum: purposefully distinctive	3 (48)	4 (60)	6 (74)	1 (13)	2 (24)	1 (11)	1 (10)										240
Student selection procedures		4 (60)	4 (56)	2 (26)	3 (36)	2 (22)	2 (20)										220
A statement of philosophy and objectives	9 (144)	1 (15)	2 (28)	1 (13)					1 (8)								208
Staff orientation	1 (16)	6 (90)	2 (28)	1 (13)	1 (12)	3 (33)			1 (8)								200
A plan of evaluation					4 (48)	4 (44)	2 (20)	1 (9)	1 (8)		1 (6)		1 (4)				139
Administrative responsibility		1 (15)	1 (14)	2 (26)	3 (36)	1 (11)	1 (10)			1 (7)		1 (5)					125
Guidance services				1 (13)	2 (24)	1 (11)	3 (30)	1 (9)	1 (8)								95
Ability grouping and/or acceleration				2 (26)	1 (12)	2 (22)	1 (10)	1 (9)	1 (8)			1 (5)					92
Special equipment and facilities				3 (39)	1 (12)	1 (11)				1 (7)			1 (4)				73
Use of community resources			1 (14)					2 (18)	1 (8)	1 (7)				1 (3)			50
Early admission				1 (13)		1 (11)		1 (9)	1 (8)								41
Community interpretation						1 (11)		3 (27)							1 (2)		40
Supplementary expenditures				1 (13)		1 (11)					1 (6)	1 (5)					35
A program of research				1 (13)					1 (8)					1 (3)		1 (1)	25

Note: — The seven write ins, each receiving one vote, and their total rank values, are as follows: Community Support for Quality Education, 10; Morale and Esprit de Corps, 9; Student Assessment and Reassessment, 9; Student Performance, Evaluation, and Reporting, 10; Interpretation to Parents and Selected Students, 9; Small and Flexible Groups, 13; and Pupil Interpretation, 13.

Numbers in parentheses denote the weighted value of each frequency, i.e., the frequency multiplied by its rank value.

A MODEL FOR ADAPTING

Bloom's Taxonomy To A Preschool Curriculum for The Gifted

Donald B. Bailey and Judith Leonard

Gifted-Handicapped Program
University of North Carolina
Chapel Hill, North Carolina

Abstract

Curriculum modification has been suggested as one means of providing appropriate educational experiences for gifted children. While several models have been suggested at the level of junior high and above, little has been done in terms of a structured approach at the preschool level. The present article suggests a model for adapting Bloom's taxonomy to a unit approach at the preschool level. Rationale for the model is presented, model objectives are provided at each level of the taxonomy, and an example of how the model can be applied to a specific unit is suggested.

Special programming for gifted children has long been suggested as essential in the effort to insure appropriate educational services for all children. Reasons for such programming include advantages to the society, such as the appropriate channeling of leadership skills, and advantages to the individual, such as realization of personal potential or the reduction of boredom and frustration as a result of inappropriate or unchallenging programming.

Recent publications have called for increasing efforts directed towards the early-identification of gifted and talented children so that alternative or supplementary activities can serve to foster unusual abilities in the formative years (Martinson, 1974; Starkweather, 1971; Spicker, 1976; Malone, 1974). Suggested alternatives at the preschool level have included grouping according to ability, early admission to public schools, enrichment activities to supplement existing programs, open classrooms to encourage self-directed investigations, and the provision of differentiated educational experiences through modification of curriculum content and teaching processes.

While research involving optimal programming for gifted children at the preschool level is inconclusive, there seems to be a general consensus that there are distinct advantages and disadvantages to each of the above approaches. The approach or combination of approaches selected by a given educational unit may be influenced by a number of factors, including public school policy, financial considerations, the needs of individual children,

and the values and goals of individual teachers. The purpose of this paper is to examine curriculum modification as one programming alternative and to suggest a model for adapting Bloom's (1956) taxonomy to a preschool curriculum based on the unit approach.

The Unit Approach

A curriculum model has been described as "an ideal representation of the essential philosophical and pedagogical components of a grand educational plan" (Evans, 1975, p. 15). While numerous curriculum models have been suggested, the structures of each offers a basic design and provides the objectives for the ongoing instructional program.

The basic design chosen for the purpose of this paper is the unit approach. Within the unit approach, instruction is organized around a central theme or concept. Topics may be oriented around subject matter, special events such as holidays, or they may be of a more general nature such as transportation, fruits, or pets.

Advantages of the unit approach center around its popularity and flexibility. Many existing preschool programs organize daily activities within a unit framework, typically spending one or two weeks on specific topics of interest to young children. Such an approach allows for correlated activities to reinforce the learning of basic concepts. For example, if the unit is *pets*, the language lesson could involve naming common pets, the fine motor lesson might consist of following a path from the pet to his house, and story time could involve sequencing the steps in the growth cycle of a frog.

In addition, the unit approach both allows for and facilitates individualization of instruction by providing a general framework for all children within which activities can be planned and sequenced at various levels of complexity and integration. For example, while everyone may be studying pets, one child may just be learning to name each pet, another may be learning the similarities and differences in various dogs, and a third may be building a bird feeder using tools and a complex set of instructions.

Thus the unit approach provides an existing framework upon which a curriculum geared towards the needs of gifted children can be built without imposing major changes in other programmatic variables. New activities for children with high cognitive skills can be incorporated simultaneously with more traditional activities that are used with other children.

Bloom's Taxonomy

In addition to offering a basic design for a program, a

curriculum model should provide a framework within which educational objectives can be established. While the design of the unit approach suggests a basis for program orientation, it does not provide a model for the specification of objectives.

Proponents of special programming for gifted and talented children have criticized existing curricula approaches for failing to provide adequate high-level objectives for children with correspondingly high cognitive abilities. Suggested adjustments for gifted children have included teaching problem-solving skills, teaching children to become independent learners (Kaplan, 1974), training for creativity (Parnes and Brunelle, 1967), teaching for understanding rather than knowledge (Bloom, 1956), and teaching the basic structure of a discipline rather than specific facts (Gallagher, 1975). These suggestions assume that gifted children can learn rapidly, advance to a higher degree of complexity of content, work with abstract concepts, and create or generate something new when provided with ample opportunities for growth and experimentation.

Bloom (1956) has suggested a model which insures the specification of objectives and the development of skills at a number of different levels of conceptualization and expression. The six major classes of objectives within the taxonomy are Knowledge, Comprehension, Application, Analysis, Synthesis, and Evaluation. Although not mutually exclusive, this ordering is somewhat hierarchical in nature, with objectives in one class being built upon behaviors or objectives found in preceeding classes of the taxonomy.

Such an approach has advantages in that it can be used in a variety of settings, it can apply to almost any subject matter of a cognitive nature, and it can facilitate individualization of instruction by specifying objectives at a variety of levels of difficulty. While not specifically designed for gifted children, the use of such a model can aid in the development of high-level objectives which involve teaching those behaviors commonly associated with terms such as understanding, concept function, and creativity (Vargass, 1972).

Preschool Model

While several models such as Bloom's taxonomy exist, few teachers systematically plan for activities at varying levels. Reasons for this may include lack of training, time factors in lesson planning and preparation, the seeming ambiguity of some categories, and resistance to the specification of objectives for gifted children. It would seem reasonable that a model which translates taxonomical objectives into activities could serve to facilitate such planning.

Current curriculum adaptations of Bloom's taxonomy have not dealt with activities which are appropriate for the very young child. Examples in the handbook itself (Bloom 1956) deal with content at an advanced level. A guide for questioning children in grades four through six has been developed (Pattersen, 1973) but there seems to be a real need for a preschool model.

Table 1 is an example of such a model adapted by the authors to a unit approach. Column 1 *Level Description*, is a brief description of each level in the taxonomy. Column 2, *Model Objectives*, gives models for several objectives at each level of the taxonomy. Model objectives are designed in such a manner that they can be used with a wide variety of unit topics. Column 3,

Sample Objectives, provides a description of how each model objective might be applied to a unit on musical instruments. (Table 1 suspended for space reasons: Please write the authors)

Discussion and Conclusion

Although the use of a hierarchy of thinking or cognitive skills, such as Bloom's taxonomy of educational objectives, is usually included within any compilation or summary of possible curriculum models for gifted education, some criticisms have been voiced about such a model. One major objection is that the model presents a framework which is too rigid for practical application. In actuality, the taxonomical framework provides only for process selection, leaving a great deal of flexibility in the selection of content. The unit approach demonstrates how the process can be applied to very diverse content. Furthermore, the amount of instruction planned at each level can vary greatly depending upon the needs and interests of individual children. The intent behind the model is not to emphasize six discreet levels of functioning but rather to suggest a continuum of skills which includes adequate high-level objectives and a broad-based approach to instruction.

A second criticism of the taxonomy as a model is that it focuses narrowly on cognitively-oriented skills. The authors wish to stress that this model is recommended as a part of larger program and does not constitute the total activities in which a child may participate. For example, a talented child may receive therapy or lessons directed towards a remediation of disabilities; and all children will probably participate in recreation, music, art, and play activities in addition to those based on this core curriculum.

Also included within the larger total program should be room for the process of discovery learning, an approach often preferred for gifted children. A number of activities at the levels above the knowledge level lend themselves well to discovery and exploration by the children. Even materials used in structured teaching situations, should be available at other times for the child's exploration and experimentation. It must be stressed however, that the individual nature of curriculum planning often requires that even discovery experiences must be planned or "guided" to some extent. A gifted child, who is also disadvantaged or handicapped, may have the ability to do higher level activities but not possess the basic knowledge to actually perform such activities. The very nature of the taxonomy indicates that creative activities, primarily at the synthesis and evaluation levels, depend upon the adequate development of skills in knowledge, comprehension, application, and analysis. Thus, the amount of structure or freedom must be individually prescribed. One of many centers that might exist in a preschool class might be a "measurement center," with sticks, rulers, weights, a balance and many other tools of the trade. Many creative and imaginative activities can result from the availability of such materials to young children, but if a child never learned rules and fundamentals of their use, he will be quite limited in the extent to which he can benefit from this freedom and exposure. The developmental nature of the taxonomy provides a guide to establish a child's level with regard to skills in a particular area and can help teachers plan appropriate activities with or without positive identification as gifted.

As for the fear that the taxonomy may be too theoretical to be practically applied at the preschool level, this model is currently in use and being field-tested by the authors in a preschool program for the gifted. The sample unit in Table 1 shows the practical objectives that can be generated. In conclusion, the model presented is seen by the authors, not only as a truly workable one, but as an alternative framework for programming for young, gifted children, without necessarily requiring specific identification, acceleration or labeling as **gifted**.

131

Creative Teaching Techniques for the Gifted Child

The extreme importance of a stimulating academic environment for the gifted child is now universally recognized. Stifling educational settings in which traditional, outmoded teaching techniques are employed can certainly not serve as a breeding ground for creative thought development. It is evident that when placed in such an environment, the academically gifted child can only become increasingly frustrated in his attempts to achieve his academic potential. As more emphasis is now being placed on appropriate programming, teachers of these children are looking for innovative techniques to inspire creative thinking, intellectual functioning, and social-emotional development. The gifted child must be provided with activities which allow for individual growth.

The following section outlines several teaching techniques which serve to inspire creative thought and uninhibited development on the part of the academically gifted.

ART THEY CAN EAT

BY KATHY STERLING

Why limit student creativity to pens, crayons and paint? Consider food as an art medium. Food lends itself to expression. It is familiar and accessible, and its color, form, texture, smell and taste combine to provide stimulation. For many children there is the added attraction of at last being allowed to touch, in fact to play with, his or her food and to be praised not punished.

Food-art is not intended to encourage waste or destroy the nutritional elements in food. On the contrary, an integral part of the experience is the joy of consumption—nothing is to be thrown out! You can even use leftovers from the school lunch program for some of your art "supplies." And you can easily bring in some basics of sound nutrition.

Working with food-art can be creatively integrated into many areas of the curriculum. Just reading recipes, for example, brings in reading, math and the ability to follow directions. Cookie puppets can be used as a takeoff point for creative drama and will encourage participation from normally shy children. Writing and speaking about their projects can provide children with an experience that is both educational and fun.

For children of all ages, a food-art experience is a combination of simplicity and new excitement. It is an experience of joy, fun, expression and even more, it's pleasing—both aesthetically and gastronomically.

Kathy Sterling, a former classroom teacher, is now a partner in Think-Ed, an educational consulting firm. The projects contained in this article resulted from research for a book by Ms. Sterling and Pat Pring.

Almost any fruit or vegetable can be used for this project. Here are some suggestions:

lemons • pears • oranges
dried fruit—raisins,
apricots, prunes, apples,
figs • maraschino cherries
marshmallows
green peppers
unshelled peanuts
potatoes • almonds

knife • toothpicks (to be used to put together the parts of our animals, it is our "glue")
needle • thread
The possibilities for creating figures out of fruits and vegetables are limitless. These two examples are just a starting point.

This is the project that requires the use of a stove. After it is baked, the puppet can be decorated with anything that looks great and is good to eat!

¾ cup melted butter
1 cup sugar • 2 eggs
1 tsp. vanilla
2½ cups sifted flour
1 tsp. baking powder
1 tsp. salt
raisins, chocolate bits, lollipops, licorice, confectioners sugar

2 mixing bowls
small pan (to melt butter)
ice cream sticks
measuring cups and spoons
rolling pin • sifter
mixing spoons

PROCEDURE:

1. Melt enough butter to make ¾ cup.

2. Place melted butter in a mixing bowl. Add 1 cup sugar, 2 eggs and vanilla. Mix well. Set aside.

3. In another bowl, sift flour, baking powder and salt.

4. Stir the flour mixture into the butter mixture, a little at a time to produce a ball-like mixture.

5. Chill dough for at least one hour.

6. While the dough is chilling, draw the shape of the cookie puppet you want to make on a piece of aluminum foil or wax paper.

7. When you remove dough from refrigerator, set oven at 400°.

8. Roll out the dough mixture on a floured hard surface.

"Art They Can Eat," Kathy Sterling, *Teacher*, Vol. 92 No. 7, March 1975. ©1975 Macmillan Professional Magazines, Inc.

LEMON PIG

1 lemon · raisins
pieces of dried apricot
pieces of marshmallow
radish slice · toothpicks

ORANGE CLOWN

pear · slices of dried apple
orange · raisins · peanuts
marshmallow
slice of lemon skin
maraschino cherry

EDIBLE JEWELRY

The children can make necklaces, bracelets, belts or any other kind of jewelry they might like to eat!

FOOD:

Once again, this is only a sample selection of possibilities to use. Experiment with whatever materials are available.
thin strings of licorice · peanuts (unshelled)
almonds · sliced radishes · sliced carrots
cherries · marshmallows · dried fruit
pretzel rings

TOOLS:

string or colored yarn · needles with large eyes
(wool needles are usually good to use)

PROCEDURE:

Assemble all materials on a large table.
String materials on either a licorice string or yarn (and wool needle). The wool needle is best with hard food, but try the licorice necklace with marshmallows, pretzel rings and other foods with holes.
Tie the ends together, leaving a large enough opening to go over the head.

With a small knife, or your hands, form the shape you want. Place the pieces on the drawing you have made. Firmly press the individual pieces of dough together.

2. Place an ice cream stick in the bottom, at the most secure place. Decorate your cookie puppet.

3. Carefully place the aluminum foil with your puppet on a large ungreased cookie sheet and bake 8-10 minutes.

FRIEZE ART:

Start same recipe as for cookie puppets.

PROCEDURE:

1. While the dough is chilling cut out a brown paper bag to the size of a cookie sheet. Remove dough from refrigerator.

2. Place the dough mixture in the center of the brown paper. Sprinkle a little flour on top and roll dough out to fit the paper.

3. With toothpick, draw a design on the surface of the dough.

4. Decorate. (Use chocolate bits, raisins, etc.)

5. Prick the dough with a toothpick all over, before placing it in the oven. Bake 10-12 minutes.

6. When done, remove from oven, and when cool add icing to the design. Cut into squares before eating.

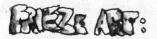

4. CREATIVE TEACHING

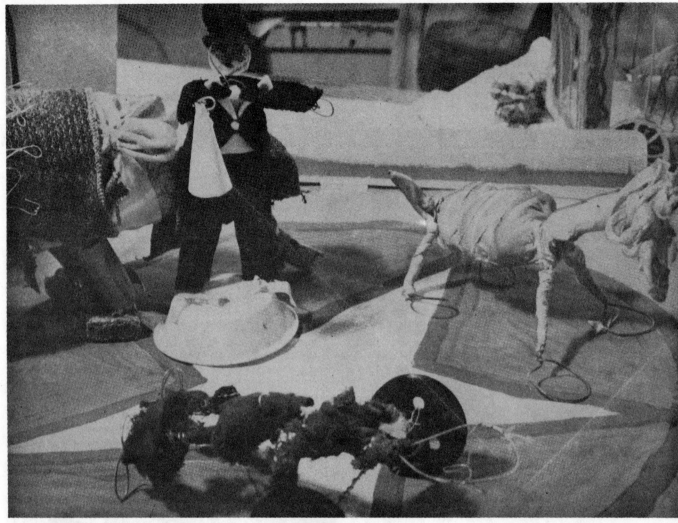

Playful wire structures are reminiscent of Alexander Calder's Circus.

Children can redesign traditional wooden blocks.

Take a ride on the MTA.

TOY DESIGN AS AN INTRODUCTION TO SCULPTURE

Dr. George Szekely
Professor of Art and Education
The College of Staten Island
Staten Island, New York

THE best way of introducing children to sculpture is through play with shapes and toys. The child's initiation to sculptural forms starts early in life and may form a natural basis for further interest and explorations by the art teacher. These early beginnings may be seen in the youngsters' fascination with three-dimensional forms as they move above the crib or in being able to control their movements. They may be seen in the child's playing as he becomes interested in putting forms and shapes together, in taking objects apart, or in putting things of various shapes in his pockets and collecting them merely because they feel good or look interesting.

Toys which the child may create or those brought by the parents may form the raw materials of play and the creative beginnings of the young three-dimensional designer. The interest in spatial construction may relate to both the child's fascination with the way forms look as well as with the potential of these objects to create new ideas and shapes which may resemble objects he might see in the world around him.

The adult sculptor, designer, or architect is also interested in materials, in the collection of objects, in the manipulation of three-dimensional forms as a way of visualizing and thinking through ideas. Both the sculptor and the child realize the difference between their small scale world and other realities, yet they are capable of dreaming on this scale and seeing its potential. All artists may be players

Toy carousel has moving parts.

Three-dimensional play forms that aren't ready made or preprogrammed.

4. CREATIVE TEACHING

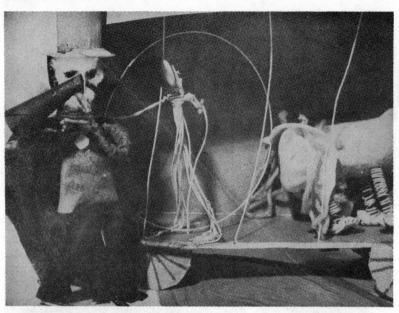

More from "The Circus," the daring young man on the flying trapeze.

who use scaled down forms, objects, and spaces to elaborate on bigger or more universal visions and ideas. The child who plays with blocks fights gravity, stacks and assembles, takes apart, tries different formations, considers new patterns or systems, and is not far removed in thinking from the architect.

The child, like the adult designer, is fascinated by the three-dimensional existence or the physical reality of his playthings. After all, his toys exist in the same space and setting as he does or as all other objects in his environment do. When a new form is created —be it toys or adult sculpture—there is a direct participation (or a feeling of it) in putting something concrete into the world. In a sense, one may be gaining a little say or control over the world.

With the abundance of store-bought toys for children and the ready-made world of entertainment (toys programmed to perform for the child), few incentives remain to create three-dimensional forms for one's own creative playing. With today's toys, overemphasis on educational function or programmed learning of school-related skills, there is a neglect of the toy as a playform, an object which does not attempt to relate a set of facts to the child but is something that he can control and bring his experiences to at each encounter. With a great consumer

zeal for safety, today's toys are made so well that a child would have great difficulty in taking them apart to see how they work and in attempting to put them back together again. The plastic molded toy doesn't lend itself to construction or destruction. Therefore the child often finds that playing with household objects, sorting, stacking and arranging them, is more interesting than playing with store-bought toys.

It is, therefore, most important today that children in the art program have the opportunity to create their own toys as a basic pre-sculptural experience. The following sections describe three areas of toy making that may be considered in an elementary art program.

1. Redesigning Children's Blocks

Toys in the form of blocks serve as tools for the child to sort out, to examine and create models for new ideas. Playing with blocks may be considered as a sophisticated device for generating new ideas that the child and the adult artist have in common. These three-dimensional forms, which can be quickly assembled, dismantled, and rebuilt become visual sketches and models for the creative designer. Children may soon note many of the limitations of commercial school blocks in terms of shapes, colors, materials, and textures and formulate their personal solutions

by creating their own set of modular forms. Inventions may include the addition of planes, lines or new colors and materials; thus cardboard planes and wood dowelsticks of various thicknesses and shapes, blocks of different scales and textures, may formulate a wide range of sculptural and architectural games. Areas of play or construction can be further defined by conducting block play experiments within a certain established space such as a taped area on the floor, on a base, or inside a container or box. Problems of the interior designer, the architect, or sculptor may be dealt with depending on the different spatial definitions.

2. Toys that Roll, Fly, or Float

Children's interest in toys and in three-dimensional forms tends to reflect their own energy, speed, and movements in play. A great deal of contemporary toys as well as modern sculpture can be described as being concerned with action and movement, in the design of quickly changing patterns and forms. Sculpture has always involved movements because of its three-dimensionality, creating the need to walk around it in order to see it from all sides.. Movement may be suggested in the stance of figurative works or actual motions demonstrated by movement in kinetic sculpture. In considering the design of toys that move, one may be inspired by the child's own variety of movements. Objects may be created based on jumping, running, pushing, pulling, turning, etc. Another approach may explore the variety of existing objects that move on the ground, in the air or in the water, with the aim of inspiring the creation of new, unique forms in each category.

The physical qualities of different objects, their weights, density, or size may suggest different motions, sounds, and sensations. Toys may be created by hanging, balancing and/or suspending forms in order to create varied patterns of movement.

3. The Circus

Alexander Calder's Circus consisted of sculptural figures which were not carved out of marble or wood but put together from wires, strings, and cans. Instead of traditional sculptural processes such as carving, this "circus"

Children bring new experiences to toys at each encounter.

Creation of high wire act requires ingenuity, skill, and finesse.

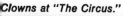

Clowns at "The Circus."

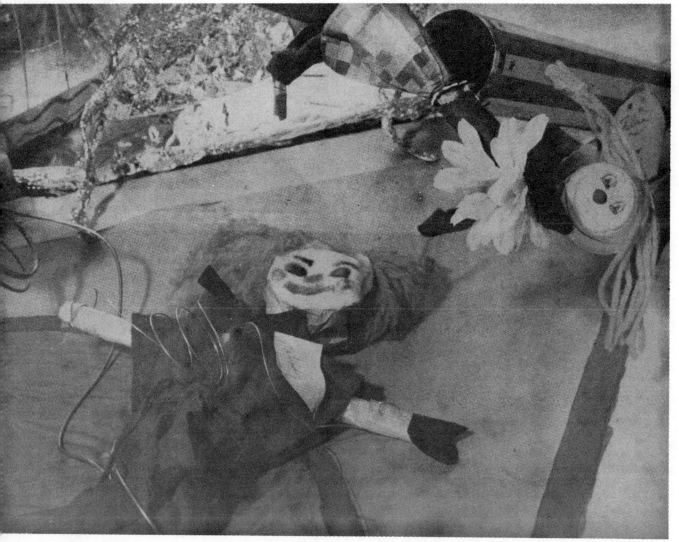

4. CREATIVE TEACHING

was assembled in a way in which forms were stacked, wound or wrapped together. Figures were not made to be stationary as in traditional sculpture but were the forebearers of his mobiles. They were each made to "perform," to be movable, and to be played with. This is perhaps the best example of a new approach in teaching sculpture to children, creating forms and figures in the form of toys—objects which are "playable" yet require all the ingenuity, finesse, and skills demanded by adult sculptural works. What we are looking for, in essence,

is a connection in toys between the child's sculptural interests and an adult sculptor's works. Children can create circus figures from many types of materials and recreate them each time by performing with their figures, planning their actions with the aid of stage, lighting, and sound effects. These toys, like other successful sculptures, may strive for expressions and ideas of movement in their designs which reach far beyond their scale.

Through their subject matter and

familiarity, toys may inspire and help to continue the creative play of the child who likes to work with objects and forms both in an observing and imaginary way. Children may invent ideas through their toy design which often parallel our existing world of objects, yet create it in a fresh and new way. Through toy experiments, the child becomes the designer, inventor, craftsperson, performer, and collector of objects and forms, demonstrating all essential traits of the adult artist working in three-dimensional forms.

From a Speech on Creativity..

STEVE ALLEN

I am always ill at ease when talking about myself, so before
doing so perhaps I should say a word or two on the subject of
pride and/or humility. I experience what I assume is the
normal emotion of pleasure, first, when I produce something
that I feel is worthwhile, and second, when what I have created
is publicly praised. I enjoy receiving the compliments, but in
a sense I don't think I truly deserve them, not because I am
more humble than the next fellow, but because my creative
abilities seem to me to have been built into my machinery
from the outset, in the same way that the color of my eyes or
other physical features were largely determined at the moment
of my conception. If it comes so easily, then it is a fair question
whether I am entitled to be proud of it. I happen to be able —
for example — to do a trick called playing the piano by ear.

In these remarks I refer largely to my own experience in
discussing the mystery of creativity. But I take it as understood that my creative achievements, according to the highest
critical standards, are noteworthy from the standpoint of quantity rather than quality. I am no genius, as my wife or children
would be the first to tell you. Nevertheless the process by
means of which I, or any other second-rate thinker, conceive
of a fresh idea is probably the same as that by which truly
great minds turn the trick.

A word on the subject of *inspiration* would be in order.
The word in its original sense apparently was meant to convey
the idea of a visitation by a consciousness outside one's own. If
a man had a startling and valid new idea, it was supposed
that God somehow *breathed—inspired*—the idea into him. On
the other hand, in the Middle Ages those who introduced
radical scientific ideas were frequently suspected of owing
their inspiration to the devil. There is little point in debating
these possibilities, since there seems to be no one left who
believes in either of them.

When we use the word "inspiration" today, we mean to
suggest that a creative person is so seized by an emotion that
he expresses it in some artistic form. It is apparently a popular
conception that creative people must somehow be inspired to
work. But this is not an either-or question. A creative idea
may arrive under a variety of circumstances. A man may
write a poem so that he can sell it and support himself from
the proceeds. Or he may pick up some grain of sand in his
environment—an overheard phrase, an unusual rhyme accidentally noticed, a scenic vista observed, a whiff of perfume—

almost anything can be the starting point around which a creative work may be woven.

An example. One day in Los Angeles, as I was looking at an
incredibly tall, thin palm tree, it occurred to me that it had
taken perhaps half a century to form very much the same
design in the air that is formed in an instant by the ascent and
explosion of a rocket. First comes the long, narrow perpen-
dicular line and then the umbrella-like outcropping at the top.
Such an observation may, as I say, serve as the starting point
for a poem. Unfortunately there is no necessary connection at
all between the validity, sensitivity, or beauty of the original
observation and comparison on the one hand, and the end-
product on the other. There are atrociously bad poems based
on very sound or sensitive ideas, just as there are delightful or
moving poems that start from a rather light premise.

The starting point, again, may be trivial, in either case.
I recall one time thinking about *darkness*, not in the sense of
evil or mystery, but merely in the strict sense of absence of
light. I remembered experiencing that fear of darkness common
to children and probably never totally overcome by any adult
save those born blind. Now that is certainly a flimsy enough
point of origin; yet a poem can grow out of picking up something common, but finding something fresh to say about it.
My contribution was to observe that, contrary to what is
widely supposed, most of what takes place on this planet takes
place not in the light, but in the dark. This is the poem:

Darkness

When I was very young I feared the dark,
But now I see it's the more natural state.
We come from an *eternity* of it,
Blink briefly in the light, and then *return*.

Most of the earth's best work is done in darkness.
And only *surface* things can know the sun.
The *oil*, the *diamonds*, the *coal*, the *iron*
Come from the undercrust's eternal night.

The *sea's work* is done equally by night.
And all *beneath* the wave is lightless gloom.
The sun has never penetrated *seeds*;
It touches but the outer skin of *fruits*.

And you, the best part of you is a stranger
That light nor I will ever know.
It's dark beneath your dress (facetiously)
And darker still beneath your *skin*. The *bones*.
The *heart* work blindly, and the cells
Grope sightlessly among the veins for *food*.
The *blood* indeed's *so* fearful of the light

4. CREATIVE TEACHING

That at the very *sight* it *starts* and *freezes*.

The *Bible* tells us that the dark came *first*.
And also that it shall come *last*
And when it does the cause may be
That of a sudden there was too much light.

As another illustration of the sort of fragment of experience that can lead to the creation of a poem, I refer to an evening several years ago when, lying half-asleep in my apartment on upper Park Avenue in New York, I was suddenly startled by that always unnerving sound of tires screeching in the street below. After my initial reaction — wincing, waiting for the sound of a crash — it occurred to me that not only I, but scores, perhaps hundreds of others in the neighborhood must have heard that same sound floating up out of the warm, still summer's night. The combination of the sound, and the reaction to it, led to these lines.

THE SOUND OF TIRES

All night long, on Park Avenue,
The braking tires screech
Freezing the heart,
Suspending the activity in a thousand apartments,
Shrieking like Mandrake roots the size of a redwood's,
Screaming like the first angel that tumbled into the pit.

With a horrible high fidelity
The squeal cuts sharp across the consciousness
Of diners with pale teacups poised,
Sleepers who make of the sound a lost
    heart's weepy plea for love,
    a nightmare monster's close blood-thirsty shout,
    lovers who are either given
    momentary pause or wildly
    cry harmony back to the
    night's intrusive bleat.

The eye winces, the spirit's shoulders hunch.
The sound has strings. In the dark
    apartments see the puppets twitch.

The *songwriter*—in any event, if he is seriously professional—could not long function solely on the basis of inspiration; this is particularly true of the lyricist, who often must turn out a product almost in the way that a tailor turns out a suit of clothes, to fit. If you are writing a musical show you must include songs of various types: a peppy opening number, an amusing novelty number, a rousing, rhythmic number, a tender song of love, and so forth.

Sometimes, in fact, it stimulates the creative juices if you are *given* a fairly specific assignment, as contrasted with just sitting around waiting for an idea to come out of the blue. Some of my best lyrics, I think, have been written to order, to melodies created by other composers, and with titles that originally seemed to me to have a somehow off-center ring.

I don't think any songwriter would ever hope to come up with a number titled *Picnic*, for example. It's just not a good title for a song, all by itself. In the unlikely event that you wanted to write a song about a picnic at all, you might come up with a title like "Picnic in the Park," or "I Met You at a Picnic." The simple unadorned word "Picnic" just seems wrong, for the same reasons that would preclude your writing a song called "Ocean" or "Walk" or "Parade." But I was stuck with the title when I wrote the words for the main theme from the motion picture based on William Inge's play "Picnic;" there

was no way out of it.

Picnic

On a picnic morning
Without a warning
I looked at you
    and somehow I knew.
On a day for singing
My heart went winging;
    a picnic grove was our rendezvous.
You and I in the sunshine,
We strolled the fields and farms.
At the last light of evening
I held you in my arms.

Now when days grow stormy
And lonely for me
I just recall
Picnic-time with you.

Another peculiar title is *Gravy Waltz*. Ray Brown had written a jazz waltz by the title, and jazz instrumentals almost invariably have abstract titles that tell no particular story and paint no particular picture. But somehow the very oddity of the title forced me to come up with a lyric that I think has a certain freshness—if only because it takes a title that has no meaning and infuses a meaning into it.

Gravy Waltz

Pretty mama's in the kitchen this glorious day,
Smell the gravy simmerin' nearly half a mile away.

Lady Mornin' Glory, I say good mornin' to you.
Chirpy little chickadee told me that my baby was true.

Well, she really ran
To get her fry-in' pan
    when she saw me comin',

Gonna get a taste
    before it goes to waste.
This honey-bee's hummin'.

Mister Weepin' Willow, I'm thru with all of my faults,
'Cause my baby taught me to do the ever new
    Gravy Waltz.

Lastly, there is indeed inspiration of the sort supposed to be common. Strong emotion — love, despondency, patriotic fervor, sympathy, anger — will sometimes lead a man to express himself in the form of a poem or song or essay. If, that is, the man is a poet, composer, or essayist.

I suppose I really should not be equating songs and poems and essays and novels or what-have-you in this way. A poem rates higher on the artistic scale than does a popular song, although in our culture a man may earn a hundred thousand dollars from a song that will shortly be forgotten, while he is unlikely to earn 50 dollars for a poem that might be remembered for centuries. This is odd, too, when you realize that very few men can create a really good poem, whereas the woods are full of songwriters.

One night about 20 years ago, singer Frankie Laine and I got into an argument, subsequently widely publicized, over whether or not I was able to write 350 songs in one week, a feat I thereupon was forced to perform by sitting every afternoon for six days in the window of Music City, a record store at the corner of Sunset and Vine in Hollywood. As I have

142

admitted elsewhere, the wager on this stunt was a publicity device — although there was an honest disagreement between Frank and myself as to whether I could write the songs. The original purpose of the scheme, frequently overlooked in press comment on the story, was to demonstrate the hopeless plight of the amateur songwriter.

"The difficulty is," I said to Frank, "that there's a market for only about 400 songs a year (very few of which make big money), while there must be about four million people in this country who can write a song. Consequently, even if every one of them had the talent of a Cole Porter, the situation would be generally hopeless. *Writing* the song is the easiest part of it all. I could write 350 songs a week. The trick is to get the tunes published and recorded *after* you write them."

Frank took exception to what he regarded as an exaggeration. To prove my point, I agreed to get into Music City's window and compose the melodies in full public view. What was not publicly revealed at the time (because it would have made the stunt sound phony) is that each day's quota of 50 songs was actually written, not in a day or an afternoon, but in an hour. I simply turned on a tape recorder and, ad-libbing tunes at the general rate of one per minute, played until the reel of tape had run out.

This ability extemporaneously to create melodies is probably related to the ability to create jokes spontaneously, but I have not the slightest idea what psychological mechanisms are involved. Of course, creating combinations of musical notes is more mysterious matter than creating combinations of words. Words, after all, are merely symbols for things or concepts, whereas music is not essentially symbolic at all. It may be associative, but in essence it means *itself*, so to speak.

It is rarely difficult for me to tell where I have gotten the idea or inspiration for a lyric, since one idea leads to another by a generally unmysterious process. But where melodies come from, heaven only knows. When I create them I sometimes figure them out more or less mechanically at the piano, but more often I suddenly hear them in my mind without having made any conscious effort to call them into being. When I am brushing my teeth or driving to work or waking up in the morning I start to hum or whistle or even just *think* of a melody, and there it is. Another new song has been delivered to me, from an unknown source.

Obviously the environment of musical conditioning has something to do with it. A composer tends to create music of the type to which he has been exposed; a Chinese composer composes Chinese music, an Indian composer creates Indian music, and an American composer writes American music. But to say as much does not explain the process of creation; it merely limits the field of inquiry. I assume that the creation of music is some sort of semi-automatic mathematical process that the qualified brain engages in when it has been stimulated to a certain necessary degree. Pour numbers into a mathematician's head and they come out in various new and different combinations. Pour music into a composer's brain and he eventually pours it out again, taken completely apart and reassembled into a variety of forms so potentially enormous that their extent cannot be comprehended by the average mind.

Because my mind "delivers" so many songs to me unbidden, it sometimes happens that I cannot tell whether I have created a new melody or am merely remembering something written earlier, either by myself or another composer. I once wrote a number, put a lyric to it, and had it recorded. Only several months later, while I was listening to the bridge of Johnny Green's beautiful standard "I'm Yours," did I realize that the bridge I had written had not been created at all but only recalled. Fortunately, the lyric and main theme of the number were original, and since Mr. Green was a personal friend and the recording did not enjoy large sales there were no repercussions.

Another interesting fact about the creative musical process is that my mind seems to build up a sort of tension if I go for several days without relieving myself, so to speak, of the music that is perhaps floating just below the threshold of consciousness. The similarity between this particular creative process and the human procreative function is obvious enough — though this is not to say that there is any connection between the two. But if I let a week or two pass without having written a song I find that I am almost *driven* to the piano, and that when I finally release the compressed creative energy that has accumulated, what bursts forth is usually not just one song but several. At such times the songs are of the best quality of which I am capable. If circumstances prevent my reaching a piano the songs eventually burst forth anyway; I suddenly find myself humming new melodies and jotting down ideas for titles or lyrics.

Although my abilities as a pianist are far below my abilities as composer, I have noticed that here, too, a period of abstinence charges my creative battery. I usually play with more emotion and originality—if not technical finesse—when I have gone for several days without playing.

It is a common assumption that there is a great deal less creative thinking today than in ages past. When we consider creative giants in the arts, for example, we almost invariably think of the great painters, musicians, sculptors, authors or philosophers of past centuries. And, if asked to name a dozen famous inventors, again we would refer largely to history for our examples: Edison, Fulton, Franklin, da Vinci, the Wright Brothers, Whitney, etc.

As regards the arts—while Saul Bellow is not the equal of Shakespeare, Leonard Bernstein not the equal of Beethoven, or Jackson Pollack the equal of Vincent Van Gogh—nevertheless there is far more creative work being done in the arts today on a quantitive basis, not only in simple numbers but in terms of the more meaningful consideration: percentage of the total population involved.

In the technical and scientific areas, while there would be no point in demeaning the achievements of Edison or Steinmetz, nevertheless the level of sophistication at which our best scientific and technical minds are working today is such that the famous inventors of earlier times would be quite lost if they were to return to earth and be introduced to the new physics and mathematics and the hardware to which they are giving rise.

I must say that I am enormously pleased that we are taking a formal interest in the subject of creativity. Think of it; on the one hand the world has progressed almost entirely by the individual creative ideas of a rare handful of inventive men, men who refused merely to accept what was handed down to them but insisted on questioning what they had been taught, and committed the further radical and dangerous sin of *adding* to the body of common knowledge. Those civilizations prospered and progressed which had a good supply of creative individuals, and permitted them to create and discover.

In this historic context it is interesting to consider the popular American attitude toward creative thinkers and intellectuals generally. They are distrusted, called "eggheads," and sometimes accorded precious little respect. Who are we hurting?

FOCUS...
THE CREATIVITY OF GIFTED CHILDREN

DRAWING BY:
Adam Larabee, Woodbury, Connecticut Age: 10

My Little World

My little world is an empty one. And sometimes I can hear a sound of an animal walking toward me. The next morning I thought it was for real but I realize it was a dream. But the dream I had I cannot forget. But a dream like that I cannot forget.

Lucille Perez

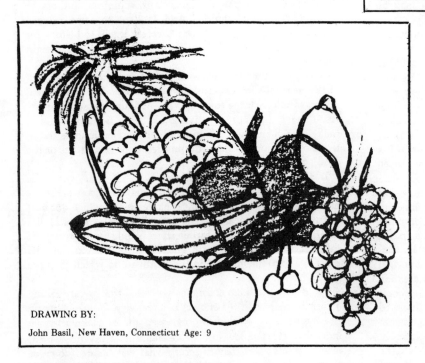

DRAWING BY:
John Basil, New Haven, Connecticut Age: 9

The Fruit School

I am a boy of bananas. I go to a school of apples. My teacher is made by oranges. My students are berries. The desks, they're cherries. The floors are whiskey and some are soda. The principal is a blackberry. The vice, blueberry. The library is redberry! My name is made out of grapes, my friends, it's a scrape. Know I am a boy, a plain own boy.

José Lopez

DRAWING BY:
Debra Ward Verona, New Jersey Age: 7

144

The Dawn of Me

was born nowhere
And I live in a tree
 never leave my tree
t is very crowded
 am stacked up right against a bird
But I won't leave my tree
Everything is dark
No light!
 hear the bird sing
 wish I could sing
My eyes, they open
And all around my house
The Sea
Slowly I get down in the water
The cool blue water
Oh and the space
 laugh swim and cry for joy
This is my home
        For Ever.

Jeff Morley

A cat's paw touching grass sounds like a cloud floating
A person's whisper is like a soft pillow.
Black ink is dark as midnight.

Lisa Jill Braun

How thirty-seven gifted children learned to read

EUNICE H. PRICE

GIFTED CHILDREN often enter school already knowing how to read, many having taught themselves. Adults working with these children may never find out how they went about teaching themselves to read or what circumstances fostered their progress.

In Palm Beach, Florida, where there is a full-time program for gifted children in the public schools, it was possible to explore the methods which had been used by a group of gifted children in learning to read, as well as their preschool experiences related to reading or reading readiness.

Children selected for the exceptional child program in Palm Beach read at least two years above grade level and range in IQ from 125 to 155, as scored on an individual Stanford Binet or Wechsler Intelligence Scale for Children.

In order to gain information about preschool experiences of these children, questionnaires were submitted to the parents of twenty-two sixth graders, eighteen fifth graders and eleven fourth graders. Thirty-seven questionnaires (73 percent) were returned.

Of these thirty-seven children, twenty-eight (76 percent) were reading when they entered first grade. All were reading almost immediately after entering first grade, except one student, whose mother reported that "the boy lacked initiative in independent reading until age nine."

Table 1 reports the children's pre-first grade reading readiness experiences. Table 2 shows parents' responses concerning the method used to teach their child. Table 3 represents data about where the child learned to read. All data in the three tables were reported by the children's parents.

One father said he taught his daughter to read using a combination of phonics and sight words. This father stated that "all three of my girls have been in libraries since birth, from California to the Midwest and finally to Florida."

Another parent reported that the child was taught to read at age three and a half or four by the family because of the high interest shown by the child.

SYSTEMATIC AND INCIDENTAL

A third child was reported to have been systematically taught at age four by his family using sight words in Dr. Seuss books.

The six who learned incidentally were reported by parents to be very persistent in asking names of letters and words. Examples quoted were magnetic letters, words on books at

"How Thirty-seven Gifted Children Learned to Read," Eunice H. Price, *The Reading Teacher*, Vol. 30 No. 1, October 1976. ©1976 The International Reading Association, Inc.

home, and words on packages in stores. When one mother noticed that her child was reading names of products on TV without seeing the products, the mother and grandmother then taught the child to read at age three and a half to four.

One father said his child had constant exposure to books and just eventually read. Another child recognized words on TV commercials. After noticing this the mother made a list of such words as "Jello," "Ivory," and "Coca-Cola" and put them on the family room door. When tested for kindergarten in a private school, the headmaster reported to the parent that this child had developed his own phonics system.

Of the nine children whose parents reported that they learned to read from a combination of home and kindergarten, no systematic teaching was reported. They did report high motivation on the child's part, that the child read cereal boxes and road signs. They reported that family members helped the child when he or

Table 1
Gifted children's readiness through pre-primer level experiences

Activity	Age	No. of children
Knew alphabet by sight	1½ yrs.	1
	2 yrs.	2
	2½ yrs.	1
	3 yrs.	10
	4 yrs.	14
	5 yrs.	6
	no answer	3
Wrote alphabet from memory	3½ yrs.	1
	4 yrs.	12
	5 yrs.	16
	6 yrs.	3
	never	1
	no answer	4
Read sight words	21 mos.	1
	2½ yrs.	1
	3 yrs.	1
	4 yrs.	11
	5 yrs.	13
	6 yrs.	5
	no answer	4
Read pre-primer level books	3½ yrs.	1
	4 yrs.	8
	5 yrs.	13
	6 yrs.	9
	no answer	6

she showed interest, but that when interest lagged the home teaching was dropped. All of the children had very good memories. Seven of these children reportedly learned to read using a combination of sight words

and phonics. Two had learned using only phonics.

Three children learned to read in nursery school, two in Montessori schools. One of these children went into first grade at a progressive private school at age four and a half and into second grade in public school at five and a half.

Of the nine children who learned to read in first grade, six reportedly learned by the phonics-sight word combination; two parents listed phonics. One mother of six gifted children said her child "had much less family teaching than the older children and that she felt the joy of

Table 2
Methods used to teach gifted children to read

Method	No. of children
Phonics	11
Sight words	3
A combination of the two	21
No answer	2

Table 3
Where gifted children learned to read

Place	No. of children
At home	9
Systematically taught	3
Learned incidentally	6
Kindergarten (private)	8
Nursery school	3
Combination of above three	8
First grade	9

learning to read in first grade overshadowed any advantages of earlier reading." She strongly adheres to reading to the child, pointing out words, pictures, and discussing books. She says, "Even though my younger children received less home teaching, they were reading as well as their older siblings were after several weeks of school. They had an excellent teacher, which I am sure helped!"

Another mother reported that she was taking a reading methods course in college at the time her child was two, and that she attempted to teach him to read using the Doman-Delacato method. He managed to learn "mother," "father," "sister," "brother," "John," "Roberta," and a few parts of the body. His mother reported, "Really, he couldn't have cared less. I thought it was a big waste of time to try to teach a two

year old to read." She also reported, "This child went to nursery school and kindergarten in a private school with an excellent readiness program. Though he has all the usual children's books and magazines at home, in the fifth grade, he still does not read as much for recreation as the rest of the family."

Another mother, an elementary school teacher, stated: "I don't believe in teaching children to read before formal entrance to school, but my child was constantly read to at home and in nursery school, which he attended when he was three years old. Upon entering first grade, it seemed he was reading immediately; before that time when he was read to from many different, familiar books, not one word could be omitted without his correcting it. At that time it seemed a matter of memorization rather than his reading it."

Even though the children in this study were reading when they entered first grade, all twenty-two parents who answered a question about the type of school reader used reported that their child had used a basal reading program in first grade.

Fifteen of the seventeen parents who answered a question on first books listed Dr. Seuss books as the first their child read independently. Two of these parents said their children read many, many books at age four.

All thirty-seven parents answered this question: Were these gifted children read to at home and from what ages? Although one child was not read to and two were seldom read to, most of the other thirty-four were read to from birth, or when they were able to sit up, until the present time. One parent answered one to three hours daily; one stated that the child was read to constantly. One mother, whose child is in the 154 IQ range, said, "The child had such an active, exploring nature that being read to was the only way he was ever still and happy until age four."

Mothers were listed most in answer to "Who read to them?" Only on one questionnaire was the answer "Father." However, twenty-three listed fathers in addition to mother. Others who read to the children were grandparents, siblings, housekeepers, and baby-sitters.

OTHER SKILLS

Durkin (1963) concluded that early readers walked and talked at earlier ages. According to Mussen, Conker, and Kagan (1970), the average child generally says his first word sometime around the end of the first year, but the expression of short sentences or meaningful language typically occurs between the ages of eighteen and twenty-eight months. Wheatley (1966) gives twelve to fifteen months as the age children commonly walk. Table 4 represents the data collected from the parents in this study.

Consistent with Durkin's (1963) and Plessas' and Oakes' (1964) findings, the majority of these children walked and talked early.

One parent said the first words her child put together were "I do" on his third birthday. Even though he didn't talk, this child showed an extremely early interest in letters and numbers, but no effort was made to teach him early. He learned the letters from alphabet blocks before he could talk. A family member would name a letter and he would get the block with that letter. They also noticed that when he looked at picture books he would seemingly study the page number instead of looking at the pictures. His favorite book was an old typewriter instruction book which he would look at for hours. At age three and a half his father taught him to count to 100 and beyond. This child knew the alphabet by sight at two, learned to write the alphabet in kindergarten, and learned to read in first grade. He was one of the three children who was reportedly not read to very often.

Another parent reported that her child spoke very early and distinctly and that the only sound he ever mispronounced was "l." His conversation at age two was adult-like and four days before his second birthday he announced (in a restaurant at lunchtime) in a loud, clear voice, "Would someone please take these diapers off and take me to the bathroom?"

Durkin (1961a) found evidence

Table 4
Personal data of 37 gifted children

Activity	Age	No. of children
Walked	9 mos.	7
	10 mos.	4
	11 mos.	5
	12 mos.	11
	13 mos.	4
	14 mos.	2
	16 mos.	1
	17 mos.	1
	18 mos.	1
	no answer	1
Spoke words	6 mos.	5
	7 mos.	2
	8 mos.	2
	9 mos.	2
	10 mos.	4
	11 mos.	3
	12 mos.	11
	14 mos.	1
	15 mos.	1
	18 mos.	3
	24 mos.	1
	no answer	2
Spoke in sentences	12 mos.	5
	14 mos.	1
	15 mos.	3
	16 mos.	1
	18 mos.	9
	20 mos.	1
	22 mos.	1
	23 mos.	1
	24 mos.	9
	36 mos.	2
	no answer	4

that having a sibling two years older, who likes to play school, plays a role in early reading. This study did not substantiate this. Only one child had a sister who was three years her senior.

Tables 5 and 6 show ordinal positioning and the number of siblings in this study. Many of the children are only children or the oldest child. In cases of the youngest child, most have five or more years between them and the next sibling. Could this indicate that the mother had more time to spend with the child in his or her preschool years?

These children entered first grade in the fall of 1967, 1968, and 1969. Four of them had been retained by their parents when under Florida law they could have entered first grade a year earlier. Three had entered a year early or had been double promoted before entering the gifted child program.

It was the original purpose of this study to explore methods used to teach reading to gifted children. This

study indicated that these children did receive instruction in phonics in most cases. The majority of these children read when they entered public school. In the cases where the child did not read prior to first grade, the parents deliberately postponed teaching reading, as they felt that the child would profit more by learning in the first grade.

It was surprising that four of these children who possessed high intellect

Table 5
Ordinal positioning of gifted children

Position	No. of children	Mean of difference in age to nearest sibling
Oldest	15	3
Youngest	12	5.4
Middle	5	3.8, 3

Table 6
Siblings of gifted children

No. of siblings	No. of children
None	5
One	14
Two	12
Three	4
Four	1
Five	1

were retained by their parents, although they could have entered first grade a year earlier. Three of these four were reading when they entered first grade. Equally surprising is that the school put even these children, who were bright, a year older, and already reading, into a basal reader program upon entering first grade.

While this sampling of gifted children is small, it suggests that parents of gifted children see their children as having persistent drive and almost a compulsion to learn at early ages. They list instances of the children's active imaginations, curiosity and problem-solving capacity.

There is evidence here that would encourage parents' putting books into each toy box, reading to a child while rocking, and investigating the possibility of volunteer readers for those children whose parents cannot provide the service. Reading to a child at an early age can provide opportunity for children's own intelligence to go to work on reading.

The Role of Music in the Total Development of the Child

Throughout history, music has been taught and learned for a wide variety of reasons, often for reasons peripheral to what musicians would consider its principal functions. According to Plato, for example, the importance of music in the curriculum of ancient Greece lay in its usefulness as a medium for the moral training of the guardians of the state, while Quintilian denoted the practical utility of music in the training of the Roman orator.

From the rise of Christianity until the modern era, music was taught and learned in Western civilization primarily because of its usefulness in the church. Lay participation in the liturgy, an essential feature of the Protestant churches, required that every member of society learn to sing as well as to read, and paved the way for the singing school of eighteenth- and nineteenth-century America. When music was introduced into the public schools of Boston in 1838, it was justified on aesthetic grounds. Between World War I and World War II, when school music in the United States was expanding more rapidly than at any other time in history, music was typically justified on the basis of its contributions to the so-called Seven Cardinal Principles of Education rather than on the basis of its aesthetic contributions.

During the critical examination of American education that followed the launching of the first Soviet Sputnik in 1957, however, it became apparent that the usual arguments supporting school music were often ineffective and unconvincing. Recognizing that they could not adequately justify aesthetic, cultural, and artistic learning experiences on the basis of nonaesthetic, noncultural, and nonartistic educational outcomes, arts educators increasingly turned to the inherent and unique values of the arts as the basis of their rationale for arts education.

Music is taught and should be taught in the schools primarily because it represents one of the most magnificent manifestations of our cultural heritage, because it brings joy and solace to mankind in the myriad activities of daily life, and because it elevates and exalts the human spirit. Music and the other arts should be taught primarily for their own sake.

Yet music is an extremely complex and diverse phenomenon. It can be many things to many people. It can serve many functions other than entertainment and pleasure, and these functions are not mutually exclusive. It has long been recognized, for example, that music can have therapeutic uses in the treatment of certain mental and physical illnesses and can contribute to the development of handicapped persons. Music can influence human behavior in various ways that have yet to be fully understood.

As schools have come under increasing financial pressures in the 1970s and administrators have been forced to cut back on educational programs, the administrators have faced the frustrating task of setting educational priorities and determining which learning experiences are most important. These circumstances have focused attention on the belief that music can make important contributions to the development of children in areas other than music itself. Some persons are convinced that music can serve as a methodological tool in teaching children academic skills such as reading, language arts, and mathematics; that the study of music can help to make the learning process itself more effective and appealing; that music can contribute to the emotional and social development of the child; or that an integrated arts program can yield benefits beyond those of the individual arts. Although much of the research that might confirm such hypotheses either lacks proper controls or is otherwise technically inadequate, the hypotheses themselves are not without merit. Current interest in these matters is sufficiently widespread to warrant further examination of the available evidence.

The position of the Music Educators National Conference is that music is basic in education, that music, along with the other arts, deserves a prominent position in the curriculum of the elementary and secondary schools, and that the important contributions of music to the aesthetic and cultural objectives of education are more than sufficient to justify that position. At the same time, the Conference recognizes that music can make other contributions to the educational and personal growth of the student and that these ancillary contributions may be highly valued in some communities. The diverse benefits of music instruction will accrue to the student regardless of the motivation that initially led to the inclusion of music in the curriculum and regardless of the relative values placed on the various outcomes.

"The Role of Music in the Total Development of the Child," MENC's National Executive Board, *Music Educator's Journal,* Vol. 63 No. 8, April 1977. ®1977 The Music Educator's National Conference.

Hands On!

Craftspeople in the Schools

Bobbi Katz

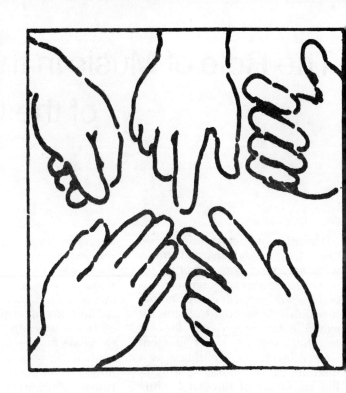

One way to make self-worth evident to the kids we work with is through tangible self-work. In this age of plastics, TV dinners and mass production, it is easy to forget the potential of the human hand to work with the human brain to create. Yet from Alaska to Florida there is a growing group of people who have rediscovered their hands. They are craftspeople.

In Bergen County, N.J., students, teachers and even parents are joining the movement. They are discovering that each person can use the same materials to make objects of infinite variety. They are having a "hands-on" experience with crafts! Over the past several years, expert craftspeople have been coming into the schools, working with kindergartners through high school students and conducting special workshops for teachers and parents.

The Bergen County program, "Craftsmen in the Schools," was developed by IMPACT, a division of the North Jersey Cultural Council, in conjunction with the New Jersey State Council for the Arts and the National Endowment for the Arts in Washington. The idea for the program grew out of the request of one teacher. Suggestions at the end of this article show how to go about initiating a similar program yourself.

Here's how the program works. With input from an educational panel, IMPACT screens and selects craftspeople who are recommended or apply on their own. This year a potter, a printmaker, a puppeteer and a sculptor were chosen. Each school pays a total of $300 for 10 all-day visits from each person.

Every school participating in the program has the freedom to set it up the way the teachers of the individual schools decide they want it. Before the workshops with the students begin, the craftspeople visit with the teachers and administrators of each school. They answer questions, provide the teachers with resource material, become familiar with the school and explain what they can or cannot do. This allows the schools to decide just what the craftspeople will do when they arrive.

One school, fortunate enough to have a closed-circuit television system, selected student representatives from each elementary classroom. These children worked with one craftsperson, and the sessions were then televised to each classroom. The children who participated had the responsibility of teaching what they had learned to their classmates. This was supplemented by after-school workshops conducted by the craftspeople for teachers and interested parents.

Most schools, however, chose to have the craftspeople work with several grade levels. They generally accepted the suggestion of most of the craftspeople that it would be better to give a small group of children an in-depth personal experience than to try to reach every student superficially.

I visited with several of the schools participating in the program and talked to the kids, the teachers and the craftspeople. Although I went to observe and take notes, I found my fingers rebelling. Despite my intentions, I couldn't resist having a "hands-on" experience myself.

Printmaking

Shirley Veenema Smith is a printmaker. Her work is exciting and beautiful. And, as one fifth grader commented, "It sure is a neat way to make a living!"

Smith is pleased that the Smith School in Tenafly lets her work with a single class at a time for rather long periods of an hour and a half. The smaller groups result in a relaxed atmosphere in which the children are free to ask questions. The time period allows each child to make several prints, to experiment, to work carefully and to improve. It also gives ample time for the children to clean up the room for the next class, a subtle lesson in consideration of others.

The class gathers around Smith. As soon as they see the samples she has brought, the children are interested. "I design something called a plate," she tells them. "A plate can be made of just about anything with high and low areas." Without overwhelming the children with details, she shows them the different types of plates that have been used to create the prints she has with her. There are metal plates, linoleum plates, plates made of embossed wallpaper mounted on cardboard and plates of layered plywood. The children get a chance to handle these and ask questions.

Smith has also brought a small portable printing press. She explains that the plates are always printed backwards, resulting in a mirror image. After putting some washable printing ink on a board made of acrylic plastic, she shows the children how to ink the plate. First the ink is applied to a brayer, or small roller, and then the brayer is rolled across the plate. The color is deposited on the raised surfaces—the only surfaces that will print.

Explaining the parts of the press and the need to protect it from ink, Smith rolls out a print. The children are delighted with the result—a purple circle that could be a landscape, a moonscape, the sea. She repeats the process with another type of plate and another color, emphasizing the need to keep her hands clean and to use another brayer that has no traces of the ink she used before. Then she makes a composition by inking another plate, printing it on the same

piece of paper and repeating the process using a third color. The oohs and ahs crescendo. She shows the children how to hand print without the press by placing white paper over an inked plate and rubbing with a flat wooden knob. The children are ready for "hands on!"

Groups of children are assigned to separate tables for each color. Wonderful colors! Fuchsia, purple, brilliant red, silver—everybody's favorites! She explains that everyone will have a chance to use all the colors by moving from table to table. This avoids clamors, such as "I want red!" It also teaches the children a basic rule of color separation in the printing process: Only one color may be used on a brayer.

The children choose plates from a variety Smith has brought along with her and settle down to inking and, with Smith's help, printing them. Next they choose a second plate and a third. They decide where each plate should be printed in relation to the others and what colors they will use. Traffic moves smoothly from the printing press to the sink to the pile of plates to the worktables. The children are obviously so pleased with what they are doing that they seem to monitor themselves. No one wants to use a dirty plate. They wash and dry the plates carefully and return them to the pile without pushing or shoving. The children are involved in the magic of the printing process.

As they wait for their turns around the press, the kids pose some interesting questions, such as: How do you get to be a printmaker? How much does a print cost? Why does a printmaker have to cancel a plate? What is a studio? How do you know how much to charge for a print? How come you still take courses if you're an artist already?

They are learning about another life-style—about the mechanics and practical realities of a new profession—and something about values, on several levels. They see that the working artist does not depend on rare moments of creativity, but that creativity comes in the course of steady, hard work, experimentation and decision-making. It can be ruined by sloppiness and carelessness. The children have a chance to understand that craftspeople are growing people, improving through the process of their own work, expanding their skills through study and enriching their visions through interactions with other craftspeople. They are also learning values that relate to themselves and to each other. The most impor-

tant lesson is realizing "I can do it! I am a person capable of making something."

In the process of making choices and decisions, the children have a direct experience with cause and effect. The results are immediate. Their progress is evident: "My first print was sort of OK. But this one! It's going to be for Mom's birthday!" The results of carelessness are equally manifest: "The purple was just on my fingers. It seemed dumb to wash my whole hands and waste time. It's just I forgot about the purple when I got busy printing red." A classmate suggests that maybe the smudges can be cut off with the paper cutter. Off the two of them go to see if they can save the print.

The students are learning something about aesthetics, too. One boy decided to print the same plate, a rectangle of grillwork, three times in the same color—silver. The resulting composition was stunning. "It's a funny thing," the child said thoughtfully, "sometimes you get more by planning to do less."

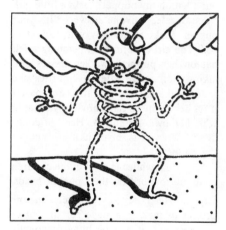

Puppet Making

Eileen Divone, a former art teacher, is now a puppeteer. Her professional life centers around creating puppets, researching the history and vast variety of puppets and teaching the art of puppetry to adults and children.

Upon arriving at a school, she usually makes a presentation to several grades at once. Out of one battered suitcase comes a profusion of puppets: simple string puppets made from scraps of felt, paper or found objects and suspended from a stick by a string; rod puppets made out of almost anything—from pipe cleaners to plaster of Paris—and held by a piece of dowel while moved up, down and around from below the stage; tiny finger puppets made out of the rounded sections of egg cartons, papier-mâché and even peanut shells; a variety of hand puppets made from socks—socks combined with paper bags, boxes, plastic bottles and paper envelopes—and many more!

Divone's presentation at the Lincoln School in Wyckoff, N.J., was followed by three successive sessions with separate classes of the grade levels the school had chosen. One group of fourth graders are making tube puppets, a type of rod puppet in which a cardboard tube section from wrapping paper, serving as the body of the puppet, is painted and costumed. A wooden stick slides through the tube and is attached to the puppet's head, which, in this case, is a plastic foam ball. A cast of characters, from absurd monsters to glittering princesses, emerge as the kids do their own thing with bits of wool, felt, fabric scraps, steel wool, feathers, buttons.

As the children work quietly, chatting with each other and delighting in each other's creations, Divone is there, giving technical assistance and encouragement. But she carefully avoids making any creative decisions for them. "Should I put a hat on my puppet?" asks a little girl. "You decide," Divone answers. "It's your puppet. Make it the way you want it to be." The girl experiments, perching a felt hat on her puppet's woolen tresses and taking it off again. After several tries, she festoons the hat with a feather and pastes it on her puppet's hair, obviously pleased with her own resolution. Her self-confidence increases as she plans a costume for the puppet.

Meanwhile, as most of the children continue to work on their puppet heads, Divone starts several children on the project of making a stage curtain out of an old sheet. It will be hung diagonally across one corner of the classroom, and the puppeteers will stand behind it. A simple scene that allows holes to be integrated into the design will be drawn or painted on the sheet. Four or five puppets can poke through the holes at the same time. The design could be a flower garden, an underwater scene—anything simple enough for the children to draw.

This group decides to draw a high-rise apartment house with lots of windows. The puppets will be able to pop through the windows to talk to their neighbors. This kind of stage allows the children to be as inventive as they want. Another advantage is that many children will be able to participate in the performances.

And perform they will! As I wander around the classroom, I eavesdrop on play writing in progress. The kids are busily discussing possible ideas for dramas starring their puppets. One child's idea feeds another's imagination. The creative process is snowballing.

Pottery and Sculpture

Gene Ebersole has a master's degree in pottery and a bachelor's in elementary education. He has an obvious rapport with kids, talking with them comfortably as he demonstrates the art of throwing pots on the wheel. During his demonstrations, he chats informally about the history of pottery and the qualities of clay. As he gets into instruction with smaller groups, Ebersole feels the most important thing he can give students is the capacity to imagine a finished object, to see it with an inner eye before it exists. As a "hands-on" experience, the students make coil pots. They experience clay as a manipulatory material they can bend, form and shape to conform to the object they have imagined.

Sculptor Judith Insler puts priority on giving the children a concept of the third dimension—working with and in space. What is it? How does it differ from two-dimensional space? How can the kids create it in their work? The third dimension is what differentiates sculpture from painting.

While her own work is executed in marble, metal or wood, Insler adapts materials the kids can use more easily. For example, the day I visited a class she was working with, the children were using cardboard boxes to simulate the type of wood constructions used by sculptor Louise Nevelson. Each class chose a general theme. Then, inside a shoe box, each child pasted a variety of projecting materials, such as cotton, foil and wooden spools. When completed, the boxes were painted one color and mounted in an interlocking fashion to form one huge, three-dimensional construction.

Craftspeople and the Curriculum

During my visits I spoke with classroom teachers about the crafts program. They were all enthusiastic, saying they found it stimulating and useful. Like many schools faced with budget problems, some of the Bergen County schools have lost their full-time art teachers. The Craftsmen in the Schools Program is partial compensation for this enormous loss, at a fraction of the cost. Ideally, of course, it would be an enriching supplement to a full-time art program.

One particularly impressive aspect of the program was the careful preclass organization of materials and the thoughtful traffic flow. These elements are applicable to any art activity and have provided Bergen County classroom teachers with help in setting up their own projects.

The teachers are most excited, though, by the ways in which what they and the children are learning can be integrated into the curriculum. Printmaking immediately lends itself to language arts, giving students a new technique for illustrating their own books, compositions or poems. Haiku and cinquain, short poetry forms that are often used to start children writing poetry, are especially compatible with the simplicity of a print. I found a print that I made was a jumping off point for writing a fable.

The possible uses of puppets are even more diversified. The transition from creating puppets to creating situations for them to perform was a natural one for the children and a super stimulation for creative writing activities. Classroom teachers intend to have the children use puppets to make situations in social studies and history lessons come alive and to add zip to a spelling lesson and fun to math. On the secondary level, the language classes are using their puppets for practicing conversational French and Spanish. The same technique can be used for any situation involving dialog.

Perhaps the greatest value that puppets afford is a projective method for working out interpersonal relationships. Divone stresses this aspect of puppetry in her after-school workshops with parents and teachers. All of us have had experiences with unpleasant situations developing in the classroom or at home: a physically aggressive child, a very shy child, a child who is susceptible to teasing, a child who is unable to share. Teachers and parents are finding that puppetry is one way to work through such problems.

For more ideas on puppetry and puppet making, see "Puppets on Parade," TEACHER, Dec. '75, p. 34 and "The Pleasures of Puppets and Poetry," Oct. '74, p. 66.] Puppetry and printmaking seem to have more practical and broader applications than pottery and sculpture, but all the craft experiences develop hand-eye coordination, imagination and appreciation of individual differences.

Here's how you and your students can have a hands-on experience, too. You can start small. There is no need to think in terms of many craftspeople and many schools. What you want is to give the kids and yourself an in-depth experience. Start with one or two carefully chosen craftspeople, unless your state arts council is willing to take over administration of a more complex program.

Think in terms of your local human resources. Imagine the value of a crafts program that exposes children and teachers to Native American crafts, Eskimo carving, Appalachian quilt making and the people who practice them.

Look into different sources of funding. The IMPACT program brought four craftspeople into each school for a total of 10 days and arranged parent-teacher workshops for only $300. P.T.A. groups may provide the necessary money, although some school budgets include special funds for enrichment programs.

IMPACT arranged matching funding through the New Jersey State Council on the Arts and the National Endowment for the Arts, which is set up to encourage projects such as this.

This year IMPACT took advantage of the Department of Labor's Comprehensive Employment Training Act, which allows a government agency, such as the Arts Council, to hire marginally employed people. The Arts Council pays several of the craftspeople annual salaries. The per diem pay of the craftspeople not on salary is $50. Bergen County is an affluent area on the fringe of New York City. Costs will vary according to locality.

Seek out local craftspeople. Perhaps you know or have seen the work of good craftspeople in your area. If not, ask your library for *Contemporary Crafts Marketplace*, compiled by the American Crafts Council and published by R.R. Bowker Co. (1180 Avenue of the Americas, New York, NY 10036). This book gives specific dates and places for every state's major craft events. It also lists the major craft centers or organizations in each state, sources for all sorts of craft supplies and a comprehensive bibliography of craft books.

The American Crafts Council (44 W. 53 St., New York, NY 10019), another excellent resource, is the largest national organization focusing on contemporary crafts. It has developed slide collections and biographical information on outstanding craftspeople according to geographical area.

State universities are also good sources of craftspeople. They all offer craft courses. Faculty members who teach craft courses or advanced students would probably welcome a chance to visit your school.

Contact your state arts council. Every state has its own arts council with a professional staff (see addresses in the alphabetical listing on p. 75). A letter to the director asking for help in getting craftspeople into your school can be the initial step in getting your council to help work out a program that fills the need of your school and section of the country.

Bergen County, N.J., is an area of high population density. IMPACT was able to develop a program involving many schools in a limited area. From 12 schools initially, the program grew to include 33 schools the following year. Naturally such a complex program requires administrative effort and expense.

In more rural areas, your state arts council might be willing to sponsor a program for a much larger geographical area or just help you with funding and let you go it alone. In any event you'll be in for an exciting, rewarding experience.

We Write the Songs

Leslie Kandell

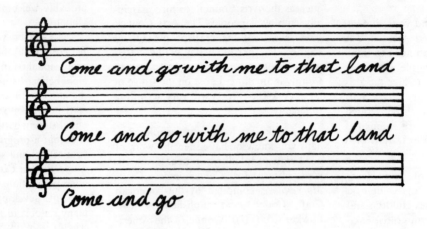

Finger-snapping, toe-tapping music is a prelude to penmanship practice

When younger children need help with penmanship, a little selective singing can go a long way. You may say to yourself, what's it got to do with teaching handwriting skills? Many songs are made up of simple words and phrases that are repeated many times. Kids who balk at everyday penmanship practice will gladly write the same phrase three or six times because they know that's how the song is sung.

The approach is relatively simple. All you have to do is choose a song, have the children sing along and then ask them to carefully write out the lyrics in their best script. They'll not only improve their handwriting but also their spelling and reading skills. An added bonus is the relaxed feeling that a musical environment can provide.

Sing Out Loud

To begin, choose a collection of songs with clear, simple words and easy-to-sing tunes. Folk, country and western, popular and work songs, spirituals, seasonal tunes and rock hits are all possibilities. (Ballads don't seem to work as well because there are few, if any, repeating lines.) No elaborate research is necessary. Just look through your school or public library for songs that you feel will appeal to your students.

For example, "Come and Go with Me to That Land" is a spiritual with repeating lines, simple vocabulary and a rousing tune: "Come and go with me to that land./ Come and go with me to that land./ Come and go with me to that land where I'm bound, where I'm bound./ Come and go with me to that land./ Come and go with me to that land./ Come and go with me to that land where I'm bound." Other well-known songs with consecutive repeating lines are "Comin' Round the Mountain," "We Shall Overcome," "Skip to My Lou," "Lonesome Traveler" and "Shoo Fly."

After you have made your selections, teach one of the songs to the children orally. Have them practice singing it a few times until everyone knows the tune and words. This is essential for the next step.

Chalkboard Lyrics

Write the lyrics on the chalkboard. Don't hand out typed copies of the words, since you want the children to practice their handwriting. Even though word endings are frequently left off in songs, as in *comin'* and *rollin'*, write the full spellings. This will familiarize the children with the words as they should be written. But they will "correctly" mispronounce them, of course, when they sing so that the sound and spirit of the song won't be affected.

You may want to avoid songs that include extreme examples of poor grammar, such as "I Ain't Gonna' Study War No More." By the time you "correct" that one, it would lose something, to say the least.

When you're finished writing the lyrics on the board, you may want to make a few comments about the punctuation, the grammar and the meaning of the words or supply some historical background information. Ask a volunteer to read the first verse aloud while everyone follows along silently. Next, have all the children read it aloud together. Then, you read the lyrics out loud and verbally emphasize that each line is the same as or very similar to the next one and ask

"We Write the Songs," Leslie Kandell, *Teacher*, Vol. 94 No. 6, February 1977. ©1977 Macmillan Professional Magazines, Inc.

everyone to sing the whole song with spirit.

Copy Writing

While the kids are still lustily snapping their fingers, thumping their desks and humming, distribute sheets of lined paper and suggest that everyone make a copy of the lyrics for individual music folders. To make them, staple two sheets of construction paper together on three sides or use business file folders. Then insert one sheet of paper inside or attach it to the outside to use as a table of contents. Point out to the students that the copy they write will be included in their music folders, so neat, careful handwriting is important.

Some tunes are so catchy that the children may be tempted to sing to themselves as they copy the lyrics. Since they invariably sing faster than they can write, they may get bogged down, sidetracked or make writing mistakes. Instead, they can sing the song softly to themselves to check for any omissions when they're finished. As a spelling check, the children can exchange papers.

When everyone completes this exercise, have them enter the song title on the table of contents and then sing the song together again. The children will glue their eyes to their papers as if they were seeing and hearing the words for the first time! After a while, young songsters will love flipping through the thickening sheaf of neat papers in the folders, all of which they can now read.

Audience Participation

A second kind of repeated line song that encourages even more singer participation is the type in which the children can substitute their own words, phrases or names. This provides added incentive to learn to spell and write.

For example, introduce a song like "Driving Steel": "Driving steel,/ Driving steel,/ Driving steel, boys, is hard work, I know./ Driving steel,/Driving steel,/ Driving steel, boys, is hard work, I know."

After you have taught the children this tune, ask them what they consider hard work. Homework? Washing dishes? Whatever the task, have the children insert that word (or words) in the song. After you solicit a wide range of variations, the children can vote on the verses they want to copy for their folders.

Other songs of this type are "Kumbaya," in which the verb changes, and "Train Is a-Comin'," in which the children can insert their own names as the train workers. For sing-alongs, the kids can use as many verses as they want, but for the copied version, you may want to choose children's names that begin with the capital letters you are emphasizing.

With older students you might use songs like "Oh, Freedom" or "If I Had a Hammer." The words are a little harder to spell and read, but the messages could be lively discussion starters. What is significant about these songs is that the words are not repeated in consecutive lines, only in consecutive verses. This means you may have to spend more time helping the children learn the lyrics. In a still more advanced lesson, you can choose a song that has different verses but a repeating refrain, such as "Goodnight, Irene."

If a chorus of sighs and grumbles greets your everyday penmanship lessons, try singing and "scripting." Cacophonous complaints can turn into a harmony of fun and skills.

Leslie Kandell is a music critic, singer and former elementary school teacher.

BIOLOGICAL
SELF-MEASUREMENTS

**Developed in Cooperation With
Chronobiology Laboratories and
Center for Educational Development
University of Minnesota**

You are about to begin a self-study for the purpose of identifying the nature of some of your circadian rhythms. To start, try to find a spot where you can sit and take measurements without being disturbed. On the data sheet provided, record the date and the time. No data is better than bad data. If you are too busy or too tired to take a complete set of measurements, then take what you can – but don't hurry or just guess at measures. Remember this is an original investigation and requires a personal commitment and a high degree of dedication.

Oral Temperature. Measurement should be at least ½ hour after anything that would affect oral temperature: hot or cold drinks, strenuous exercises, singing, being in a sauna or out in the cold. Ideal times would be immediately upon getting out of bed, before lunch, after coming home from school, after supper, and just before bedtime. Some students even set their alarms for 2:00 A.M. so they can make a measurement at that time. This really makes their parents happy. Shake the mercury column in the thermometer down below the 96° F mark. The bulb is fragile, so be careful not to hit the bulb against obstructions. Place the bulb as far back under your tongue as is comfortable and leave it there for at least five minutes. The other measurements can be done while you are sitting there with the thermometer in your mouth. After five minutes or more, read the position of the mercury column and record the value to the nearest 0.1 degree.

Mood and Physical Vigor. Both of these ratings use a seven-point scale, where 1 is very depressed or tired, and 7 is elated or full of vigor.

The Mood rating is how you feel mentally: happy or sad, optimistic or pessimistic, eager or bored, etc.

The Vigor scale is how your body feels physically: your strength, energy, coordination, reaction time, etc.

Don't look at your previous data before you make either rating. It is possible that your expectations might influence your rating.

MOOD and VIGOR SCALE

MOOD	PHYSICAL VIGOR
1. Depressed, blue, very sad	1. Inactive, tired, sluggish
2. Somewhat depressed	2. Somewhat inactive
3. Slightly less cheerful than usual	3. Slightly less active than usual
4. Your usual state	4. Your usual state
5. Slightly more cheerful than usual	5. Slightly more active than usual
6. Quite cheerful	6. Quite active and energetic
7. Happy, elated	7. Very active, full of pep (able to leap a tall building in a single bound)

INSTRUCTIONS FOR GRAPHING:

All of your data can be plotted on the graphs of the next page. Use a different color or different plot symbol for each day – such as M, T, W, Th, F, Sa, Su. When all of the data have been plotted, you can then draw in the **average** for several days (if you have made measurements at about the same time every day). The average is likely to be more regular than the separate days, because irregularities will tend to cancel each other out. Draw the line smoothly trying to keep as many points above the line as below it.

Time Estimation. Start a stop watch (or let a sweep second hand on a wallclock or wrist watch reach precisely 12.). Look away from the dial and wait for what seems like exactly one minute to go by. (You may count to 60 at as nearly a one-a-second-pace as you can.) Stop the watch (or look quickly back at the position of the sweep second hand) and record the actual number of seconds that you estimated "minute" took. If you don't have a stop watch you can use any clock, preferably electric, with a sweep second hand. Be sure to remember where the minute hand is before you begin otherwise you may confuse the time estimate.

Pulse or Heart Rate. Place two fingers firmly over the brachial artery in your wrist or against the carotid artery next to your windpipe. (Don't use your thumb, because it has a pulse of its own.) Count the number of beats in a full minute and record this value. Don't use a shortcut method of counting for only a half or quarter of a minute and then multiplying – this would reduce your accuracy considerably. For example, if you make one or two errors at the start of the counting period

"Biological Self-Measurements," *Conn-Cept II Differentiated Curriculum for the Gifted and Talented in Science and Mathematics.* ©1978 Connecticut State Department of Education/Special Education Services.

NAME _____

| DATE | | | TIME | | MOOD, | PULSE | BLOOD PRESSURE | | EYE-HAND COORDIN- | 1-MINUTE | ORAL |
| year | month | day | hour min. | | VIGOR | | systolic | diastolic | ATION | ESTIMATION | TEMPERATURE |

4. CREATIVE TEACHING

and you count the pulse for 10 seconds then multiply by six, you will introduce an error of 6 to 12 heartbeats.

Blood Pressure. First place the stethoscope (with the ear pieces bowed forward) in your ears. The reason for this configuration is that your ear canal runs toward the front of your head and downward. Tap softly on the probe to be sure it works properly. Wrap the cuff snugly around your upper arm, about 1 inch above the crease where your arm bends. (If you have your own cuff, you can leave it wrapped and save time by just sliding it off and on.) Lay your forearm flat on the table, palm up, so that it lies about heart level. Since different arm heights will give different results, you want the measuring situation to be as consistent as possible. Slide the cuff around to the correct position—most cuffs have a patch or some arrows that should be lined up with the top of the arm. If there are no such marks, be sure that the rubber bladder of the cuff is on the inside of the arm.

Now locate your brachial artery. With your arm flat on the table palm up, your elbow should be in such a position that the hollow in the joint is facing upward also. Press firmly around in this soft area with your fingertips until you feel a pulse. Find the position where the pulse is most distinct. Generally this is on toward the inside part of the arm. It is here that you place the probe of the stethoscope.

Inflate the cuff, using the *opposite* hand to squeeze the bulb. If the hand that pumps air into the cuff is on the arm wearing the cuff, your pressure values will be driven very high in that arm. Pump air into the cuff until the gauge is at least 10-20 pressure units ("points") above what you expect your blood pressure will be. If you do not know, pump the cuff up to about 150mm Hg. (one hundred and fifty milli-meters of Mercury) The purpose of the cuff is to press on the brachial artery until the blood flowing through it stops, thereby cutting off any pulse sounds.

Switch the bulb to the hand of the arm being measured and use your free hand to place the stethoscope probe lightly but firmly over the artery in the bend of your arm. Open the bulb valve slightly to allow air to leak slowly out of the cuff. (About one scale or 2mm of Hg. division per second is right.) As the gauge needle gradually drifts down, you will start to hear tapping noises caused by blood getting through during the peak pressure of each heart beat. The scale value you see as these sounds start is your systolic blood pressure. Remember this value and continue to let the pressure drop.

You will continue to hear the tap, though the sound will become softer. Eventually, blood can get through smoothly even between heart beats and all sounds fade away. The scale reading you see when you hear the sounds disappear completely is your *diastolic* blood pressure. Record both the upper and lower pressure values.

If you have left the thermometer in your mouth while making the blood pressure measurement, be careful that you don't knock it out with the stethoscope or bite on it while you are squeezing the sphygmomanometer bulb.

If there have been any special circumstances that occured before or during the measurement session that might have artificially affected any of your measures, make a note of it on the data sheet.

To avoid irregularities that might distort your natural pattern of variation, it is a good idea to keep a fairly regular schedule of sleeping and eating times over the days that you are making measurements—and for a few days before you start.

Tell Me, Teacher

HENRY P. COLE

Teacher, teacher, tell me true,
Tell me what I ought to do!

Teacher, teacher, where's my book?
Tell me where I ought to look!

Tell me what to feel and how to think,
When to eat and what to drink.

Tell me what is good and what is bad
When I'm happy and when I'm sad.

Tell me, tell me, what to do,
Tell me, tell me, what is true.

Make me learn and make me know.
Watch me closely as I come and go.

For I am small and I am weak,
Without your permission I cannot speak.

I cannot learn except by your decree,
Please, I beg you, give knowledge to me.

I am stupid and you are bright.
I am wrong and you are right.

I am bad and you are good.
I must do what you say I should.

Oh teacher, teacher, look what you have done!
I don't believe I'm anyone.

Oh teacher, teacher, can't you see!
Look at what you've done to me!

A few years ago, Lee Cronbach pointed out in a book on educational psychology that one of the most serious and common problems in the classroom is the over-dependent and submissive child. I remember reading this and thinking about it, but not being especially moved by the statement. A short time later, while I was teaching science to seventh and eighth grade students, I came to understand what Professor Cronbach was saying.

Activity in my classroom was frequently less formally organized than is usual. Pupils often spent entire class periods in the completion of some carefully planned activity or experiment while I tried to stay out of the way and watch. Usually, the children worked in groups of two or three. Many of the children enjoyed these "laboratory" periods; even those with reputations among the teachers as troublemakers didn't get into trouble in such situations, and were generally quite productive and well behaved. The room was usually noisy as excited children shared observations, ideas, and techniques. Many came back after or before school to continue or expand upon the activities they had been engaged in. In a short time, there were so many kids hanging around after school to "mess around" in my room and the rooms of two or three other teachers that the maintenance staff complained about not being able to clean up the building on schedule. Subsequently, a regulation was made that all pupils had to leave the building immediately following the end of the school day unless their teacher requested that they stay.

During the four years I taught in this manner, I regularly encountered children who were anxious and ill at ease during the activity periods. They caused me no trouble, but they were unhappy and sometimes miserable. There were always more individuals of this type at the beginning of the year than at the end, especially in the seventh grade classes. It generally took about six weeks for most pupils to learn to to work comfortably and productively in these non-directive activity periods, but some never did learn to stop being dependent upon me or upon directive fellow pupils during these activity sessions.

Joann was a good example of this type of student. She would follow me around the room saying, "What do you want me to do?" "Tell me the answer." "Tell me what you want me to see in the microscope." "Tell me what you want me to write in my notebook." One day, the task for the children was to classify a group of animals in any way they wanted, as long as they used observable characteristics and could explain their classification system to others. Each pair of students received a tray of 14 preserved animals including such things as an earthworm, a snail, a crayfish, a beetle, a grasshopper, a small fish a starfish, and a spider. In several earlier sessions devoted to classification activities, groups of pupils had classified arrays of common objects in multiple ways, using different characteristics and rules. Common classification systems including the telephone directory and the Sears-Roebuck catalog had been examined, and the children had suggested other systems that could be used based on characteristics other than the first letters of common and proper nouns.

During all these activities, Joann appeared unhappy. She didn't enjoy this game of classification. She became upset when she learned that things could be classified in three, four, or five very different ways, and even more upset when I refused to say which way was "the right" way. Finally, during the classification of the animals, she began to cry. I thought she found the worms and spiders frightening; but this was not the problem. The trouble was that she knew there was a *right* way to classify them. She didn't see why she had to fool around with these silly animals and waste time trying to figure out how I wanted them classified! She wanted me to tell her how to group the animals; to state the rules for the classification procedure so she could memorize them. She felt she had learned only when she had memorized a truth presented by the teacher, a book, or some other authority. Her mother felt the same way and so did some of her other teachers. Her happiest moments in my class were times when I was being very explicit, such as when I was explaining the parts to the microscope and how to use it. During such sessions, she would take notes and ask many questions about what I had said to insure that she had it just right. She would then memorize these bits of wisdom until she could recite the microscope's parts and the rules for its use by heart, but that was the end. She had no interest in using the microscope and no inclination to apply the rules for its use. She never did use the microscope by herself, not because I wouldn't let her but because she couldn't.

I haven't done a good job of explaining the serious nature of Joann's problem in these last few paragraphs. My comments only begin to describe the setting in which this experience took place. Perhaps the poem at the beginning better communicates the problem. I can't claim that the lines are original; virtually every one of them has been spoken to me many times by Joann and other students like her. Those words have haunted me for many years. All I have done is write them down.

Although Joann may have been an extreme example, I have met many children like her, and there are many more in our schools today. How did they get this way?

In their search for answers to this question, many scholars have found that formal education practices may frequently facilitate the development of children like Joann. In separate and independent observations, Carl Rogers and Neil Postman with his colleague Charles Weingartner have noted the real assumptions that underlie educational practice. These include:

The student cannot be trusted to pursue his own learning.

Presentation equals learning.

The truth is known.

The aim of education is to accumulate brick upon brick of factual knowledge.

Constructive and creative citizens develop from passive learners.

The voice of authority is to be trusted and valued more than independent judgment.

Feelings are irrelevant in education.

Discovering knowledge is beyond the power of students and is, in any case, none of their business.

Passive acceptance is a more desirable response to ideas than active criticism.

John Goodlad's direct observations of many schools and classrooms confirm that these assumptions do indeed exist and adversely influence educational practice. Numerous other studies have shown that formal education frequently tends to inhibit or destroy the child's curiosity and will to learn. In short, schools often help children to become less than they are capable of being.[1]

Process education[2] rejects as immoral, unhealthy, and completely inappropriate educational practice that either facilitates or ignores the development of individuals like Joann. The assumptions of process education demand the learner be an active and expressive creator of knowledge and experience; that he make his *own* viable meaning from that knowledge and experience. Dominated, submissive, dependent children will have little chance to reach such a goal and perhaps little opportunity as adults to be healthy and productive members of our society.

REFERENCES

COLE, H. P. *Process Education: The New Direction for Elementary-Secondary Schools.* Englewood Cliffs, NJ: Educational Technology Publications, 1972.

COMBS, A. W. (ch.) *Perceiving, behaving, becoming. Yearbook 1962.* Washington, DC:Association for Supervision and Curriculum Development, 1962.

CRONBACH, L. J., HILGARD, E. R. & SPAULDING, W. D. *Educational psychology.* NYC: Harcourt, 1963.

GOODLAD, J. I. The schools vs. education. *Saturday Review,* 1969, *52 (16),* 59-61, 80-82.

POSTMAN, N. & WEINGARTNER, C. *Teaching as a subversive activity.* NYC: Delacorte, 1969.

ROGERS, C. R. The facilitation of significant learning. In L. Siegel (ed.), *Instruction: some contemporary viewpoints.* San Francisco: Chandler, 1967, 172-182.

RUBIN, L. J. (ed.) *Life skills in school and society. Yearbook 1969.* Washington, DC: Association for Supervision and Curriculum Development, 1969.

TORRANCE, E. P. *Rewarding creative behavior.* Englewood Cliffs, NJ: Prentice, 1965.

WILLIAMS, F. E. (ed.) *Creativity at home and in school.* St. Paul, MN: Macalester Creativity Project, 1968.

WILLIAMS, F. E. *A Total Creativity Program for Individualizing and Humanizing the Learning Process.* Englewood Cliffs, NJ: Educational Technology Publications, 1972.

ALEX HALEY

gives INSTRUCTOR his tips for
launching family history projects.
Then read about "Roots" projects in
schools in New York and California.

*"The oldest people in this country
today, those who provide us with our
legacy and heritage, will be gone in
a years. If we let them get away
without knowing what is in their
heads, we will have lost more than we
could ever know. They are a resource
as important to us as energy . . . ."*

That's "Roots" author Alex Haley
speaking with INSTRUCTOR editor Sally
Reed. Haley took time from his con-
tent-hopping schedule to share his
thoughts about family history projects
in the schools. He tells you why they
are important and how you can successfully launch them in your own
classroom . . . .

**SALLY REED: Mr. Haley, why is the
study of family history so important?**

ALEX HALEY: Fundamentally, all
human beings have a psychic need to
know who they are. This is one of the
common denominators that helped
"Roots" do what it did. Many people

had never considered the fact that
they had families. So when the issue
was raised, it didn't matter who you
were or what your ethnic background
was, you just started thinking, "What
about my family? How far back do
I go?"

For students and teachers there are
other benefits. Teachers seek to find
activities which genuinely involve students' interests. Family history projects
do this well.

Almost overnight a student takes on

a new position within the family. That student becomes the "family historian," a very special role. The students will probably find that almost unconsciously family members begin to regard them differently. As a result, students often assume a greater sense of responsibility—because we all tend to react as we are perceived.

REED: What advice would you give to teachers embarking on family history projects?

HALEY: First, I'd go to any reputable genealogist. He or she will give you basic questions students should ask, plus directions to the best local resources, libraries, and files. It's also helpful if students have a familiarity with basic genealogical practices and a family tree chart made up for them ahead of time. (*See* INSTRUCTOR'S *family tree chart.*)

Next, I'd tell teachers: See how much you can gather about your own genealogy! For example, if you are fortunate to have old people in your family, talk with them. Sit down with your grandmother, grandfather, great-grandmother, great-uncle, whoever, and ask them what they remember about their family. You will be amazed at the things you discover—things you never bothered to ask before, things that occurred before you were born. You realize that you really are a genetic product of several generations. It gives one cause for thought. It is a very rich experience.

REED: Once teachers have done this, though, how do they begin a family history project with their students?

HALEY: Using this same process, teachers should in turn ask students to query their elders. They should start with their parents and then get to the oldest people in their family. Have them find out all they can.

It's as simple as suggesting students begin, "Grandma, I was just thinking about what life was like for you when you were my age . . . ." The subject, broached in this manner, lets the person go back to that time with a nostalgia and fondness for the youngster asking that question.

Let me digress for a moment to tell you why I think this is important. Today we have these expressions, "the generation gap," and "I am trying to find myself." Both reflect a sense of rootlessness.

It used to be that a family would get together evenings. The elders would talk and the young would listen. Now, it's rare for whole families to get together at one time, any time. If the different generations do get together, students will acquire a sense of roots and close the gap between those of other generations.

So, to get back to your original question, students should seek out the older members of their family. Ask them to recall things they heard when they were young. Questions shouldn't focus on just people or important events but every possible detail and anecdote. For instance, have them describe their homes. Where did they live? Is there anything unusual about the clothes they wore? Did they ever live on a farm? What animals did they have? What crops did they grow?

The interviews should then be written up, either at home or at school. They should be typed, if possible, copied, and circulated or sent to every unit of the children's family.

The second step is related to the first. Students should locate and preserve those old trunks and boxes in closets and attics. We should consider these precious family heirlooms. These are actually each family's personal archives.

Third, once students locate various family units, they can play valuable roles in setting up a family reunion. This provides a way for families to get together, talking and sharing their stories.

REED: Are there dangers or pitfalls teachers should avoid?

HALEY: Teachers should explain to pupils that they might encounter some difficulties. For instance, sometimes older people are unwilling to talk about a specific individual, which very frequently is the case with an out-of-wedlock birth. This was considered quite a stigma in yesteryear. It still is, for that matter, but not as much as it used to be.

I would explain to students that there is no such thing, biologically, as an illegitimate child. Every child has a father and mother, and hence two family lines. That particular word *illegitimate* is one of my favorite annoyances. Our society has let it stigmatize and cause more grief to people than any other single word I can think of.

REED: Since the National Education Association has suggested "Roots" be part of classroom curriculum, family history projects have sprung up around the entire country. What impresses you most about the projects already in operation in the schools?

HALEY: What has particularly struck me is the immense receptivity to the projects. I have sheaves of letters from teachers and students. They just bring tears to your eyes. They really do.

In Texas, I told an audience, "Just go up and hug your grandparents and thank them for what they have done for you." One young fellow later told me, "Look, I want to tell you that for the first time in my life I saw my grandfather cry. I had just hugged him and told him I wanted to thank him." It moved me very much that this happened. And that's the big impression I have had—the strength of the receptiveness to this whole idea of researching our heritage.

Family history moves students because it gives a sense of self, a sense of dignity, a sense of worth, and a sense of being part of . . . . It helps students understand who they are in terms of ethnic groups. And many psychologists and psychiatrists have come up to me and said, "I can't tell you how much you've helped our work by stressing people's self-perceptions—both young and old."

REED: Sociologists claim that the big success of "Roots" was in terms of what it did for black Americans. What exactly do you think it has done?

HALEY: Think about the image of Africa everyone grew up with—both historically and culturally. It was "Jungle Jim." What "Roots" has done is provide us with a new, better, more positive image, and, incidently, an incredibly more accurate image. Up until recently black people were ashamed of their past. Black people were not proud of slaves shuffling around. Hopefully "Roots" enabled us to see slaves as heroic—they survived. That's the most important thing "Roots" has changed—the image of the black past.

One of the things that kind of tickles me though is that black people have the totally erroneous impression that the great majority of white people an trace themselves back to William he Conqueror. That's far from true. Most white people in this country on't know much more about their ast than other people do.

EED: What do you think the pursuit of roots will do for us as a nation?

HALEY: It will make us a stronger people if we have a sense of who we are and where we come from. In schools it is very important that while individual students pursue their own family history, it should also be a means to study each other's cultures. The more people know about each other —proud of who they are and where they came from—the less hostility we will have. Hostility is usually born of ignorance.

Family history projects are in schools coast to coast

"Rootsmania" hit the American schools last spring and has picked up once again this fall. Just how are elementary teachers tackling family history projects today? Read two reports to find out: Dorothy Levenson talks about her project in an elementary school in New York while Bruce Davis reports on a project in California.

NEW YORK: "I want a sister, but my mother's not married and she doesn't want any more children," Lucy said angrily. During the first three weeks of our "family history project" that was *all* Lucy told us. She finally relaxed the morning we had Hot Cross buns. The class had been talking about family foods and as Lucy ate she made casual remarks about her family. Perhaps the food represented all the pleasant and warm feelings one associates with family life. But from then on Lucy was the project's most enthusiastic contributor—she brought an old family scrapbook to class, she painted a family tree (including her father), and she loved to explain our program to visitors in the classroom.

This "family history project" was set up for gifted children in the fourth, fifth, and sixth grades at the Stephenson School in suburban New Rochelle, New York. But it could be implemented with any group of children. The program was designed to explore basic historical concepts plus develop skills children need to express their feelings and experiences.

The greatest benefit of the program was that children learned that history is not just something that happens in books—it is life, it is what happened to them yesterday, and to their mothers, fathers, and grandparents before them. Students also learned to deal with primary sources—people they interviewed, family birth certificates and Bibles, letters to and from relatives, family photographs. . . . They learned to organize raw material into records that made the information available to others. Here's how our family history project worked.

Overall picture

We planned our project long before the television production of "Roots." But, by coincidence, our first session was a few days after Kunte Kinte swept through America's living rooms. For weeks newspapers and magazines were full of stories about "Roots," and we set aside a bulletin board for the clippings. The children referred to them often. "Roots" was a story of people with intense feelings—of joy and pain, of happiness and grief. The children found these same emotions in their own families.

What were some of the activities we did in our family history project?

● Another teacher in the same school visited the class and talked about her search for roots. She had scoured the Pennsylvania countryside for family records and lost cousins.

● We talked about the origins of family names. One girl told us that her family name had been given by an immigration officer who couldn't spell her grandfather's name and labeled him with the name of the man ahead of him in line. The black children in the class could relate to that after watching Kunte Kinte's struggle to retain his identity.

● As teachers we became thoroughly involved. I grew up in Australia. Theo Cunningham, my team teacher, grew up in the American South. We'd both lived in houses with wood stoves, outdoor toilets, and grandmothers full of stern folk wisdom. In class we talked about our own childhoods.

Understanding time

It's difficult for children (and even adults) to understand the concept of *generations* or *hundreds of years*. To develop a sense of time we asked students to make a list of 10 things they liked to do—chew gum, watch TV, or ride a bike, for example. We then asked them to think back to when they were in kindergarten, and check off on their list the things they liked to do when younger. Next they thought ahead to when they would be 20 years old and checked off the things they might like to do then. They did the same thing for age 50. Finally, when I mentioned 80 years of age, they couldn't imagine being old and doing anything! They agreed, however, that they might still watch television or go swimming.

The students took this exercise home and interviewed family members about what they liked to do as children. Through this activity students began to see parallels and understand the passage of time in the lives of real people.

Family trees

MY ROOTS

KIDS: Here's your very own family tree chart to record your ancestors. Fill in the blanks to the right. Next, write the names of your parents in the center. Put your father's name on the left side and your mother's name on the right side. Then write the names of their parents in the next circle, and so on, until you've gone back five generations!

YOUR NAME: ....

BIRTH DATE: ....

BROTHERS: ....

SISTERS:.............................

TODAY'S DATE ....

It was difficult for students to organize the information they had gathered about their families. They needed practice. So, we handed out mimeographed sheets with this exercise written out.

"My name is John Smith. I was born in 1967 in New Rochelle, New York. My father's name is James Smith. He was born in 1940 in Washington, D.C. He married my mother in 1960. Her name before she was married was Mary Jones. She was born in Montreal, Canada, in 1942. Her father's name was Edgar Jones. He was born in London, England, in 1920. He died in 1975 in Montreal. His wife was Jeanne Leboeuf. She was born in 1925 in Quebec, Canada, and died in New Rochelle, New York, in 1976. My father's father, John, was born in Baltimore, Maryland, in 1914. He is still alive. He married Susan Peters in 1937. She was born in Boston, Massachusetts, in 1913."

We asked students to put all the above information on a chart. We'd prepared for them listing all the generations. We warned them they would not be able to fill in all the spaces.

The children then figured out their own family charts. With these charts they were able to make family trees. For example, one set of relatives became bright red apples on a green tree. Another was a family tree for a famous family—the Kennedy's. One student traced Kunta Kinte's travels and those of his own immigrant family on a world map. Still others painted theirs with bright colors.

Families were the major source of information. The children went home and asked questions about their origins. They interviewed mothers and fathers, aunts and uncles, and grandparents. Many wrote letters to distant family members. There was a constant two-way communication.

The children's vocabularies expanded as they learned such words as *genealogy, sibling, ancestor,* and *kin.* They came up with exact definitions of familiar words as *niece, cousin,* and *grandfather.* They also completed these writing assignments:
● *"Write 10 questions that you would have liked to ask your great-great-grandmother."*
● *"Where do you think your grandchildren will live? Write a letter to them telling them what you think they would like to know about your life now."*
● *"Write a letter to your great-great-great-grandmother telling her what has happened to the family."*

Family problems

Students in the class *did not* have to make family trees or study their families. There was always a choice of projects. One boy taped a report on cats including a number of stories about the cat that was an important member of his family. A group of sixth-grade boys wrote science fiction stories about imaginary animal families. The girls, in general, seemed more able to talk about the details of family life, even when they were painful.

At first we wondered if open discussions about families would arouse feelings we would be unable to cope with in class. More than half the students in the project came from single parent families. But when one child had her brother die during the course of the program we realized that we couldn't pretend that family life has an orderly and benign process.

One girl, Joan, was gently troubled. She told us: "I can't put my father's name down. My mother hates him and she'd be angry." We told her to put down whatever was comfortable for her. No children were pressured into sharing information.

As we talked about families during the project, students expressed their anger with siblings or difficulties in getting along at home. The family history project became a project on family living as well. Our school district ombudsman, experienced at working with groups of students and adults in conflict situations, came to class. He talked about family conflicts and gave problem-solving activities.

Families and food

Food plays a large part in the physical and emotional lives of families. There are foods for special childhood days, for holidays, or for every day.

The children brought in favorite family recipes: "Curried Goat" (from Jamaica) to "Ricotta Balls." We collected the recipes and made a book. It was a great way to practice writing out directions fully and accurately so that everybody could understand them. In addition we cooked the food.

We also read legends associated with holidays. In an Irish fairy tale the word *guinea,* meaning a gold coin, came up. When one child asked: "What's a guinea?" another answered: "That's an Italian." We talked about racial epithets and the hatred and prejudice they reveal—and how families have suffered because of them.

Family night

Toward the end of the project, we invited parents to join us for an evening. The children had decided that since many mothers worked, an evening would be best. Students served dessert and displayed family trees. Lucy explained the program to the group. John read a letter from an uncle about the history of his family and its travels through several generations.

As a concluding activity the parents and children broke into three groups. The only rule was that children should not be with their own parents.

Each group was given two packs of index cards, a roll of sticky tape, and 10 minutes in which to build a house. When the time was up we talked about how the groups functioned.

One group spent a long time discussing the project but then completed an organized, cohesive structure very quickly. Another group didn't talk much. It built a rambling house to which each member added a piece. The third group quickly broke into three separate groups, each of which made its own building. One of the subgroups totally ignored the rules and the kids went to the supply cupboard and took another pack of cards when theirs ran out.

Students and parents realized that this is how families function—with a variety of organizations and structures. Our family history project became a lesson on families as well. When parents and children went home that night there was laughter *and* a new understanding. **DL**

CALIFORNIA: One of the nicest benefits of Carol Tennant's family history project in Los Angeles was the communication established between children and parents—particularly in single-parent families.

"Children started talking to absent fathers—in some cases for the first time in a long time," Carol explained recently. "It opened up lines of communication between parents and children and with so much divorce today, that's a real plus."

Carol teaches a combined third-fourth grade class at Marshall School, Garvey School District, Rosemead, California. Her students, largely of Oriental and Mexican descent, were so turned on by "Roots" last year, that Carol dropped her prescribed social studies curriculum and devoted the last quarter of her school year to family history.

"We were in the middle of a lesson on 'freedom'" she noted. "I hadn't planned to do anything about "Roots" beforehand, but it fitted in perfectly. The students kept talking about the program, wondering just why Alex Haley wanted to know where he was from. This led to wondering 'Where am I from?' It was obvious from students' conversations that they had misconceptions about their own origins and prejudices about ethnic groups other than their own. So we launched our own family history project to see what we could learn about each other's cultures.

The project's roots

Students started by taking a class poll: "Where are your ancestors from?" It turned out one-third of the students had no idea; one-third thought they knew; and another third felt fairly certain they knew where they were from.

Then the students took questions about their origins home. They asked three basic ones:

● Where was I born?
● Where were my parents born?
● Where were my grandparents born?

Students checked out tape recorders from the school library and recorded the comments of their parents, grandparents, and other relatives. In addition, they asked for family documents and other memorabilia to support their interviews.

It turned out that only five in the class of 30 had been correct about their origins. In some cases students thought they were born in Mexico but in reality they had been born in the United States. It was actually their grandparents who were from Mexico. Students uncovered a few other surprises, too.

One little boy discovered he had a grandparent who was mayor of the town of San Luis in the state of Sonora in Mexico. Another student traced her roots back to Cuba and then Spain. A third youngster discovered a city official in Madrid among her ancestors. A fourth learned that his mother was a Cherokee Indian.

One wall was covered with paper to make a large bulletin board area. Students recorded their own origins on a world map. They started in California and connected colored string to various points of the world.

Then the fun really began. Students traced each others roots, and friendships grew as a result. "Oh, you're from the same country I am!" they'd exclaim. In some cases it was even the same town. There was a commonality among students and they became very interested in other people and other ethnic groups.

Grandparents were thrilled to answer the kids' queries. "Nobody ever bothered to ask me before . . . ." they'd say. Parents, too, became involved. In a few single-parent families, parents forgot their bitterness towards each other and worked together on their child's project.

Parents of students in other classes heard about the project and asked if their students couldn't get involved, too. The master bulletin board in Carol's room became the center of attention for not only the entire school but the community as well.

The project didn't erase all the kids' prejudices and misconceptions overnight, nor solve all their family problems, but it sure went a long way in that direction.

Creative Chemistry

LeRoy W. Haynes and
David L. Powell

Changes, reactions, deductions.
Five simple experiments add new skills and excitement to science

Chemistry is seldom given an important role in the elementary school science curriculum; in fact, most children do not encounter the subject until high school. Perhaps teachers believe that it is too remote from their students' experiences or understanding or that experiments require too much equipment and time.

We have taught summer chemistry courses to children aged nine to 12, and we'd like to share with you a description of five practical, easy-to-do experiments that our students responded to with scientific interest and enthusiasm. [For more information on the complete courses, write to the authors, College of Wooster, Wooster, OH 44691.] All of the experiments can be used with fifth or sixth graders and even some fourth graders. They demonstrate that chemistry can be fun and informative without producing explosions, fires or bad smells.

As the children perform the experiments and take notes, they learn several chemical characteristics of familiar substances. They also practice some of the steps in the scientific method: experimentation (by following self-developed steps with minimum directions or by following rather specific directions), recording observations, drawing conclusions and predicting.

We usually allot at least one hour for each experiment, but they can be done in 30 or 40 minutes if the students test only a few substances. To ensure success, we suggest that you do each of the experi-ments yourself before presenting them in class.

Materials, Procedures, Safety Rules

Most of the chemicals and materials you will need can be purchased at supermarkets, hardware stores or drugstores, and some are familiar household items. Small plastic cups or baby food jars can be used instead of test tubes for mixing ingredients. Wooden applicator sticks, also obtainable at a drugstore, can be used instead of glass stirring rods.

When testing or mixing solid ingredients, students have a tendency to use too much. Point out that a little less than a quarter teaspoon of a solid by itself or dissolved in about one-half ounce of water is sufficient for the tests. All lumpy solids should be ground to a powder first. If you use tap water, test it with litmus paper to make sure it's neutral. If not, use distilled water.

The experiments are designed with safety in mind, and small amounts of the chemicals are not toxic. But warn students beforehand that no chemical should be tasted or eaten and that hands should be washed carefully at the conclusion of an experiment. Encourage the children to wear an old shirt backwards as a lab coat to protect their skin and clothes. Also, your state may require that the children wear safety glasses during chemistry experiments. If any chemical does get into the eyes, wash well with water and consult the school nurse or a doctor for further treatment. Although caution is important, don't be unnecessarily fearful about handling chemicals. As long as you and your students have a healthy respect for these materials, they can be used confidently.

Acidic, Basic, Neutral Substances

The following experiment helps children sharpen their skills of observation and become familiar with the characteristics of acids, bases and neutral substances. It serves to provide important background information about these substances that they'll need for the next two experiments.

Before you begin, explain to the children the major characteristics of these materials. Although taste is one of the characteristics, caution them not to try any of the substances. Acids usually have a sour taste and turn blue litmus paper red. Bases feel slippery, have a bitter taste and turn red litmus blue. Neutral substances are neither sour nor slippery and do not change the color of litmus.

The materials you will need are: litmus paper (available from a chemical supply company or your local high school's chemistry department), wooden applicator sticks, water and small plastic cups. The substances to be tested are salt, orange juice, vinegar, saliva (may produce various individual reactions), trisodium phosphate (known as TSP, or use Spic n' Span), baking soda, washing soda (sodium carbonate), talcum powder, ice-

"Creative Chemistry," LeRoy W. Haynes, David L. Powell, *Teacher*, Vol. 94 No. 6, February 1977. ©1977 Macmillan Professional Magazines, Inc.

melting salt (calcium chloride), toilet bowl cleaner, sugar and shampoo.

Have the children place a small amount of each substance in a separate jar and label it. If the substance is a solid, mix a quarter teaspoon of it with a half-ounce of water and stir. Some of the solids will dissolve completely; others only partially. Then ask the children to classify the materials under three headings—acid, base or neutral—by dipping a stick into the liquid and putting a drop of it on the litmus paper, noting the color changes. Have students record their observations for each substance.

Acids and Bases React

When young experimenters have some familiarity with the properties of acids and bases, they can observe how these substances affect other materials. The following experiment provides some examples of easily noticeable chemical changes that the children will need to understand to successfully complete the experiment after this one.

The materials you will need are: hydrochloric acid (available from hardware stores as muriatic acid, which is 28 percent acid by weight, or from a high school lab as reagent grade acid, which is 36 percent acid by weight), lye (sodium hydroxide), water and small cups. Protective eye wear for you and your students is a must at all times. The substances to be tested are: limestone, chalk, washing soda, baking soda, a penny, an iron nail, an aluminum nail, ice-melting salt, trisodium phosphate and sugar.

To begin, make dilute solutions of the acid for your students. If you are using muriatic acid, add one part acid to eight parts water. For reagent grade acid, add one part acid to 11 parts water. Always add the acid to water; the reverse procedure may cause splattering. To dilute the base, add eight teaspoons of sodium hydroxide to one quart of water. Make all solutions slowly and carefully.

Although these dilute solutions are much less corrosive than the concentrated chemicals, they should still be handled with care. If they are spilled on the skin, wash immediately with water.

Place a quarter teaspoon of the testing materials in labeled cups and slowly add about a half-ounce of the dilute acid or base solution. If the students notice no immediate change, have them stir the mixture with a wooden stick. Ask the children to note if the substance dissolves, changes color and/or produces a gas. They can test the acidic,

basic or neutral nature of any gases caused by the combinations by holding moist litmus over the container. Again, have them record their observations carefully so that they can refer to the results later.

Knowing the Unknown

One of a chemist's most frequent tasks is identifying an unknown substance. The next experiment encourages children to draw conclusions through deductive reasoning. With the information they gathered about acids and bases and their reactions to other chemicals, the students can identify an unknown substance.

Materials you will need are: hydrochloric acid and sodium hydroxide solutions, water, cups, litmus paper. The substances to test are: table salt, washing soda, ice-melting salt (calcium chloride) and trisodium phosphate—all substances the children have tested before. Supply the children with samples of these ingredients, but don't indicate what they are. Have the children dissolve the substances in containers of water, test the liquids with litmus paper and note if the results show the substance to be an acid, a base or a neutral substance. Then ask them to add a few drops of the hydrochloric acid and sodium hydroxide solutions to another set of samples of the unknown liquids, watch what happens and write down their observations. The students will be able to identify the substance by comparing the data they obtained from these two tests with that of the two previous experiments.

For example, the students may have noted before that the washing soda turns red litmus paper blue and that it bubbles when an acid solution is added. By repeating these steps with the mystery substance and looking at their notes, they can be fairly sure that it is washing soda.

Oxidation Without Oxygen

The most familiar form of oxidation is the process of burning wood, paper, gas, gasoline and so on. As we know, this produces heat and fire. The following experiment will show children that oxidation can occur in the absence of oxygen and does not have to produce a flame or discernable heat. Oxidation is a chemical reaction that can be viewed as the transfer of electrons from the material being oxidized to another substance, known as the oxidizing agent, or the electron acceptor. Doing this experiment

well means the children will have to observe carefully and be patient, an important attitude for any scientist.

The materials you will need are cornstarch, water, cups, wooden stirrers and potassium iodide (available from a drugstore or a high school lab). Note: This chemical is *not* tincture of iodine. The substances to test are liquid and solid bleach, dish detergent, clothes detergent, toothpaste (regular and brightening type), toilet bowl cleaner and cleansing powder. Also, make sure that you and your students have protective eye wear.

To start off, make a starch solution by adding two teaspoons of cornstarch to one quart of boiling water. Some stirring may be necessary to dissolve the cornstarch. When the solution is cool, add five teaspoons of potassium iodide.

To find out whether or not certain substances are oxidizing agents, add a few drops of a liquid or a quarter teaspoon of a solid to about one-half fluid ounce of the starch and iodide solution. If the substance contains an oxidizing agent, the solution will turn blue.

Separating Colors

Another aspect of a chemist's work is separating a mixture of two or more substances. In this experiment, which was the most popular with our students, the children can separate the pigments in food coloring.

Materials you will need are: a standard food coloring kit, small aluminum pans or shallow containers like petri dishes, paper circles cut from coffee filters somewhat larger than the circumference of the pans, rubbing alcohol and water.

Give each child a pan and a filter. Fill the pans with a mixture of one part alcohol to three parts water. Have the children place a small drop of food coloring near the middle of the circle, punch a hole in the center and insert a small "wick" made of twisted filter paper.

Place the circle on the edges of the pan so that the "wick" touches the liquid. As the wick absorbs the liquid and transfers it to the circle, the children will see a widening circle of moisture on the paper. As the liquid continues to spread through the paper, the colors will separate because of their different attractions to alcohol and water. The time it will take will vary according to the kind of filter paper you use.

Our students got the best results with green coloring, which separates into blue and yellow. It's also fun to mix two or more colors and watch them separate.

Bubbling liquids, paper that changes color and pigments that separate before your eyes are all part of chemistry's drama. Learning about the building blocks of the earth's materials is one way to build a solid science foundation.

Science with everyday things

Alan J. McCormack

WANT to start your intermediate science program out with a bang this year? Introduce imaginative explorations, using familiar objects and materials you and your kids can find in school and at home. Then add imagination, and you're off.

Imagination is the root of every burning electric light, every moving car, every ticking clock, every soaring rocket. Name any man-made device or material and you can be sure that sometime, somewhere, someone had a flash of imagination which, acting as a catalyst, turned known materials and ideas into impressive and exciting new creations. All of mankind's developments and inventions, which we call new, have rested upon previous ones. For example: The axe combines principles of lever and knife. Photographic film was invented when certain well-known silver compounds were adapted to new uses.

The inventor's secret is a simple one—he sees applications for known materials that have occurred to no one else. Apply the inventor's secret to your classroom science program and reap a bonus in increased motivation and creativeness in your pupils.

"How can I do it?" you ask.

It's easy! Let the following tips boost your imaginative and creative abilities. Then question, explore, and create with the kids.

Expand your conceptions of science. Look beyond your usual science activities. Become explorers—thinkers, probers, problem-solvers. Don't be just a follower of what other people have done, be a doer! Scientifically explore materials

"Science With Everyday Things," Alan J. McCormack, *Instructor*, Vol. LXXXVII No. 3, October 1977. ©1977 The Instructor Publications, Inc.

or objects—sawdust, cooking oil, paper, houseflies, dust, city pavement, even garbage. Remember, any material can be used or combined with other materials in countless new ways. The human process involved in all this is usually called *creativity*.

Forget the "I never had a new idea" syndrome. Instead, build a positive attitude and state of mind about exploring creatively. Try out your ideas. Forget the "No, it can't be done" routine. Think *yes* or at least *maybe*.

Start with materials not present content objectives. Give the traditional science method—starting with a list of content objec-

tives and finding materials and procedures to teach them—a flip-flop. Collect a good quantity of discarded materials from your home and community—cardboard boxes, old newspapers, tin cans, plastic bags, sand (almost any nontoxic substance will do). Use this cache as a springboard for idea production by both you and your children. Explore the properties of the materials, generate ideas for alternative uses, combine them with other objects, and manipulate and enjoy them.

Use simple materials to develop challenges. "Bet you can't," challenges interest and launches kids into personalized mind-trips. For example, "Bet you can't" design a

way to automatically snuff out a candle or "Bet you can't" find a way to make new paper from old newspaper.

Challenges, functioning as bricks thrown through the windows of the mind, incite questioning, manipulating, and investigating.

Blend science with other subjects. Science is not a discrete entity. Think of it as materials and a set of thinking skills overlapping into other disciplines—all learning activities which can be included in your classroom routines.

Now try the following activities which combine commonly available materials, creativeness on the part of the children and you, and an exploratory orientation toward science.

Innovative science activities

The Mystery Jar

It's time for science and you have before you a carton of old glass jars, large balloon pieces, rubber bands, birthday candles, steel wool, paper, vinegar, baking soda, aluminum foil, and so on. Take a square piece of balloon and stretch it across the mouth of a jar, fastening it with a rubber band.

"Notice," you say to the class, "that the rubber stretches to make a nice flat top on the jar. A rubber sheet will always take this flat shape when you stretch it . . . except when it doesn't!" You then go on and explain how you discovered a way to make a special mystery jar. Show your jar wrapped in foil (so no one can see inside) with a piece of balloon that is concave-shaped like the inside of a bowl (see illustration). Now zap the kids with a challenge—How could you take these same materials and produce a mystery jar like mine?

The youngsters will respond with different ideas: heat it, put an ice cube in it, burn a candle inside, take the air out of the jar with a vacuum cleaner, and so on. Once the ideas are listed, divide the class into groups. Encourage each group to produce a duplicate mystery jar based on one of the ideas.

What will they find out? Lots of

discoveries are likely: (1) there are many different methods that will succeed, (2) the trick is to somehow lower the air pressure inside the bottle, (3) the air will expand and contract in response to changes in heat energy, (4) air is interesting stuff. Meanwhile, the children have sampled

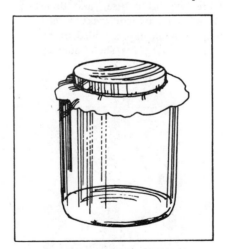

a little of the scientist's excitement—the development of an idea and devising a means to test it.

How do you produce your mystery jar? It's easy. Just seal a small piece of wet steel wool and a little water inside the jar, using a piece of rubber balloon and elastic band to cover the jar's mouth. When this is done a day

before it is to be used, the steel will accumulate some rust. The chemical process of rust being formed will decrease the pressure inside while the outside pressure pushes the rubber lid down.

Sound Sculptures

In these days of *sound* pollution, who hears the delicate sound of a wind chime, the clacking of a board on a picket fence, or the muted protest of a playground swing? Sound sculptures combine science of sound with aesthetics of music and sculpture.

First discuss the relationship between the appearance of an object and any sounds that it may make. Does it enhance, complement, amplify, mute, or dignify the object? Look at some pictures of sound-making devices (bagpipes, hunting horn, rattles). Discuss how the form of an object affects its function. Can they get any clues about the sound from its appearance.

Now, present a clatter box. To make one, mount sound-producing mechanisms (Slinky toy, popgun, bell, stones in a tin can, chain, toy animal voice boxes) on the inside of a large, heavy cardboard box with controlling levers affixed to the outside. Keep the box sealed.

4. CREATIVE TEACHING

Invite the children to move the levers and listen and imagine, making quick sketches of the objects making the sounds. Encourage them to seek out remote explanations, prompting innovative thinking. Now challenge them to construct their own sound sculptures from junk materials found at home: wire, bolts, string, pipes, corks, tin cans, nails, tubing, bottles, and so on.

Junk metal chimes

Eggciting Challenges

Through some quirk in economics, 200 good eggs deemed unmarketable were made available for use. Some zany challenges produced remarkable results.

Egg stand: Using only straws, toothpicks, and paper, find a way to make an egg stand on end.

The youngster who grabbed the brass ring on this one did it with no

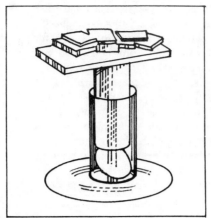

Egg strength cylinder and piston

materials other than the egg. To accomplish this, he gave the egg four or five hearty shakes. This broke the yolk, and its contents settled to one end, lowering the center of gravity so it could be balanced on end.

Egg strength: Devise a way to find out how much weight an uncooked egg can support without breaking.

One girl's device was a cylinder and piston arrangement with a shelf for holding weights. Surprise! The eggs tested could support 7-9 pounds! A related question: Is the resistance the same for brown and white eggs?

Two other challenges—**Egg Bounce Package:** Equip a raw egg so it can be bounced over a 12-inch wall (without breaking, of course), and **Boiled or Raw?** Find two different ways to determine if an egg is boiled or raw without breaking the shell. Someone

Glass bottle wind instruments

will remember the old method of finding boiled eggs by spinning them. (Boiled eggs spin much faster than raw ones due to greater internal friction of the semiliquid contents of uncooked eggs.) How else could you find differences? Does light pass through the shells differently? Do they float in the same way? Does the sound vary when their shells are tapped? Can you tell by shaking the eggs?

Be bold this year. Challenge yourself and your class and have fun while learning!

Vocabulary Scavenger Hunts

Sally Vaughan and Lee Mountain

Sally Vaughan teaches fourth grade at Thornwood School, Houston, Texas. Lee Mountain is a professor of education at the University of Houston.

Kids find it easier to remember words when they can get their hands on them

---

A scavenger hunt as a school assignment? Our intermediate-grade students thought it was almost too good to be true. We felt it would be an intriguing way for them to expand their vocabularies, so we designed a number of "vocabulary scavenger hunts" as part of our language arts program.

To prepare our students for these lessons, we ask them if they have ever been on a scavenger hunt. The response from those who have is immediate and enthusiastic, with much hand waving and comparing of good times. To clarify the idea for the children who have not, we explain that the participants in a scavenger hunt are divided into teams, each responsible for locating and gathering items on a list, and that after a given period of time, the teams' findings are assessed and scored according to the number and authenticity of the items found.

Household Variety

Then we ask how many students think they can find the following items on a scavenger hunt: a spatula, a lozenge, a chisel and a chamois cloth. It becomes apparent that not all of the students are familiar with these words. The children discuss how the members of a scavenger-hunt team might help each other find these and other household items. They also examine the pros and cons of teamwork, discussing such questions as: "If you disagree with another team member about a word on the list, what should you do?"; "How can team members decide who should bring in which items?"; "If you can't find the real item, can you help your team's score by bringing in a picture?"

After this discussion we divide the class into teams for their first "vocabulary scavenger hunt." Then we give each student a work sheet (see p. 76). Our word lists are suitable for the intermediate grades, but the procedure is applicable to a broad range of grade levels.

Each child works on Step 1 alone, first categorizing easily recognized words and then going back to try the harder ones. When this step is completed, the teams meet, compare individual lists and discuss the words on which they disagree. In each group at least one child usually suggests, "Let's use the dictionary." After the team members settle their categorizing disagreements, they rewrite the words in a second list, showing the changes made through group consensus.

Each group then divides the work of finding items among the team members. A student's initials are written next to the items she or he is to bring to school the next day. We hand out plastic bags to each child to carry the items to school and back.

The following day each team carries out Step 3 by pooling its findings

---

Vocabulary Scavenger Hunt—Household Items

Step 1 (by yourself): Read the list of items below. Write each word under the most appropriate heading.

chisel	monkey wrench	strainer
lozenge	level	tongs
detergent	whisk broom	steel wool
pliers	spatula	tweezers
screwdriver	bolt	eyecup
grater	sifter	chamois cloth
gauze	ointment	paring knife
squeegee	nasal syringe	bottle brush

COOKING	REPAIRING	CLEANING	FIRST AID

Step 2 (with your team): (a) Compare lists with the other members of your team. Discuss the words until your whole team can agree on which ones belong under each heading. Write the list that best reflects your team's thinking below.

COOKING	REPAIRING	CLEANING	FIRST AID

(b) Now decide who will bring in each item and write that person's initials next to the corresponding word in the list. Bring in a picture, drawing or tracing if the real item is not available.

Step 3 (scoring): After finding as many items as possible, get together with the other members of your team again. Go over the list item by item so that members can show what they brought. Tabulate your team score (two points for the real thing; one point for an accurate picture drawing or tracing) and share your findings with the class. As in any scavenger hunt, the team with the most points wins.

"Vocabulary Scavenger Hunts," Sally Vaughn and Lee Mountain, *Teacher*, Vol. 94 No. 9, May/June 1977. ©1977 Macmillan Professional Magazines, Inc.

4. CREATIVE TEACHING

and tabulating its score. (Two points are given for each real item; one point for an accurate picture or tracing of it.) Then the teams report their results to the whole class.

Satisfying Results

The children gain a lot more than enjoyment from their "vocabulary scavenger hunts." First, the three-step procedure involves all the students. The categorizing in Step 1 ensures individual participation. The teamwork in Step 2 involves oral usage of unfamiliar words and sharing of knowledge. The children discover that certain items are not as common in some households as in others. In addition, their interaction skills develop along with their vocabularies as they work at making accurate group decisions, dividing work fairly and functioning as a task-oriented team.

Step 3—hunting for the items (or their pictures)—is the most entertaining part of the assignment, but a keen sense of competition and teamwork are evident. None of the children forget their assignments. If a child cannot find an item, she or he brings in a picture of it or asks another team member for help.

Hungry for More

The scavenger hunt was so popular that students asked for more. We prepared additional scavenger-hunt word lists to fit the grade level of our students. We jumbled the words before listing them on the work sheets so that the students would again have to start by categorizing the items under the given headings. In order to save time, however, we used the same work sheet instructions for each lesson. Following are some of our lists.

Containers

DRINKING	TRAVELING	COOKING
mug	briefcase	kettle
stein	knapsack	teapot
tumbler	satchel	broiler
canteen	suitcase	casserole
flask	purse	skillet
goblet	trunk	saucepan

Pastime Materials

SEWING	SPORTS
bobbin	shuttlecock
pinking shears	boomerang
hook and eye	croquet mallet
thimble	horseshoe
fabric	racket

BOARD GAMES	WRITING
pawn	scratch pad
checker	slate
die	fountain pen
domino	stationery
spinner	letter opener

Shades of Color

PURPLES	GREENS	YELLOWS
violet	olive	blond
grape	grass	gold
lavender	lime	brass
orchid	fern	lemon
lilac	pea	butter
plum	emerald	straw

REDS	BROWNS	GRAYS
cherry	chocolate	silver
rose	khaki	steel
tomato	beige	lead
lobster	coffee	mouse
blood	earth	gunmetal
ruby	toast	smoke

Foods

NUTS	FRUITS	VEGETABLE
cashew	date	turnip
almond	fig	broccoli
walnut	raisin	okra
pecan	tangerine	onion

MEATS	CANDIES
bologna	brittle
frankfurter	caramel
sirloin	licorice
pot roast	taffy

One of the biggest rewards of "vocabulary scavenger hunts" was the discovery several weeks later that students retain what they learned. We asked each child to fill in another copy of the work sheet. The results showed that hands-on familiarity with an item promotes vocabulary retention of its name.

There were other bonuses. It was an unexpected thrill to see usually shy children actively participate in the discussion step. We also observed less-than-enthusiastic children returning to school the second day of the lesson with every item they were supposed to bring. Some students even brought items that were assigned to other team members, just in case someone forgot. That's teamwork in action! And that's what happens with "vocabulary scavenger hunts."

INDEX

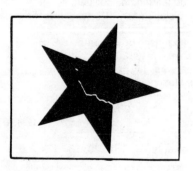

Appendix: Agencies and Services for Exceptional Children

Alexander Graham Bell Association for the Deaf,
   Inc.
Volta Bureau for the Deaf
3417 Volta Place, NW
Washington, D.C. 20007

American Academy of Pediatrics
1801 Hinman Avenue
Evanston, Illinois 60204

American Association for Gifted Children
15 Gramercy Park
New York, N.Y. 10003

American Association on Mental Deficiency
5201 Connecticut Avenue, NW
Washington, D.C. 20015

American Association of Psychiatric Clinics for
   Children
250 West 57th Street
New York, N.Y.

American Bar Association
Commission on the Mentally Disabled
1800 M Street, NW
Washington, D.C. 20036

American Foundation for the Blind
15 W. 16th Street
New York, N.Y. 10011

American Medical Association
535 N. Dearborn Street
Chicago, Illinois 60610

American Speech and Hearing Association
9030 Old Georgetown Road
Washington, D.C. 20014

Association for the Aid of Crippled Children
345 E. 46th Street
New York, N.Y. 10017

Association for Children with Learning Disabilities
2200 Brownsville Road
Pittsburgh, Pennsylvania 15210

Association for Education of the Visually
   Handicapped
1604 Spruce Street
Philadelphia, Pennsylvania 19103

Association for the Help of Retarded Children
200 Park Avenue, South
New York, N.Y.

Association for the Visually Handicapped
1839 Frankfort Avenue
Louisville, Kentucky 40206

Center on Human Policy
Division of Special Education and Rehabilitation
Syracuse University
Syracuse, New York 13210

Child Fund
275 Windsor Street
Hartford, Connecticut 06120

Children's Defense Fund
1520 New Hampshire Avenue NW
Washington, D.C. 20036

Closer Look
National Information Center for the Handicapped
1201 Sixteenth Street NW
Washington, D.C. 20036

Clifford W. Beers Guidance Clinic
432 Temple Street
New Haven, Connecticut 06510

Child Study Center
Yale University
333 Cedar Street
New Haven, Connecticut 06520

Child Welfare League of America, Inc.
44 East 23rd Street
New York, N.Y. 10010

Children's Bureau
United States Department of Health, Education
   and Welfare
Washington, D.C.

Council for Exceptional Children
1411 Jefferson Davis Highway
Arlington, Virginia 22202

Epilepsy Foundation of America
1828 "L" Street NW
Washington, D.C. 20036

Gifted Child Society, Inc.
59 Glen Gray Road
Oakland, New Jersey 07436

Institute for the Study of Mental Retardation
   and Related Disabilities
130 South First
University of Michigan
Ann Arbor, Michigan 48108

International Association for the Scientific Study
   of Mental Deficiency
Ellen Horn, AAMD
5201 Connecticut Avenue NW
Washington, D.C. 20015

International League of Societies for the Mentally
   Handicapped
Rue Forestiere 12
Brussels, Belgium

Joseph P. Kennedy, Jr. Foundation
1701 K Street NW
Washington, D.C. 20006

League for Emotically Disturbed Children
171 Madison Avenue
New York, N.Y.

Muscular Dystrophy Associations of America
1790 Broadway
New York, N.Y. 10019

National Aid to the Visually Handicapped
3201 Balboa Street
San Francisco, California 94121

National Association of Coordinators of State
   Programs for the Mentally Retarded
2001 Jefferson Davis Highway
Arlington, Virginai 22202

National Association of Hearing and Speech
   Agencies
919 18th Street NW
Washington, D.C. 20006

National Association for Creative Children and
   Adults
8080 Springvalley Drive
Cincinnati, Ohio 45236
(Mrs. Ann F. Isaacs, Executive Director)

National Association for Retarded Children
420 Lexington Avenue
New York, N.Y.

National Association for Retarded Citizens
2709 Avenue E East
Arlington, Texas 76010

National Children's Rehabilitation Center
P.O. Box 1260
Leesburg, Virginia

National Association for the Visually Handicapped
3201 Balboa Street
San Francisco, California 94121

National Association of the Deaf
814 Thayer Avenue
Silver Spring, Maryland 20910

National Cystic Fibrosis Foundation
3379 Peachtree Road NE
Atlanta, Georgia 30326

National Easter Seal Society for Crippled Children
   and Adults
2023 W. Ogden Avenue
Chicago, Illinois 60612

National Federation of the Blind
218 Randolph Hotel
Des Moines, Iowa 50309

National Paraplegia Foundation
333 N. Michigan Avenue
Chicago, Illinois 60601

National Society for Autistic Children
621 Central Avenue
Albany, N.Y. 12206

National Society for Prevention of Blindness, Inc.
79 Madison Avenue
New York, N.Y. 10016

Orton Society, Inc.
8415 Bellona Lane
Baltimore, Maryland 21204

President's Committee on Mental Retardation
Regional Office Building #3
7th and D Streets SW
Room 2614
Washington, D.C. 20201

United Cerebral Palsy Associations
66 E 34th Street
New York, N.Y. 10016

COMMENTS PLEASE:

SPECIAL LEARNING CORPORATION

42 Boston Post Rd.

Guilford, Conn. 06437

SPECIAL LEARNING ___TION

COMMENT

Does this book fit your course of study?

Why? (Why not?)

Is this book useable for other courses of study? Please ___

What other areas would you like us to publish in using this format?

What type of exceptional child are you interested in learning more about?

Would you use this as a basic text?

How many students are enrolled in these course areas?

_____ Special Education _____ Mental Retardation _____ Psychology _____ Emotional Disorders

_____ Exceptional Children _____ Learning Disabilities   Other _____

Do you want to be sent a copy of our elementary student materials catalog?

Do you want a copy of our college catalog?

Would you like a copy of our next edition?   ☐ yes ☐ no

Are you a ☐ student or an ☐ instructor?

Your name _____ school _____

Term used _____ Date _____

address _____

city _____ state _____ zip _____

telephone number _____

G/T